*Practical Politics
for School Administrators*

Practical Politics
for School Administrators

DAVID K. WILES
State University of New York at Albany

JON WILES
University of Montana

JOSEPH BONDI
University of South Florida

ALLYN AND BACON, INC.   *Boston London Sydney Toronto*

Library of Congress Cataloging in Publication Data

Wiles, David K
  Practical politics for school administrators.

  Bibliography
  Includes index.
  1. School management and organization. 2. School
administrators—Handbooks, manuals, etc. I. Wiles,
Jon, joint author. II. Bondi, Joseph, joint author.
III. Title.
LB2806.W495   371.2   80-18431
ISBN 0-205-07132-5

Printed in the United States of America

Contents

Preface

This book presents a new orientation to the field of educational administration. It has been written for those line administrators and would-be administrators in America's public and private schools who will be serving as leaders during the 1980s. The book takes a reality-based look at school conditions in an era of declining resources and prescribes action for survival.

Each year in the United States thousands of upwardly mobile educators return to school to secure an administrative endorsement. With such an endorsement, these educators aspire to enter the ranks of school administration. While many who enter succeed, many others do not. The field of school administration has a high degree of turnover. It is the contention of the authors that much of this turnover results from basic ignorance about the complexity of schools and the jobs to be done. To be candid, professional preparation often fails to prepare the school administrator for the real world of schools.

Practical Politics for School Administrators introduces the political perspective of school administration. In contrasting a political perspective with conventional presentations found in educational administration literature, the authors suggest that the local school center is actually a political arena. The principal, the focused role in this book, is presented as both a broker and a decision player in the arena. The ideas and language that presently dominate the study of politics in school administration are introduced.

The early chapters of the book illustrate how to take charge of a new administrative position, how to maintain control of the political arena, and how to make meaningful changes. The principal's "style" as a decision player is discussed in terms of three significant periods: the honeymoon, initial coalition formation, and the institutionalization of administrative authority.

The final chapters of the book deal with specific populations and problems that determine the degree of effectiveness in school administration. Relationships with Boards of Education, the central administration, parents, community groups, and students are discussed. Ways of working with school personnel, the politics of the budget, and political dimensions of curriculum, instruction, and evaluation are analyzed. Finally, a number of case stories are provided to assist the readers in internalizing concepts and making the translation to their own local conditions as administrators.

While this book is addressed specifically to the principalship, the observations should be valid for other educational leadership roles. Superintendents, in particular, will appreciate the analyses and strategies that encourage "survival" in educational administration.

It is assumed that *Practical Politics for School Administrators* will be controversial because it addresses an area of administration rarely covered in the literature—the survival of the administrator. To the degree that the reader experiences a sense of ownership in reading about the political influences that shape school administration, this book will be practical and may serve as a guide in the decade ahead. It may also serve as an aid in avoiding such situations as the one that follows.

DKW
JWW
JCB

BOARD OF EDUCATION
SCHOOL DISTRICT

Memorandum to: Principal, Dasher Intermediate School

Reference: Notice of Termination

By action of the School District Board of Education, voting 6 for and 1 against at its February 14th meeting, your position as Principal of Dasher Intermediate School will NOT be renewed. You are to vacate your office no later than 4 P.M. on June 12th.

In accordance with your contract, you do possess return rights in the district as a classroom teacher. Your assignment for the fall semester, should you choose to accept it, will be an Industrial Arts/ Remedial Skills position at Lively Vocational Technical School.

For the Board,

Ben Dover

CHAPTER I

Politics and the Principal

It is time to discuss the principalship in a real world context of the 1980s. Contrasted with broad prescriptive statements about what the administration of a local school should be, this chapter establishes some basic assumptions about what the role of the principal is. The importance of the chapter is in showing how different a political reality-based viewpoint is from most conventional presentations of the topic. We think our assumptions are realistic for the educational world of the 1980s and that principals on the firing line will have a practical understanding of this perspective. Most popular models used to explain school administration are inadequate. While the models provide convenient explanations, they are too general and are based upon assumptions of governance and control that are questionable in today's world. Worse, the present models of the school and principal's role create a dangerous illusion of certainty and stability that cannot be justified in this transitional era. It is time to rethink the concept of principal in the local school setting and tie words to reality.

THE TRANSITIONAL ERA

Few people would argue that public education today is the same as it was in the days of the Great Society in the late 1960s. The blanket assumptions of enough resources to try compensatory efforts, of stable governance arrangements where reasonable people prevail, and of people believing in the worth of schooling have been shaken to the core during the 1970s. Perhaps public education mirrors the larger societal dynamics; the Vietnam War, Watergate, the Government Services Administration scandal and so forth are the true indicators of societal transition. But within education we have our own indicators that point to the fallacy of stating that the 1970 hardships were a "passing deviation," or that the decade of the seventies was just part of another cyclical trend returning us to the "good old days." In previous times some people have lost faith in the school's ability to deliver academic achievement while other eras have exhibited conditions of financial scarcities. Yet the 1970s were different from other decades and historical periods, if in no more than the *magnitude* of educational problems and the dismal projections for the 1980s. Past eras were times when problems were perceived as "manageable" (even though difficult) and, most important, that the future *would* be a better day. Today, things seem different. In the 1980s many people doubt that our societal and educational problems can be solved. In the past, educators often argued *if* the pupil-teacher ratio was lowered significantly, learning would improve. In the past, we argued that centralization of certain services and consolidation would lead to economic savings and greater efficiency. This time around the assurances are given less often and with more qualifiers. Privately, some leading educators wonder if our problems are solvable at all.

The 1980s do not hold the automatic promise of better times. People who speculate on birth rates and fiscal conditions predict further hardships and a continuation of worsening conditions. This fact also makes the 1970s different from any other transitional era in the past. Friedmann and Hudson make the point succinctly: "It is not the uncertainty about what things are . . . but the certainty that current knowledge and today's paradigms . . . will misstate the nature of conditions tomorrow . . . ." [1]

We believe the context of the 1970s and the possibilities of the 1980s demand new perspectives about local school governance. This text is "radical" only in the sense that it attempts to be realistic about school administration in times that many educators wish were different. However, wishing is inadequate when we are trying to provide guidance and knowledge about such a crucial topic.

THE POLITICAL PERSPECTIVE

School administration has been openly recognized as political for some time,[2] yet there is little understanding about what "being political" implies. Certainly a great difference exists between the partisan politics of formal parties vying for elected offices and the politics of the principalship. However, some commonalities can be identified (even in these extreme cases) by the factors that outline a "political perspective." David Easton defined politics as the "authoritative allocation of scarce resources." [3] The seeming abstraction of such a definition dissolves as a word by word interpretation points to concrete meanings.

The word *authoritative* indicates that a primary concern of the principal is to be *legitimate*. Perhaps the major departure of the educational politics literature from the standard educational administration literature is that role legitimacy is *not* assumed. The conventional assumption of administration is that the principalship is, by definition, legitimate because of the law and formal structure of the school organization. A political perspective would argue that the law and formal organization *may* make the principal legitimate (in fact, in the overwhelming number of cases it seems to—under normal conditions) but the possibility remains that the law and organization may *not* confer legitimacy. During the social crises of the late 1960s there were documented cases of principals retaining enough legitimacy to operate only by *avoiding* conventional legal stipulations and standard operating procedures of the school system.[4] Similarly, during recent winter weather crises, with heating fuel unavailable and attendance sporadic, the issue of a principal's legitimacy to govern became a function of the ability of the person to initiate adaptive actions *without* school system guidelines.[5] The political perspective stipulates legitimacy, or being "authoritative," as a critical, ongoing concern of being a principal.

The word *allocation* indicates that the primary concern of the principal is deciding. Whether the principal is deciding how to give out additional supplies, monitoring a current pattern of allocation (supplies among departments) or evaluating and contemplating a reallocation, the political perspective emphasizes the who, how, what, when, and where of *deciding* as the critical focus.

As we will discuss in detail later, allocative decisions take different forms, each with a special brand of "politics." Lowi[6] identifies *distributive* decisions where allocations are parcelled out in such a way that "the indulged and the deprived . . . never come into direct confrontation." This type of allocation differs from *regulative* decisions where "there is a direct choice as to who will be indulged and who deprived." Both allocations differ from *redistributive* decisions, which are similar to regulative policy making in the clear choice, but affect total classes of people rather than individuals or small groups. Redistributive decisions might affect all the students or all the teachers; a regulative decision might be a selection among small numbers of individual faculty or pupils.

The word *scarce* implies the crucial condition of competition in politics. The administrator is assumed to live in a decision-making world characterized by adversary relations, shortages of desired commodities, and sanctions for wrong choices. In political terms there are winners and losers, and "winning" is not conferred automatically to those who hold positions in the administrative hierarchy.

Finally *resources* implies that political competition may center upon a variety of objects that are chosen for their perceived and/or actual value. Resources may be concrete, such as dollars or job vacancies, or resources may be abstract (ideological commitment). The crucial characteristic of resource is having enough value to be the center of competition.

In summary, the definition of politics, the "authoritative allocation of scarce resources," guides the practitioner to four fundamental issues of description:

1. What is legitimate?
2. Who controls decision making?
3. What is the nature of competition?
4. What is valued?

These four issues define the political situation and set the stage for study of the principal's role in terms of decision making.

THE SCHOOL AS AN ARENA

The school setting can be seen as an arena where individual actions can be studied, issue by issue, in a *situational* context. The arena perspective of the local school is different from the popular explanations of organization. The arena stands in sharp contrast to the pure bureaucracy model of how schools operate. The arena perspective is also different from the consensus oriented, small group view of school organization. When we are discussing models, the bottom line is which explanation *best* captures the *most* dynamics of how decisions are actually made. The arena does not replace all aspects of the bureaucracy or the small group as explanations, but places them in a secondary or supporting context. The primary explanation of how decisions are made in local schools is the arena for bargaining.

The arena perspective does not ignore the long history of school organization being assumed to be a hierarchy with fixed rules and inherent stability. Indeed, many decisions are now made according to such assumptions. *However, the critical distinction of the arena perspective is that the real meaning of decision making is determined situation to situation through an understanding of the actions of individuals.* Formal authority, such as the principal, may not dominate the decision processes in certain situations. The type of authority or power that dominates a particular decision may come from many sources and often depends upon (1) what is "up for grabs," (2) the "rules of the game" for a particular arena context, and (3) the particular "players" involved. Obviously, this perspective suggests decision situations where the formal role of the principal actually *negates* the political influence of the person acting within that role.

Another characteristic of the arena perspective is the imprecise nature of the decision process. The trading considerations of arena activity do not lend themselves to clean, clear cut relations of costs to benefits or inputs to outputs. Instead, the arena process is a jumble of conflicting psychological-behavioral actions that may merge symbolic and concrete decisions or confuse long- and short-term strategies. The arena perspective demands a tolerance for ambiguity about making decisions. More important, it does not assume that individuals involved in decision making are of a like mind or have the automatic ability to reach common understandings or agreements. Many decisions made in the arena are misunderstood, even by some of those participating in the process of choice.[7]

In summary, the arena perspective makes some strong assumptions about how decision making in schools is best explained. Foremost, it is an explanation of individual actions taken situation to situation, which implies that the perspective is issue oriented and that the arena itself depends upon choice. Thus both the rules for deciding an issue and the individuals involved in the decision are particular to that issue. It also means that the actual processes of deciding are not clear cut. The competitive trading that occurs may offer no clear delineation between the immediate and long-range objectives or between symbolic and concrete options. Finally, there is usually no automatic agreement or consensus that is reached by those involved in a choice.

Each of the characteristics of the arena perspective violates some aspect of our conventional models about how people decide in schools. Further, its shifting, ambiguous nature may well explain why most descriptions of organization and decision making seek to establish more stability and generality. The real issue of explanation may not be how *realistic* a particular perspective is but how clear cut the world of deciding is assumed to be. The arena perspective assumes that reality in schools is illusive.

POPULAR MODELS OF ADMINISTRATION

The present literature in educational administration is dominated by three arguments that purport to explain school decision making: systems theory, the bureaucracy, and the consensus-building small group. These models are generally taken as articles of faith or a litany to rationalize school operations.

Systems Theory

Lip service has been paid to systems theory in educational administration for some time, with applications of systems thinking predating the formal education of many contemporary school principals. The origins of systems thought come from the field of biology, the natural sciences, behavioral science, and engineering management. A term often used interchangeably with systems, cybernetics, emphasizes an approach to planning that assumes certain configurations of communication and control.

A system refers to a set of interrelated components that work together to accomplish an outcome. There is a dynamic relationship between the parts of the system and the system as a whole. Granger defines a system as

> ... a cohesive collection of items that are dynamically related. The term describes an interrelated network of objects and events or the symbols for such an assembly. Systems are sets of elements or parts which possess some degree of independence or identity but, at the same time, are an integral part of a larger ensemble or whole. In this assembly or network the parts function to produce some process or product which is unique to that particular organismic unit or system.[8]

Kaufman, providing a less complex definition for school contexts, defines systems as "a type of logical problem solving which is applied to identifying and resolving important educational problems."[9]

For the school principal, the central idea of a systems analysis approach is that the functional components of the school, and principal activity, are best understood if treated as a whole. The causal relationship between activities creates a work "network" that provides opportunity for greater efficiency and more predictable work outcomes. The whole of activities, and school components, is the school program.

Several conditions are assumed to be necessary for the principal to begin seeing the school, and his or her role, as a system. First, boundaries must be defined by the goal statements of the school. If the school lacks clear-cut goals, no component or behavior can be logically assessed. Second, the relationship among the parts in the school must be unified and working toward objectives. Third, the process of interaction must be perceived as an input-output situation—the children enter as uneducated students and exit as educated students. Finally, there must be an understanding that the system is a tool in use to maximize the efforts in achieving that output.

Functionally, a systems perspective can help the principal identify the goals of the school, plan for the attainment of objectives, make crucial judgments, marshal resources, and evaluate the program. In designing the system in his or her school, the principal would proceed through five basic steps:

1. Develop a description of the desired product or outcome of schooling, uncontaminated by the means for attaining that outcome.
2. Analyze those objectives to find the preconditions needed to produce the desired outcome.
3. Analyze in greater detail, describing in finer and finer language what is to occur.

4. When the smallest components are outlined by the planner, the process to produce the desired result is constructed.

5. The process is activated by principal behavior.

While systems are organized by function, they are managed by product. In managing a system in a school context, the principal can control major transformation components by his or her behavior. Among these variables that direct the development of school programs are goals and values of the organization, the structure of the organization, the psychological and social relationships within the organization (climate), and the technological or delivery mediums of the organization. Collectively, these transformation subsystems allow the principal considerable latitude in managing the school to achieve desired ends.

During the 1970s, a number of constraints acted to thwart the rationalistic planning and achievement schedule of even the most dedicated systems advocate. Among those constraints that were most difficult for individual building principals were time deadlines imposed by constant changes in school programs, an inadequate planning data and knowledge base, the interface with other elements of the school district, and the constant intrusion of forces from outside the individual school. The "tightening" conditions in public schools in the 1980s may well lessen constraints of the 1970s. Change efforts will probably be directed at less diverse outcomes. Evaluation efforts in the 1970s may have provided much of the necessary planning data. Building principals may be left on their own to a greater extent to solve local problems. And the public may have a declining (or at least different) interest in school programming. In short, the educational system as represented by the single school building may be less open. While we believe a systems perspective often creates a rationalistic artificiality, principals who try to act according to the assumptions of the systems model should have greater successes.

The principal attempting to act according to a systems model in the school must understand the relationship between process and product. This flow is outlined in Table 1.1.

TABLE 1.1

Process	*Product*
1. Assessment of need	2. Statement of intent
3. Criteria for program development	4. Program strategies and guidelines
5. Cataloging of resources	6. Development of options, ideas, and materials
7. Development of long range plans	8. Development of a management system
9. Assessment criteria identified	10. Evaluation plan employed

As can be seen, process activities in a systems approach are formalized in products that suggest further process activities. Building principals who focus administrative tasks (process) on program development (product) will find that administration has natural curricular and instructional components as displayed in Table 1.2.[10]

While much of a systems perspective makes sense, and provides a good rationale for how things are supposed to operate, many practitioners have grown frustrated with its abstraction. A closer look at school governance and choice reveals a second pervasive set of assumptions in the current literature.

TABLE 1.2   *Flow of Administrative Activities and Tasks*

Administrative Tasks	Curriculum Tasks	Instructional Tasks
1. Set and prioritize goals	Determine instructional objectives	Develop instructional plans
2. Establish standards and policy	Survey needs and conduct research	Evaluate programming according to standards
3. Provide long-range planning	Develop programs and plan changes	Initiate new programs
4. Design organizational structures	Relate programs to special services	Redesign instructional organization where needed
5. Identify and secure resources	Select materials and allocate resources	Deliver instructional resources
6. Personnel selection and staffing	Orienting and renewing instructional staff	Advising and assisting teachers
7. Securing necessary funding	Estimating expenditures for instruction by program	Dispersing and applying funds
8. Providing adequate facilities	Suggesting modifications in facilities	Overseeing specifications in facility modifications
9. Organizing for instruction	Preparing instructional programs	Coordinating instructional activities
10. Promoting school-community relations	Disseminating descriptions of school programs	Reacting to inquiries about school programs

THE ADMINISTRATIVE FLOW OF ACTIVITY

$\longrightarrow$

Source: Jon Wiles and Joseph Bondi, *Supervision: A Guide to Practice*, Charles E. Merrill Publishing Company, 1980, p. 35. Used by permission.

The Bureaucracy

The bureaucracy model is derived from a general sociological interpretation of organization that notes that every organization is a cluster of suborganizations and part of a larger organization. Further, there is never complete compatibility among the different organizational levels. Finally, the sociological interpretation emphasizes that during any given interval in an organization's history it will be growing, stable, or declining. The dynamics of this history means all organizations will face change and crisis from time to time.

This general framework, with several critical additions and deletions, forms the basis for modern organizational theory. Max Weber[11] created the ideal model of bureaucracy based upon five critical assumptions about decision making: specialization of work, authority by hierarchy, rules and regulations, emphasis on personal detachment, and employment based on technical qualifications. Others have discussed how these assumptions would characterize actual decision making in schools and other complex organizations:

1. Specialization of work is concerned with the manner in which tasks in an organization are distributed to the various positions as duties. This means that there is a clear-cut division of labor.
2. Hierarchical authority structure is concerned with the formal arrangement of superiors and subordinates in an organization.
3. Rules and regulations govern all official decisions and actions within the organization. These rules are often precise and insure a high degree of rationality for the decisions made. In addition, they maximize control through an impersonal and rational means.
4. Personal detachment on the part of officials within a bureaucracy is expected toward both clients and other officials within the organization. This requirement makes it easier for an official to make decisions beneficial to the organization, without having concern for friends, colleagues, and other personnel unduly influencing his decisions.
5. The assignment of persons within the bureaucracy is based on technical qualifications, which are ascertained through highly formalized and impersonal procedures. The benefits of this are (a) elimination of nepotism and favoritism, (b) elimination of class privilege, and (c) members have lifelong tenure, maximizing vocational security that tends to ensure their service without regard to extraneous pressure.[12]

The direct meanings of bureaucracy for school decision making are found in the following assumptions about organizational reality: (1) there is an unequal status among members, which is *hierarchically* arranged, (2) *formal* rules dominate decision making, (3) *administration* is a separate specialization, and (4) the organization is *stable* or fixed. These assumptions are so ingrained in most of us that it is hard to think of organization outside of them. Yet during the educational crises in the 1960s and 1970s, much of the crisis revolved on the inapplicability of the critical assumptions about bureaucracy. Certainly the hierarchy and dominance of formal rules suffered a variety of successful challenges. There are many "war-stories" that relate particular instances where the principal was *not* "captain of the ship" or where in the final analysis, the principal did not decide even though he or she had "the final authority." These conventional truths have been tempered by the experiences of political reality.

The same danger of assuming universal characteristics of bureaucracy also applies to some assumptions of administrative specialization and the stability of a decision environment. Administrative separation may be forced by dynamics of a labor versus management confrontation, but the bureaucratic assumption of administration *being accepted as a true specialization* is another matter. Many principals describe their daily role with words such as "middle management frustrations." In local school situations that are dominated by master contract stipulations or a waffling board policy, some principals are unsure whether they are specialized to do anything. All these factors lead to an organization that is anything but stable from a management perspective.

What can be observed? This text argues that we have overgeneralized and assumed too much about the bureaucratic parameters of both what is the school organization and what is the principalship. Today, it may be wiser and much more realistic to talk of "tendencies toward" bureaucracy but recognize the possibility of another type of organization: *the arena*.

The Small, Consensus-Oriented Group

A third popular model of organization that has been used to describe school decision making is the consensus-oriented small group. This perception of organization usually underscores *professionalization* as the reasons for consensus building and why the small group is the primary mechanism for deciding. Where the "bureaucracy" was an institutional model of formal decision authority, the consensus-oriented small group is a person-centered model. People decide because of common professional values and personal expertise or specialization. Professionalization provides a general rationale for deciding (independent of the institution's authority) while specialization focuses decision making on areas of expertise. For example, *teaching* describes the general professional value but teaching of certain specialities (e.g., English) sets the rationale for who should actually decide.

This model has often been presented as *the* alternative to the bureaucracy, and the discussion of organization and/or decision making often ends on this either-or distinction.[13] The arena perspective would argue against the small group consensus-building model on essentially the same grounds as the bureaucratic model. The assumptions about professionalism and individual rationality based upon expertise are too general to be meaningful. For example, the meaning of professional becomes a point of debate whenever an attempt to talk about specific behaviors or practices occurs. This debate occurs especially in times of crises. In teacher strikes, those who leave the classroom to take up the picket line and those who continue to teach because leaving would harm the children both see themselves as professional. Other differences exist among those who identify themselves as professional. Those who are upward mobile will comply with bureaucratic expectations; there are those who wish to be left alone to be creative, and there are those who teach only to gain resources to do other things in their lives.[14] Educators may disagree about which variation is most professional, but the fact that variation exists is the critical point.

Such overgeneralization of meaning causes difficulty with the basic assumptions of consensus building in the professional model. The rationality of the problem-solving approach and the predominant authority of expertise are both called into question. The problem-solving approach is so familiar that many educators accept it blindly as truth. This approach specifies that the problem is first defined, alternatives to its solution are listed, and the choice is made on a consideration of the particular costs and benefits of each option. Although this is the rational way to decide, many people involved in actual decision making know this is not the way many decisions are made. Sometimes people are forced to decide without knowing the actual problem. Often they select the first alternative that seems to alleviate stress as if it were the only option they could think of.[15] These are the realities of certain decision situations. These realities do not fit the classic problem-solving approach. The lack of a universal approach to problem solving illuminates a critical dimension of the assumptions about consensus building.

Likewise, the expertise by which judgments are made in the professional model fails to hold up in practice. In the consensus-building small group, education (teaching *and* administration) is acknowledged to be an art rather than a science. In spite of exhaustive effort, there is little universal agreement on what constitutes good teaching or excellent administration. Without a concrete standard to judge expertise the assumed rationality of professional choice is further shaken.

A CONTRASTING PERSPECTIVE

The arena perspective of organization stands in sharp contrast to the three popular discussions of decision making in schools. The systems approach presents a rationalistic world governed by identifiable inputs and outputs that link process and product in a systematic fashion. The bureaucratic model presents a general picture of institutional authority and stable decision-making arrangements based upon impersonal structures of rules, regulations, and standard operating procedures. The small group consensus-building model is presented as a stable arrangement of interpersonal decision making based upon professional expertise and rational problem solving. Each interpretation of school organization is artificial and paints a false picture of how decisions are actually made in today's world. The basic problem with all three popular models is that they are too general and, consequently, make organizational decision making appear too stable.

The arena perspective makes no assumption that a principal will find a stable decision environment in a local school. Although elements of potential stability are always present (e.g., organizational rules or norms among teachers) there is no automatic guarantee that these elements will influence a particular choice. Some people argue rules are made to be broken and a person has a right to change his or her mind. The arena model accounts for these possibilities by emphasizing *the situation and issue* as the determinants of choice. Organization follows decision context, not vice versa as in the conventional models. People *know* about choice and organizational decision making only as they view the present actions and processes of those involved in choosing. There is no guarantee that the past will guide the present or that current decisions will accurately project the future. *The arena model of organization is a model where change is assumed to be as likely as stability.* Tendencies and precedents can be discussed only in the context of *potential.*

Finally, the arena model is a candid admission that real decision making is messy, confusing, and often contradictory. Players and rules for deciding may be constantly changing. The actual trading associated with a particular decision may be a blur of long- and short-range objectives and symbolic and concrete options. It is not necessary that deciders agree or be like-minded. In fact, a person can influence a particular choice without even being aware of the arena for deciding. These are the realities of decision making that this text assumes and that discussions of the principal are based upon. We now turn to specific consideration of the principal in the arena.

The Principal as Poker Player

Consistent with the arena perspective of school organization is the view that the principal's role in leadership or governing the school is not fixed or stable in the traditional sense. Neither bureaucratic stipulations of authority (legal rules, delegated formal responsibility) nor descriptions of professional expertise will explain how the principal actually operates in the local school. Both formal authority and professional orientation provide some guidance concerning the management of a particular school but neither describe the dynamics of governance. *The principal's decision role is defined by the issue and the choice situation.* The general models that assume one role definition or a single portrait of how a principal decides are artificial. This statement strikes hard at several conventional models of the principalship that assume a general classification is possible. For example, a well-known model defines authoritarian, laissez-faire, and democratic behavior.[16] Each behavior has specific indicators of the leader's intent, the type of relation to subordinates, and the type of decision outcome that can be expected. The impression given by the model is that a principal can be described and classified by one of the three variations. If this assumption was ever valid, it is not so today. The situation and issue determine the type of governance behavior. For example, if an issue demands an immediate resolution and the principal must act without consultation, the behavior may be authoritarian. On the other hand, another issue and time constraint may allow democratic delegation. The problem with the traditional models is that they force overextension of the information about actual decision making and the overgeneralization of how principals are classified.

We prefer to describe the principal's role as a "player" within the arena of local school decision making. The player's behavior itself and later evaluative judgments about the decision behavior both depend upon the issue and decision context. If educators know the particular arena and the outcome of choice they can say something about how the principal operated (and even pass judgment *in retrospect* of how he or she might have operated differently). The player in a political environment does have several characteristics that can identify a particular style of play.

Many writers emphasize that all governance behavior can be discussed as desires and/or actions based upon calculation and control. In most decision situations there is a calculating and a control component. The calculating aspect includes the means by which demands are recognized, goals are identified, alternatives weighed, probabilities estimated, actions selected, and so forth. The control component considers what occurs once the decision has been calculated. Control considers the implementation, enforcement and/or enactment of the decision. Dale Mann states:

> Calculation proceeds by quantification, comparison, theory testing, making predictions, analyzing incrementally, mixed scanning, etc. Examples of mechanisms that may have their primary use for calculation occur readily: cost-benefit analysis, some forms of systems analysis, critical path methods, etc. Control on the other hand proceeds by compromise, coercion, bargaining regulation, the uses of power, in-

fluence, authority, constraint, and so on. Examples of control mechanisms are also easy to generate; bureaucratization, job codification, performance standards, incentive rates, program guidelines, and legislation are some examples.[17]

Players in a decision arena can be described by how they view legitimacy (authoritative), how they view scarcity, how they compete with others, and how they value and utilize resources. Each player may judge a particular situation differently and the only way to describe such arenas is to infer behavior from the actual dynamics of choice. For this reason, the principal's role is analogous to a poker player's in what is becoming (in some situations) a "wild" game. It is obvious that the criteria for good poker playing differ from the "conventional" criteria given for good principalship. Yet we will argue throughout this text that the practical reality of the arena makes the poker player perspective realistic and viable as a way to assess principal decision behavior. What are some of the criteria of playing good poker? In order of priority:

1. There is never such a thing as a "sure hand" in an honest game.
2. Never play a totally new game when significant stakes are involved.
3. To come out ahead you expect to win some and lose some.
4. To come out ahead you play for the long haul. Winning is rarely a one shot, dramatic phenomenon but more likely a gradual accumulation of chips.
5. (Contrasting with golf) it's how you drive *and* how you arrive. We judge "winners" in process and products of choice.
6. Each deal starts the players anew.

These general rules provide guidance in spite of the particular dynamics of play. The poker rules do not *guarantee* success for any single individual but, as some adherents of "democratic" administration have found, neither do traditional models. The poker criteria do provide standards to judge a situational perspective of school governance and a way to judge principal decision behavior. The rest of this book is based upon the "poker" perspective of real life school management.

The Ethics of "Poker"

A final issue must be addressed before discussing the actual processes of governing a local school. In many ways, the ethics or morality of the principal who adopts a poker playing perspective of school administration is the most important concern of this text. Without preaching, we feel that a person who governs according to situational interpretations and the competition of the arena has a special obligation to understand certain ethical concerns. To win, by itself, is not an adequate criterion for "poker" when the application involves people's lives and the administration of local schools. The excesses of the win-at-all-costs mentality are documented in Machiavelli's, *The Prince*[18] and in the atrocities of war when unethical applications are rationalized as an operational necessity. We feel a moral condition is imperative to a positive application of the messages of this text. The primary criterion for an ethical concern is *open* recognition of potential excesses and continuous discussion of unethical possibilities by those involved in the school governance arrangement. We believe that constant vigilance and self-scrutiny by all involved in the arena is the best guard against a self-fulfilling righteousness by a certain arrangement for control. Winning has a long and cherished history in the United States, but the dangers of excess or immoral applications in governance do not have to be documented in just the extreme cases.

In the everyday life of local school administration the safeguard of ethical concern is also mandatory. With the luxury of hindsight, it seems that much of the humanist movement, which reached a high water mark in the late 1960s, created an *illusion* of ethical concern that frustrated many school building principals. No one can fault the intent of those who call for the humanization of administrative activity or letting the people become responsible for their destinies. Most people *believe* in consensus and logic in deciding because they *believe* in respect for others and the self-determination of democracy. These are the ideals of governance in the United States and they underscore the argument for freedom with authority.

However, recent history in the United States has shown vividly that intent is not reality and that the 1960s brand of humanism failed to address some fundamental realities of organization. For example, the roots of the human relations movement that has altered educational administration since the late 1930s are traced to the Western Electric Studies.[19] These studies described the "Hawthorne effect"—that attention paid to workers will increase production. Production increases because workers know they are the subject of attention. During the 1960s and 1970s it seemed that many humanists who touted the recognition of individuals and intrinsic motivation forgot why the studies were done in the first place. The Western Electric Company, or the local school, is interested in human variability to fit a formula to improve institutional production. This carries different operational meaning for governance than the philosophical expression of free democratic choice. In fact, when there is a tendency to consider only the abstract and pretend such expression confers operational meanings, one of two things happen. Either the actual system of governance produces a set of ideological true believers out of touch with reality or the system produces guilt in those who must operate in the realities of governance.

Since the 1930s school administrators have complained about the two faces of what they do and what they *say* they do in educational decision making. Principals have been encouraged to share and delegate decisions, to balance authority and responsibility, and to build consensus without realistic consideration of operating differences between lofty intent and actual practice. The safeguard of ethical concern begins with a realistic appraisal of what humanism may come to mean in a variety of existing governance arrangements.

There is one type of recognition that helps to focus the ethics of "poker." First, the players should fully understand the differences between governance as *stability* and governance as *consistency*. There is a stability of a single, fixed position and a stability of controlled movement (the person standing still and the person running). The ethics of the arena demand consideration of the dynamic form of stability. Basic questions concern the who, why, how, and when to control the speed and type of running. That the final goal may not be apparent is the crucial issue. There is a consistency of process and a consistency of product. Consistency of product implies the same results, but consistency of process means adherence to established rules for play. The arena perspective demands process consistency in administrative behavior. Ethical concerns of process consistency focus upon the critical distinction between "the end justifies the means" and "the end allows systematic consideration of the means." Process consistency is judged by looking at particular decision-making actions and raising fundamental questions of equity and fairness in the rules for and dynamics of how choices are made. It is strongly recommended that those educators who have not read Rawl's *Theory of Justice*[20] do so for a fuller explanation of the ethics of decision making. Local school administration can be a situational "poker playing" exercise *and* also be an ethical operation of governance *if* those involved in and affected by choices appreciate certain critical meanings.

NOTES

1. John Friedman and Barclay Hudson, "Knowledge and Action: A Guide to Planning Theory," *Journal of American Institute of Planning*, January 1974, p. 12.
2. Some of the pioneers in presenting this perspective were Eliot, Bailey, Iannaccone, and Kimbrough. See Thomas Eliot, "Toward an Understanding of Public School Politics," *American Political Science Review*, December 1959, pp. 1032–1051; Stephen K. Bailey et al., *Schoolmen and Politics* (Syracuse: University Press, 1962); Lawrence Innaccone, *Politics in Education* (New York: Center for Applied Research in Education, Inc., 1967); Ralph Kimbrough, *Political Power and Educational Decision Making* (Chicago: Rand McNally, 1964).
3. David Easton, *A Systems Analysis of Political Life* (New York: Wiley, 1965).

4. David Wiles, "Community Participation Demands and Local School Response in the Urban Environment," *Education and Urban Society* 6, no. 4 (August 1974): 451–467.
5. David Wiles, *Energy, Weather & Schools: Chronology of Decision Crises* (Lexington: D. C. Heath, 1979) especially Chapters 9 and 10.
6. Theodore Lowi, "American Business, Public Policy, Case Studies and Political Theory," *World Politics* 16, no. 4 (July 1964): 677–715.
7. For extended discussions of the arena dynamics see Graham Allison, *Essence of Decision* (Boston: Little, Brown, 1971) Model III; and Irving Janis, "Groupthink Among Policymakers," in *Sanctions for Evil*, ed. N. Sanford and C. Cornstock (San Francisco: Jossey-Bass, 1971).
8. Thomas J. Sanders and Judith G. Myers, *Essentials of School Management* (Philadelphia: W. B. Saunders, 1977), pp. 397–99.
9. Roger A. Kaufman, *Educational Systems Planning* (Englewood Cliffs, N.J.: Prentice-Hall, 1972), p. 1.
10. Jon Wiles and Joseph Bondi, *Supervision: A Guide To Practice* (Columbus, Ohio, Charles E. Merrill, 1980), p. 347.
11. Max Weber, *A Theory of Social and Economic Organization* trans. A. M. Henderson and T. Parsons (New York: Oxford Press, 1947).
12. Peter Blau, *Bureaucracy in Modern Society* (New York: Random House, 1965), pp. 14–15.
13. See, for example, Ronald Corwin, *A Sociology of Education* (New York: Appleton-Century-Crofts, 1965), p. 232.
14. Robert Presthus, *The Organizational Society* (New York: Alfred A. Knopf, 1962).
15. Herbert Simon discusses bounded rationality and satisficing. See "A Behavioral Model for Rational Choice," in *The Making of Decision*, ed. W. Gore and J. Dyson (New York: Free Press, 1965).
16. See discussions in Kimball Wiles, *Supervision for Better Schools* (Englewood Cliffs, N.J.: Prentice-Hall, 1967).
17. Dale Mann, *Policy Decision Making in Education* (New York: Teachers College Press, 1975), p. 55. For the basic work in this area see Robert Dahl and Charles Lindbloom, *Politics, Economics, and Welfare* (New York: Harper Torchbooks, 1953).
18. For a modern interpretation see Anthony Jay, *Management and Machiavelli* (New York: Holt, Rinehart and Winston, 1968).
19. Raymond Callahan, *Education and the Cult of Efficiency* (Chicago: University of Chicago Press, 1962).
20. John Rawls, *A Theory of Justice* (Cambridge: Belknap Press, 1971), especially pp. 395–512, 567–588. The reader may find the text too philosophical and unrelated to education but the message is worth the effort.

CHAPTER 2

Taking Charge

The concept of taking charge relates to the meaning of being accepted in a new environment. It has special significance for a person who, by the formal recognition of a position of authority, is the head of the organization. This chapter covers the conditions by which a principal might be entering a particular local school center, the phenomenon of being "judged" before taking any actions, how to identify the direct and indirect reasons for judgment, and how to deal with the initial entry period.

CONDITIONS FOR ENTRANCE

Two major aspects of taking charge affect the type of political conditions a principal might find upon entering a local school. One aspect is whether it is the principal's first job as local school administrator. Regardless of the number of years as a teacher or how extensive and varied the professional background of the principal, the key criterion in the minds of many people is the amount of experience as an administrator. A first-time principal may be judged a "nice guy" or as possessing "exceptional potential," but he or she is still "unproven." The key guidance for a first-timer is that the burden of proof rests with the principal who carries the double burden of being acceptable *and* gaining the crucial ingredient of experience. People often feel more comfortable with proven products (even if the proof is superficial) so their skepticism or show-me attitude should not be taken as a personal insult.

There are two ways a principal may enter his or her first-time principalship. Usually the first-time principal has completed an apprenticeship as an assistant administrator or as a participant in a training program or (most likely) as a combination of both. The new principal should rely on this background as a means to legitimize his or her background as an administrator. Many faculty place much more confidence in a local school level endorsement of administrative ability than a central office pronouncement.

A second way a first-time experience might occur is in an emergency. A teacher assumes an "acting" principalship (usually of an elementary or small "special" school) for a temporary assignment. Depending upon the type of emergency the temporary assignment becomes permanent. The teacher turned administrator may run back to graduate school to obtain the appropriate certificate and credits but will remain a full-fledged principal to those at the local school site during the interim. In an unexpected way, the emergency conditions may be the best asset of the first-time principal. The new administrator can be forgiven many mistakes and problems due to the unusual situation. If these conditions are emphasized, the principal's lack of experience may become less important to his or her critics.

Another major aspect of taking charge is whether the principalship is to govern a new environment. For experienced administrators at the local school level of governance, there are two types of new environment. One is the result of a lateral move. For example, an inner city junior high principal becomes principal of a suburban junior high. The other new environment is the result of a vertical move. An elementary principal with several years experience becomes a junior high principal. Of course, lateral and vertical movement are often combined in this aspect of new environment. For our purpose, the particular type of new administrative environment is less important than the fact that experience is not an automatic, transferable property. The outstanding principal with several years at P.S. 142 may be treated with skepticism and reserve at P.S. 37.

One final aspect (which may have been a major feature on entrance ten years ago, but seems to play a diminishing part in public schools today) is whether the principal is an outsider to the local district. Scarcity of administrative positions and an oversupply of highly qualified, certificated people have restricted many candidate searches to within the district. Although private schools may well continue national, regional, and statewide searches for headmasters, the public schools will do much less of this practice during the 1980s. The advantage at entrance is that no principal (first-time or transfer) will be a complete stranger to the problems and dynamics of a local school. The principal's personality and style will fit the local school environment because of the reciprocal knowledge within the district.

In conclusion, there are two major aspects of entry: previous administrative experiences and whether occupying the principal's office was the result of a lateral or vertical move. Each presents different problems and advantages for an individual taking charge of the school.

Perhaps the most important thing to understand in taking charge of a new school is that the new principal will probably be judged before beginning the job. Further, the judgment may well be upon appearance or conjecture rather than reality. Whether as harmless rumor or a calculated effort to discredit, a principal might expect to find himself or herself prejudged as a hard guy or wishy washy, a central office stooge or the school's advocate. When expected as natural, these judgments are not too traumatic, but the extent of their pervasiveness does indicate the amount of effort the new principal will have to expend in coping with symbolic identification. Symbol and image of leadership are at least as important as actual performance and behavior.[1] Think of what the words *charisma* or *good morale* imply. Obviously, there is an important performance aspect, but symbolic identification is a critical component of both phenomena. The new principal must identify and deal with symbolic identity in taking charge. Some of the reasons for image are obvious and can be easily identified. How was the process of hiring conducted? Did those in the local school gain the impression the process was fixed, or a setup for a particular candidate? What is the image of the experience of administrator vis-à-vis his or her record of past performance? The obvious reasons for symbolic judgment should be dealt with openly and directly. Until the issues are clarified there is a risk that symbol will contrast with or outweigh the individual's initial efforts to perform as a principal.

Indirect reasons for symbolic identification are harder to detect and deal with. The next two subsections assess why people make indirect image judgments, and who the principal might identify as the source of such judgments.

THE SYMBOLIC IDENTIFICATION

Klapp presents an interesting typology of social roles[2] that are the basis of symbolic judgments. He identifies types that people associate with the words *hero, villain,* and *fool.* Beyond the general characteristics that may be used in the symbolic identification of a person, Klapp points out how a general sympathy of a particular environment can heighten the distinction between what is considered the hero versus the villain and the fool.

There are five subcategories of hero: the winner, the splendid performer, the socially acceptable person, the independent spirit, and the group servant. Klapp cautions that it is a very fine line between the image of hero in each of these five categories and being perceived as villain or fool for the same characteristics. For example, the winner hero is competitive, self-assertive, invidious, and oligarchic. It is a role of power, but the abuse of power in winning makes the individual a villain, while the pretense of power makes an individual a fool. In poker, the winner is admired if he or she does not "rub it in" or boast without actually performing. Intellect is valued in winning if tied to practical results and/or outsmarting others in a bad situation. On the other hand, intellect that identifies an individual with abstract dreaming (egghead) is a fool's role and intellect that gains unfair advantage is a villain. In sum, people identify winners with power that also carries the impression of fairness and being humble.

People also identify positively with splendid performances. The crucial aspect of this symbol is performance before an audience. People admire a person who can succeed in spite of adversity. Again, being the villain or fool is a small step away. The showoff is not admired. The critical distinction is performance for others versus the image of self-aggrandizement.

Interestingly, positive images can be created for conformity and social acceptability or for nonconformity and an independent spirit. We like people who have a desire to be accepted and belong but not to excess. The overconformer is an object of contempt, so being liked for the sake of being liked is not enough. Other symbolic values must be evident. The same is true for independence. People admire individualists not so much by their achievements but by their courage to follow their convictions. Yet excess creates the negative image of snob or social deviant. The key distinction of positive, independent action is the image of standing alone on a social frontier where others are interested in being themselves.

Finally, a person can have the winner image as a group servant working for cooperation and solidarity. However, loyalty is a tentative image in this era of post-Watergate skepticism. The crusader, benefactor, or even martyr are often viewed positively if the group judges the servant role as authentic. But it is an especially difficult image to maintain when the individual is in a superordinate position vis-à-vis the group. Many principals have tried to be democratic to increase feelings of solidarity and loyalty only to be judged pseudo-democratic.

Klapp notes two aspects of the villain image. First, under some circumstances people admire a villain. In times of uncertainty and scarcity people are likely to admire the rebel or the troublemaker who challenges established authority, especially if villainous acts are identified with group gains (e.g., Robin Hood).

A second message about villains is the general suspicion that any group has of strangers. A new principal can expect to be considered an intruder. The group fears that the intruder will upset the established practices. This impression can be gradually overcome beginning at the time of entry into the new situation.

There is no viable fool image that can create a positive symbol of the principalship. Fools are in five basic categories; (1) incompetents (clumsy, rash, weak, dumb), (2) people who claim more than they have (the has-been, the small minded, the pompous, the upstart), (3) the extreme nonconformist (the strange or antic fool). (4) the overconformist who suffers comic rebuke because he or she has been too enthusiastic about complying (the yes man, the faddist), and (5) the fanatic (both the leader and follower of the cult).

In summary, a person entering into a new principalship will have to cope with symbolic identifications. Klapp presents three basic types of symbolic image that people identify with leaders; the hero, the villain, and the fool. Obviously, the preferred symbol for the principal is the hero and not the villain or fool. The following list should help in planning strategies to facilitate a positive symbol:

1. The distinction between hero and villain or fool is a thin line, usually defined by excess and whether actions have a group identification.
2. Newcomers can expect some intruder image of the villain role at first.
3. Special circumstances of uncertainty or scarcity may make the villain role of rebel temporarily viable.
4. The hero image is related to five categories: the winner, the splendid performer, the socially acceptable person, the independent spirit, and the group servant.
5. The particular combination of hero categories depends upon the preferences of a particular environment.

THE INDIRECT JUDGES

Another aspect of taking charge is identifying and being able to understand who is doing the judging within the local school. Two general schemes are particularly valuable in the initial identification effort.

In a classic study, Gouldner[3] identified people that he called *locals* and *cosmopolitans* based upon their *loyalty* to the particular environment (in this case, the district and especially, the local school· center). Locals and cosmopolitans break down into six subunits:

1. *The Locals*
   a. *The dedicated.* These people are the true believers who attach much importance to the goals and philosophy of a specific organization. They stress commitment to the institution, rather than to the technical competence of colleagues; they tend to see themselves primarily as members of the faculty and only secondarily as professional specialists; they stress consensus and internal harmony; and they comprise an inner reference group in the organization—the loyal and reliable group.
   b. *The true bureaucrats.* They resist outside control of the institution, and their loyalty is not so much to the ideals of the school as it is to the idea of the school, or the place itself. Sensitive to external criticism, true bureaucrats are willing to make changes in traditional institutions in order to ameliorate it. They do not favor lighter workloads to provide more time for re-

search and writing. Finally, as true bureaucrats, they tend to favor formal regulations.

c. *The homeguard.* These people tend to be second echelon administrators, mostly women. They have the least professional specialization and attend few conventions. They are not committed to the distinctive values of the organization, nor to its community; many of the homeguard in Gouldner's study were people who had graduated from the schools they worked for.

d. *The elders.* These people are the oldest locals and have been with the organization for the longest time. Generally in their fifties or sixties, elders are deeply rooted in the informal organization; they look forward to retirement and tend to evaluate the present situation in the organization in terms of past events they have experienced.

2. *Cosmopolitans*

a. *The outsiders.* They have little involvement in either the formal or informal structure of the organization, little influence in the faculty—and do not want more—and are not likely to stay with the organization permanently. Such cosmopolitans are highly committed, not to the institution, but to their specialized professions. Their outer-reference orientation is expressed in their feelings that they do not get much intellectual stimulation from their colleagues; they read many journals and meet with fellow specialists at meetings and conventions that they often attend in various locations.

b. *The empire builders.* These comospolitans are similar to outsiders but are integrated into the formal structure of the organization (although not into its informal structure). Their affiliation to their department is strong, and they favor strong department autonomy. Like the outsiders, the empire builders feel they can easily find jobs outside the institution; they are economically and professionally independent. They would accept an appointment at an institution with higher professional prestige.

The importance of this identification for the new principal is to recognize underlying bases of loyalty and potential reasons for symbolic conclusions. Locals desire the security and stability of what has been the school's precedent in governance. *Their primary concern is the status quo of the governance system itself.* Their nervousness will be related to the general system of rules, regulations, routines (formal and informal), and standard operating procedures.

On the other hand, cosmopolitan loyalty rests with *the decision markers that are transmitted by the governance system.* They are concerned with the issues that define specific distributions of rewards, payoffs, and sanctions. The environment is important only to the extent that it defines the issues and the opportunities to compete. The new principal should try to identify all members of the local school by this gross classification. (Chapter 3 will discuss the local-cosmopolitan preference that has a major role in the maintenance of control.)

A second scheme that should provide a useful basis for identification is presented by Presthus:[4]

1. *Upward mobiles* generally accept "the system"—its goals and values, its authority and demands. This acceptance is genuine and, which is significant, the upward mobile sees his or her superordinates in a good light—as friendly and sympathetic.

2. *Indifferents*, however, largely ignore the organization and find their satisfactions away from the job. They work to "make a living" (or, often in the case of women, to make a little extra money), but they rarely are involved in the organization more than is necessary.

3. *Ambivalents* are tempted by the attraction of power, authority and the prestige of success that accompany promotion; but they are not organization men, for they value their own individuality and their friendships more than the rewards the organization can offer.

To the degree that the new principal represents the organization and the access to institutional regards, the Presthus scheme represents a second type of loyalty measure. It is important to identify the type and intensity of organizational involvement among the members of the local school.

THE HONEYMOON

A final phenomenon in the initial taking charge period is known as the "honeymoon."[5] This is a period of time when a newcomer has a license to prove himself/herself as the members of the local school adopt a wait-and-see attitude. Caplow[6] suggests that strategies for using the honeymoon period are a function of whether the predecessor was strong or weak and whether the new principal was selected from within or is perceived as an outsider. He suggests that an *insider* following a strong predecessor should make no major changes during the honeymoon, but one following a weak predecessor should introduce sweeping changes to announce a "new day" in governance. For the new principal *from the outside* the best honeymoon strategy following a weak predecessor is to make no major changes but if the predecessor was strong he or she should introduce sweeping changes.

PUTTING THE PIECES TOGETHER

Now the various pieces of assuming a new principalship can be put together in a general strategy for taking charge. Foremost, recognize that the issue of initial acceptance is largely an exercise in symbolism and imagery. Further, most prejudgments are based upon impressions and conjectures about the unknown, *not* personal references. The new principal should expect people in the local school to have initial fears and unfair perceptions of him or her. The inexperienced administrator or the one who has a "bad track record" in another location should expect the process of taking charge to be a process of proving himself or herself by creating an acceptable image of authority.

We emphasize the generalized image of authority as the most important in initial encounters. A principal can be judged hero, villain or fool for a number of reasons (not all justified). Being a hero blends strength with compassion, winning with benefits for others, and intelligence with practical payoffs. In extremely uncertain environments a little dose of rebel villainy may be used as a temporary measure. There is no situation where the fool image is successful.

A basic task of the new principal is to identify other members of the local school environment, particularly those critical to judging and creating the image of governance. Gouldner's classification of local-cosmopolitan gives a rough measure of organizational loyalty and preference for the status quo. Presthus's classification identifies those people who want to be involved and those who (for several reasons) want to be left alone. If the two schemes can classify the people in the local school who are inclined to see the new principal as hero (or villain or fool) and want to be involved, those people have identified their core support (or opposition).

The honeymoon period is a key time in the taking charge period. It is the time for action based upon assessment of needs discussed previously. It is a time when principals can initiate actions and gain commitments from superiors simply because they are establishing themselves. Caplow suggests the dimension of weak or strong predecessors should structure the type of action taken. In many cases, the *same* initiatives can be taken either as the continuation of past practices or as a demonstration of bold new departures. The keys are both in the objectives to be realized and in the mode of presentation.

The specific pieces of information about taking charge can now be related to symbolic themes that the new principal may wish to try to initiate. Two themes that seem promising are the projected images of creativity and positive outlook. The following example presents a rationale and specific steps toward achievement of these images for the interested administrator.

John Gardner has identified a series of acts that can assist a school in renewal and development. The conditions that will allow a school to experience creative and positive growth unhampered are as follows:

1. The organization must have an effective program for the recruitment and development of talent. People are the ultimate source of renewal.
2. The organization must have a hospitable environment for the individual. Organizations that have killed the spark of individuality for their members will have a greatly diminished capacity for change.
3. Organizations must have a built-in provision for self-criticism.
4. Organizations must have a fluid internal system, responsive to the problems of the moment.
5. Organizations must have an adequate system of internal communication.
6. Organizations must have a means of combating rigidity in the form of rules and procedures.
7. Organizations must have a way to combat vested interests.
8. Organizations must be oriented to the future, not what has been.[7]

Note that most of the conditions outlined by Gardner seem antithetical to the conditions for schools that we predicted. While we agree with the desirability of such openness and flexibility, we feel that the achievement of such conditions in the 1980s will be difficult. However, there is no question that such ends will be desired as symbols by those working in educational institutions, and it will be expected that school administrators will work for such conditions. Again, we believe that in the initial stages of taking charge the process of working toward these ends will be more important than the actual achievement of the ends. Understanding how the environmental factors or school climates affect behavior should be an integral part of school administration in the future.

School climates can be defined as the quality of the organizational environment as subjectively perceived or experienced by the organization members. Litwin and Stringer describe climate in the following manner:

> Climate is made up of expectancies and incentives which interact with a variety of psychological needs to produce aroused motivation and behavior directed toward need satisfaction. Climate is assumed to be influenced by a variety of factors such as the physical situation, nature of the activity, needs of the people, group norms, and behavior and leadership of formal and informal leaders.[8]

Through their research at Harvard University, Litwin and Stringer have identified nine variables that are important to the establishment of a climate, variables that can be emphasized and manipulated by the building principal toward the images of creativity and a positive outlook.

1. Structure—the feeling that employees have about the constraints in the group, how many rules and regulations there are.
2. Responsibility—the feeling of being your own boss, not having to double check all decisions.
3. Reward—the feeling of being rewarded for a job well done, emphasizing positive rewards rather than punishments; the perceived fairness of pay and promotion policies.
4. Risk—the challenge in the job, the emphasis on taking risks as opposed to always playing it safe.
5. Warmth—the feeling of good fellowship that prevails in the work atmosphere; the prevalence of informal social groups.
6. Support—the perceived helpfulness of the superiors; emphasis on mutual support from above and below.
7. Standards—the perceived importance of goals and performance expectations.
8. Conflict—the emphasis placed on getting problems out into the open, of hearing different opinions.
9. Identity—the feeling of being a member of a working team.[9]

On the basis of their organizational studies, Litwin and Stringer hypothesized that by emphasizing certain variables in the environment, particular types of motivation and behaviors could be aroused in either individuals or groups. They stated their deductive reasoning in the following manner:

1. Individuals are attracted to climates that arouse their dominant needs.
2. Those climates are made up of incentives and experiences.
3. Climates interact with needs to arouse motivation toward need satisfaction.
4. Climates represent the most powerful lever available to managers in bringing about change in individuals.

Stated another way, symbolic leadership can, through its actions, affect the perceptions and experiences of individuals in an organization. The collective perceptions of leadership behavior form a climate that tends to influence change in the organization.

Litwin and Stringer identified three primary types of motivation that might be encouraged in an organization by varying leadership style: (1) achievement motivation, (2) affiliation motivation, and (3) power motivation. By emphasizing certain of the nine variables, then, a leader might encourage certain types of change and attitudes toward the school. (See Table 2.1.) Although this approach may seem manipulative, the following observation might be made:

> ...the manager will...first, have to sit down and carefully assess the basic needs of his people. Then he will have to stay up nights dreaming of ways to manipulate the tasks, the climate, and *his own leadership style* to satisfy certain of these basic needs in order to generate the desired behavior. In fact, the real question is, who is really being manipulated in this approach? [10]

The authors feel that school principals can approach climate building in a number of ways, any one of which will contribute to image. The approach may be as calculating as that proposed by Litwin and Stringer, or climate building might be approached by developing certain themes of administrative style. Such themes can establish a mind-set in the organization that will begin to unleash the potential of the school and enhance the image of the school leader.

TABLE 2.1   *Relationship of Climate and Motivation Types*

SUMMARY OF HYPOTHESES AND PRELIMINARY EVIDENCE
REGARDING THE RELATIONSHIP OF CLIMATE DIMENSIONS
AND ACHIEVEMENT MOTIVATION

Climate Dimension	Hypothesized Effect on Achievement Motivation	Findings	Hypothesis Support	Revised Hypothesis
Structure	reduction	mixed	moderate	—
Responsibility	arousal	consistent positive	weak-moderate	—
Warmth	no effect	some negative	moderate	—
Support	arousal	positive	moderate	—
Reward	arousal	consistent positive	strong	—
Conflict	arousal	mixed	very weak	—
Standards	arousal	mixed	weak	—
Identity	no effect	negative	none	arousal
Risk	arousal	some positive	weak-moderate	—

SUMMARY OF HYPOTHESES AND PRELIMINARY EVIDENCE
REGARDING THE RELATIONSHIP OF CLIMATE DIMENSIONS
AND AFFILIATION MOTIVATION

Climate Dimension	Hypothesized Effect on Affiliation Motivation	Findings	Hypothesis Support	Revised Hypothesis
Structure	reduction	consistent negative	strong	—
Responsibility	no effect	zero order	strong	—
Warmth	arousal	consistent positive	strong	—
Support	arousal	positive	strong	—
Reward	arousal	consistent positive	strong	—
Conflict	reduction	weak negative	moderate	—
Standards	no effect	some negative	very weak	reduction
Identity	arousal	positive	strong	—
Risk	no effect	some negative	very weak	reduction

SUMMARY OF HYPOTHESES AND PRELIMINARY EVIDENCE
REGARDING THE RELATIONSHIP OF CLIMATE DIMENSIONS
AND POWER MOTIVATION

Climate Dimension	Hypothesized Effect on Power Motivation	Findings	Hypothesis Support	Revised Hypothesis
Structure	arousal	strong positive	very strong	—
Responsibility	arousal	positive	strong	—
Warmth	no effect	weak negative	moderate	—
Support	no effect	weak positive	moderate	—
Reward	no effect	zero order	strong	—
Conflict	arousal	consistent positive	strong	—
Standards	no effect	weak positive	moderate	—
Identity	reduction	weak positive	none	no effect
Risk	no effect	negative	very weak	reduction

Source: George H. Litwin and Robert A. Stringer, Jr., *Motivation and Organizational Climate*, exhibits 5.9, 5.10 and 5.11 (Boston: Division of Research, Graduate School of Business Administration, Harvard University), 1968, pp. 90–91.

Individuals possess undeveloped potential for development, and so do organizations such as schools. Because schools are uniquely human organizations, the real product of education results from the interaction of people. To the degree that individuals in an organization are growing, the school will take on a dynamic quality. Miles refers to this condition as follows:

> Schools turn out to be filled with innovative people (each of whom thinks he is a minority). This feature of social systems has been dubbed pluralistic ignorance.[11]

Whether a school as an organization turns out to be a growing and developing place does not have to be an accident. Collectively, people who work in a school possess the power to control their environment through the visions they have and through their ability to pursue desired alternatives.

The building principal is the key to whether people in the school regard their roles as jobs or whether they see the school as a place where their needs for professional creativity can be met. Professional inservice, for example, is an area where many teachers feel that the experience is less than enhancing. The meaning of the experience is determined by how it is approached. As Jackson observes:

> The first of two perspectives from which the business of inservice training might be viewed is found in the notion of repair and remediation. For this reason I have chosen to call it the "defect" point of view. It begins with the assumption that something is wrong with the way practicing teachers now operate and the purpose of inservice training is to set them straight—to repair the defect—so to speak. The second approach, the "growth" approach, begins with the assumption that teaching is a complex and multi-faceted activity about which there is more to know than can ever be known by one person. From this point of view, the motive for learning more about teaching is not to repair a personal inadequacy as a teacher but to seek greater fulfillment as a practitioner of the art. The central goal of inservice from the growth perspective: to help teachers become progressively more sensitive to what is happening in the classroom and to support their efforts to improve on what they are doing.[12]

The building principal needs to believe in the potential of his or her staff. There should be an expectation that any staff member can make a creative contribution to the program if given proper support. The creativity of members of the organization should be seen as coming in many forms, not simply as a demonstration of good teaching or the development of a highly visible product:

Creativity has long been regarded as a special endowment bestowed on a chosen few. There has been an aura of the mysterious connected with creativity. The word creative has also been subjected to myriad interpretations. It has often been used to describe the commonplace, the ordinary, the usual. Traditionally, creativity has been associated with products—paintings, inventions, literary masterpieces, music. Tangible evidence was the criterion—something to hold, to see, or to hear. Not too much thought was given to the process. We still search for and encourage the tangible, but the concept of creativity has been enlarged to include ideas, decisions, relationships, problem solving—results of man's cognitive powers. The product, whatever form it may take, would not evolve without the process. The growing realization of the universality of creativity, of man's heretofore unsuspected capacity for creativeness, places the idea of creativity in a new perspective.[13]

The building principal must seek ways to release the collective potential of his or her staff; the establishment of a climate appears to be a promising route. If the principal is successful in establishing themes of leadership, themes that may draw out the talents of the staff, the image of the principal will be enhanced. Even under the constraints already outlined as probable in the 1980s, the principal can establish and posture such themes through his or her personal behavior. The following two strategies with prescriptive behaviors show strong promise for establishing the symbol of a creative climate within the school.

A Supporter of Creativity

Most teachers fail to exhibit creativity on the job because either their initial displays of creative work go unnoticed or there isn't a system to follow through on creative activities. Principals can get into the creativity role and make the development of human talent a legitimate concern by starting activities such as the following.

- Developing an incentive program for "better ideas" in operating the school. Such rewards could be small token money awards, release time, or special training opportunities. All awards should be highly visible, and there should be a school-wide nominating committee to involve as many people as possible in looking for the new ideas.
- Dissemination of a special newsletter that highlights innovative techniques and practices in the district.
- The organization of an ad hoc committee of teachers and other personnel whose sole job is to study problems and make policy recommendations to the principal. The committee should be open to

anyone who wishes to serve, deal with only one problem at a time, and be regenerated each time a new pressing problem comes to the attention of the principal.

- Initiating a league of schools in the district or across the district boundaries. Schools in the league would sponsor teacher exchanges, joint inservice programs, collective textbook evaluations, and other information exchanges worthy of dissemination.
- Sponsoring pilot programs to demonstrate or test novel concepts in instruction, evaluation, communication with parents, or other areas of interest.
- A program of idea bombardment where the principal routinely routes suggested practices to teachers in the school. Such suggestions could be reinforced by periodic, but not regularly scheduled, brainstorming lunch sessions.

AN ACCENT ON THE POSITIVE

Events of the past five years in public schools have caused many classroom teachers to shift their perception of what they do each day from that of a profession to that of a job. Many social forces have acted to reduce the autonomy of the classroom teacher and regulate instructional interaction. The result of these events has been to reduce the amount of introspection among teachers about what is happening in their classrooms. Their interest and enthusiasm about school operations have been reduced. The intrinsic rewards of the profession have been diminished. Administrators, and no one but administrators, can reduce this trend by their behavior. Through regularly planned activities that highlight the positive aspects of teaching, they can give hope and stimulation to individuals within the organization.

- Regularly summarizing positive achievements in the school through a personal letter to teachers, parents, or students.
- Sponsoring inservice opportunities for teachers that feature enthusiastic people who are having successful experiences in implementing programs.
- Developing a "Dear Abby" type of response mechanism to connect the classroom teacher to the district office where policy is determined. This format should specialize in solving small but important personal problems otherwise lost in the bureaucratic shuffle.
- Annually sponsor a conference on the future of something, bringing new ideas and hopes to all educational personnel.

These themes are not intended to be exclusive but to suggest the types of things an administrator can do to establish the symbolic image of a creative climate in the school. The particular theme an individual administrator chooses should be one that he or she can be comfortable with. The hoped for result of such administrative activity is not the complete renewal of the particular school in which the administrator works. Conditions in the 1980s will make such a situation difficult, if not impossible. Rather, the goal of such activity is to *project* an image that this principal is alive and competent and to allow teachers in the building to project that same image to others in the district.

If a well-thought-out symbolic impression is established during the taking charge phase of becoming a principal, many of the issues of maintaining control over time will be lessened.

NOTES

1. See Erving Goffman, *Relations in Public* (New York: Basic Books, 1971), especially pp. 62–94 on supportive interchanges. Also Murray Edleman, *Symbolic Uses of Politics* (Urbana: University of Illinois Press, 1967).
2. Orin Klapp, *Heroes, Villains and Fools* (Englewood Cliffs, N.J.: Prentice-Hall, 1962).
3. Alvin Gouldner, "Cosmopolitans and Locals: Toward an Analysis of Latent Social Roles," *Administrative Science Quarterly* 2, 3 (December 1957): pp. 281–306; 2, 4 (March 1958): 440–480.
4. Robert Presthus, *The Organizational Society: An Analysis and a Theory* (New York: Alfred A. Knopf, 1962), pp. 164–202.
5. Thomas Jefferson is supposed to have written the following while contemplating the presidency, "the honeymoon would be short.... and its moment of ecstasy would be ransomed by years of torment...."
6. Theodore Caplow, *How to Run Any Organization* (Hinsdale, Ill.: Dryden Press, 1976), pp. 14–16.
7. John W. Gardner, "How to Prevent Organizational Dryrot," in *Managing People at Work,* ed. Dale S. Beach (New York: Macmillan, 1971) pp. 12–13.
8. George H. Litwin and Robert A. Stringer, *Motivation and Organizational Climate* (Boston: Division of Research, Harvard University, 1968), p. 110. Reprinted by permission.
9. Ibid., pp. 81–82. Reprinted by permission.
10. Ibid. Abstract of work (Boston: Division of Research, Harvard Business School).
11. Matthew B. Miles, *The Development of Innovative Climates in Educational Organizations,* ERIC 030 971 16.
12. Phillip W. Jackson, "Old Dogs and New Tricks," in *Improving Inservice Education: Proposals and Procedures for Change,* ed. Louis Rubin (Boston: Allyn and Bacon, 1971) pp. 21, 26.
13. Arthur W. Combs, ed., *Perceiving, Behaving, Becoming,* 1962 Yearbook of the Association for Supervision and Curriculum Development, (Washington, ASCD, 1962) p. 142.

CHAPTER 3

Maintaining Control

Chapter 2 concerned the dynamics of initial acceptance and, consequently, strategies that emphasized the symbol or image of the principal to the local school This chapter assumes the principal has successfully breached the problems of initial acceptance, is taking charge, and has identified the members of his or her local school center in a rough but effective fashion. At the minimum, the principal should know which people are oriented to replicating the past and which people are looking for a new day. More important, the principal should know who are looking for symbolic leadership and who want the "evidence" of actual decision behaviors. Finally, the principal should have a rough inclination of people's attitudes toward his or her administration, whether those attitudes are positive, neutral (a "wait and see" posture) or negative. In most cases, the principal will not know his or her own specific reasons for a general impression during the take-charge period. The principal must trust his or her "sense" of a particular individual or group and be ready to recalculate as new information becomes available.

At the bottom line, the new information should be a function of the actual processes and products of decision making. Only through running a local school will the principal be able to make political judgments about members of the school and maintain control over time. Few people can maintain a positive image in the face of negative actions. For example, remember the distinctions raised about Richard Nixon, the President *versus* Richard Nixon who occupied the Office of the Presidency. Ultimately the principal's actual decision actions, not symbols, will be the basis for how people respond to his or her leadership attempts. The political scientist, Friedrich,[1] discusses the "law of anticipated reaction" regarding how a decider will structure his or her action on the basis of what might happen when those affected by decisions do not comply. Schools with self-contained classrooms offer a vivid example of the type of environment where Friedrich's "law" must be taken into account. If the teacher can close the door and ignore the mandate, the principal's real control is a papier maché fantasy.

For strategy planning the principal needs four critical pieces of information to operate successfully; he or she must calculate (1) the resources available, (2) the basic power structure(s), (3) the natural dynamics of large and complex organizations, and (4) the extent to which stability and certainty are valued in making decisions.[2]

RESOURCES AVAILABLE

Many of the educational decisions of the 1980s will be restricted by the lack of crucial resources. It is imperative that a principal understand the general condition of availability[3] for his or her local school and any special limits that are part of major policy determinations.

Dahl[4] defines resources as anything that might be used to sway the choices of others. Money, expertise, formal positions, rhetorical ability, friendships, and ideological commitment are some obvious examples. The principal must identify critical resources in conflict situations. In general, the more extreme the actual or perceived shortage of a resource the more intense the conflict.

The political interpretation of the principalship assumes competition for scarce resources and that unlimited resources are not found in real choice situations. However, there are three times when *the impression of unlimited resources* can influence a decision situation. If a particular decision context allows (1) no declaration of concrete features, or (2) declarations of faith, or (3) a priori presentation of certain unquestioned givens, the image of unlimited resources may occur. An example of no concrete features may be discussions of education being "good for all." A faith type of example might be a declaration of "all children are capable learners." An example of a priori "givens" might be, "we've always had so and so in the past and it would be unthinkable to have a local school without so and so." The commonality of the three examples is the lack of any grounds for testing the assumptions. To the extent *resources* are discussed as a decision *property*[5] in this manner, the principal may find the concept of unlimited resources. *The principal may find it useful, from a symbolic perspective, to discuss unlimited resources (along with "tomorrow will be a brighter day"), but strategy planning should focus upon identifying the actual, limited resources.*

Limited resources can be described on a continuum from abundance to nonexistence with six major intervals. First, in the 1980s conditions, expanding resources or even the stability of status quo may well be seen as abundance. These conditions of availability seem more accurate as descriptions of the Great Society "feast" days of the late 1960s. Unfortunately, current administrative theory and thinking about school organization is still dominated by assumptions of abundance. This view has some dangerous outgrowths. For example, it is one thing to resolve a conflict or diversify a curriculum by adding more resources to an existing base of allocation, and quite another to redistribute a shrinking amount.

Another condition of resource availability occurs when the decision system *first* copes with shortage and a slight diminishing of critical resources. In the usual reaction to this condition people try to improve the organizational efficiency of how resources are allocated. In the extreme, the stretching of efficiency in processes for allocating may subvert the initial goals of the school. The luxury of asking *why* we are doing things in a certain way may be lost in a growing preoccupation with *how* things are done.

The condition of "make do by doing it better" is often followed by scarcity due to drastic curtailment. This situation dominated many school systems in the late 1970s. Further, the paradox of drastic curtailment can affect both the supply and the demand for resources. In some cases, the numbers of students available represented drastic curtailment and problems of *too many* empty classrooms and teacher *oversupply*. At the same time, certain curricular programs and extracurricular activities were severely curtailed for costs or lack of demand. Drastic curtailments raise fundamental questions of "who is to survive" and a sharpening of conflict between "haves" and "have nots" for control of *basic* allocations. Conflict over the distribution of resources based upon the *margin*[6] may change (of allocating five or ten percent of the unaccounted for resources) to fights to be included in what is to be considered *basic* or the *core* of essential allocations for the local school or school system.[7]

Another condition of resources is temporary unavailability. "Temporary" may represent a day, a month, or a year but it is a period of time when the school is to operate without certain resources. In this condition, the expectations of regaining lost resources are present. From an administrative standpoint, the expectation of regaining lost resources is coupled with a growing skepticism of management techniques and rational planning as guides to the school center decision processes. There is a growing feeling that management and planning *per se* will not "guarantee an adequate supply of honest business people, noble legislators, true patriots or humanists on one hand nor enough electricity, new housing or food on the other."[8] This realization usually generates heated debate of whether the "cause" of failure in governance is an issue of technical and institutional capacity ("we put men on the moon so *if* we shift priorities...") or professionalism and morality (we can't just *forget* the disadvantaged child...").[9]

Another important implication for management under conditions of temporary unavailability in decision making is the direct challenge posed to conventional meanings of economic efficiency and production.[10] One challenge is to the assumptions of growth and "bigger means better." Efficiency measures begin to consider both economics and *diseconomies* of scale (i.e., when growth itself or even "steady state" are *costs*). Related to the challenge of growth is the increasing policy orientation toward "small is beautiful" [11] for those decisions involving known *finite* ("when the supply is gone that's all") resources.

What these three implications mean for decision making in many local schools is that the poker game is becoming an uncertain and volatile process. Much of the decision focus is on the parameters of making choices (the rules) and *not* on the issue of availability itself. There is still an expectation of regaining what was lost but the decision making is also becoming a shooting gallery for many conventional meanings of administration, planning, efficiency, and production. A major focus of the following chapters is on the politics of decision making in conditions of drastic curtailment and temporary unavailability.

Where temporary unavailability holds the hope that shortages ultimately will be alleviated, the sixth and final condition assumes no future resources. Most citizens of the United States do not know this condition as a continual way of life and can only speculate upon its impact to the public schools as institutions and the administrators within local school centers. Where the condition of temporary unavailability is likely for many school jurisdictions during the 1980s, permanent loss of what are now considered critical schooling resources is beyond the scope of this text. Certainly the essential assumptions of organizational decision making and role of educational administrator would be transformed. For example, no students could mean no *compulsory* institution called schools. No fiscal aid to schools could mean no professional employment structure called public school teachers. It is not our purpose to discuss school governance under the voucher type of client choice or whether learning networks[12] could be operated in real life. We do, however, note the Malthus-like implications to decision making that are inherent in the sixth condition of resource availability.

In summary, an absolutely essential part of maintaining control in a local school is knowledge of resource availability. The principal in control must identify the critical resources for his or her school environment. Second, the extent that resources are considered unlimited must be considered for possible symbolic identification with the administrator role. Finally, the general condition of availability must be calculated and future control strategies must take the present (and projected future) situation into account.

THE POWER STRUCTURE

Power structure is a term that has been popular for several decades and is usually associated with attempts to describe the community or external environment of the local school. Through the decades there have been heated debates about the concepts assumed for the meaning of power, the methods used to identify the structures of power, and the findings in particular communities.[13] Several general conclusions can be drawn from the debate. First, there is no single configuration of power, so a certain structure must be identified within a particular environment. Second, power is stratified so there are pyramids of influence but this does not automatically mean a single and/or pervasive pyramid. Third, personal power in decision making is probably a combination of an individual's general reputation and specific actions of participation. Finally, power may either be general to a stable pattern or specific to the resolution of particular issues.

A principal can borrow from the classification of community power structures to gain a rough measure of the members of the school community. Table 3.1 is adapted from a typology development by Kimbrough.[14]

While it is dangerous to stereotype, *a monopolistic elite* situation probably reflects a large percent of Gouldner's locals described earlier. Further, they are probably a "pure" variety such as all being homeguards or elders. This situation is rare today (e.g., small, rural elementary schools) but may become more prevalent if the expected retrenchment of the 1980s causes faculties to "age in place." The *multigroup noncompetitive* situation might also be a school environment composed of locals but with two distinct subgroups, such as the homeguard and the true bureaucrats. These subgroups share the same general perception about "our school" but differ in specific interpretations, such as how the principal should govern.

A *competitive elite* situation is stable enough to identify various subgroups of power, but the groupings are characterized by degrees of antagonism toward each other. This might be a situation where there is a cluster of locals and a cluster of cosmopolitans in the faculty. Despite lots of rhetoric about being professionals and being concerned for the children (both probably true), the subgroups will be in sharp disagreement and will struggle for dominance in power situations.

Finally, the *segmented pluralism* situation is so unsettled by competition that stable subgroups have not formed. The particulars of the issue under consideration dominates the configurations of power among various school personnel.

Obviously, each of the power structure situations defines the arena for deciding, the role of various players, the type of competition, and the strategy of the principal differently. The meaning of *good strategy* is contingent upon appropriate identification and adapting to the particular mix of a situation.

TABLE 3.1 *Types of Power Structures*

Monopolistic Elite	*Multigroup Noncompetitive*	*Competitive Elite*	*Segmented Pluralism*
1. Single pyramid of pervasive power	1. Two or more pyramids which share power	1. Two or more pyramids in competition for power	1. No stable pyramids of power
2. Issues contained, 80–100% overlap	2. Minor issue competition, 70–80% overlap	2. Major competition on issues, 50% or less overlap	2. Issues determine power arrangements, no overlap
3. Communication up and down within group	3. Communication to guarantee consensus	3. Communication with satellites, little with competitors	3. Little communication, function of issue

LARGE COMPLEX ORGANIZATIONS

Principals who administer large local schools or work in mammoth school systems should also take into account some natural laws of deciding in large, complex organizations. Cyert and March[15] identify four conditions of a decision process they call bureaucratic bargaining. First, that conflict is not resolved completely or rationally. For example, a quasi resolution of conflict is accomplished by subdividing a school-wide issue into subparts, not for rational consideration at all levels of the organization but, *to avoid the conflict of a centralized decision.* The impact of deciding by subunits is that the process of choice becomes sequential with no simultaneous consideration of objectives or needs. Each of the parts is decided separately without overall comparisons or coordination.

A second characteristic of bureaucratic bargaining is to avoid uncertainty. This avoidance may be achieved by the use of rules, regulations, and standardized operating procedures that promote stability, regardless of whether they make sense for a particular decision process (the Catch 22 phenomenon). A modification of uncertainty avoidance is to use the assumption of base allocation to fix the type and extent of decision-making possibilities. Many school budgets *start* with given restraints that limit change to less than 5 percent of the total allocation.

A third condition of deciding in a large organization is called problemistic search. The best decision is the one that will *first* satisfy a particular need or stress. The actual dynamics of choice are short-run, immediate resolutions of present problems, not long-range considerations of the local school's future.

The final condition, known as *organizational learning,* relates to how changes are made. The basic rule is that all new or different allocations will be resisted until existing patterns are satisfied. For example, people will react to an anticipated school-wide cut by first trying to maintain the relative positions of the existing have and have nots. If this fails they will focus cuts in areas that lack a long school history or cannot demonstrate immediate, tangible returns.[16]

It is especially important for principals in large schools to identify the extent to which these natural laws guide school decision practices. In a complex bureaucracy, the conditions may have become so ingrained as a way of decision life that the players react automatically. While difficult to deal with, knowledge of this automatic reaction among players is imperative for strategy planning. There are ways to overcome such a bureaucratic stance but they are different from a strategy of rational convincing or an attempt to persuade by personal appeal. A player governed by the natural laws is part of the structure of the institution and *not* a political decider within an issue-oriented arena. The principal must identify those individuals who have the marching orders of the bureaucracy.

DYNAMICS OF THE ARENA

Between the lines of the above discussion is the basic issue of strategy planning when organizational conditions are stable and planning when they are not. In order to maintain control the principal must know about and set strategies to cope with differences in the availability of resources, the power structure of local school members, and the natural laws of bureaucratic decision making. The decision arena itself and the meaning of good play by the principal depend upon these understandings. *Bluntly, what works in a stable situation may be the opposite of what works in an unstable situation.* A principal is most likely to find a stable arena when resources are abundant, when the power structure is a single pyramid of influence, and where natural decision laws of the bureaucracy are a way of life. At the other end of the continuum, the most unstable arena would be where there is a famine of available resources, where the power structure shifts with the issue and has no other ongoing stability, and where each of the natural laws of bureaucratic choice has been challenged openly. It is doubtful if many principals will encounter the extremes of stability or instability, but the tendencies either way will be found in all local schools.

There are concurrent, identifying characteristics of stability and instability that are part of the actual dynamics of choice within the arena.[17]

The Stable Arena

In a stable arena, the players normally act as representatives of their particular interest groups rather than as independent individuals. This means that their decision-making activities take into account those with whom they associate in a political manner. Obviously, the representation of players does not have to follow formal expectations of the local school structure. For example, a department chairperson in a large high school may be a member of a critical decision arena because of the institutional position, but politically represent the interests of the homeguard or old timers.

In a stable arena, a player's representation tends to be conservative, based upon parochial priorities and perceptions. The primary message for the principal is that decision actions are guided by the protection of political interest, not by classic interpretations of personal reason or rationality. The dynamic of the pecking order and the relative relationship of haves and have nots explains the conglomerate arrangement of the stable arena. Rewards, sanctions, rules, and regulations promote the stable political arrangement. The ultimate concern of most players is the health of their interest within the organization through control of resources that affect budget, manpower, and territory. Conflict is usually found in decision areas where "boundaries are uncertain, control is ambiguous and changing or issues constitute new territories. In these instances, decision making is dominated by colonizing activity." [18]

Finally, player concern in a stable arena is more oriented to control or implementation of resources than the formulation of new policies or generation of new ideas. As one veteran of political wars put it, "you be the idea man all you want. Define the problem, list alternatives and make decisions. If I control implementation and evaluation, I control the arena." [19]

In a stable arena, the safest bet for a principal wanting to succeed is to go with the winners and not rock the boat. As noted earlier, stability is the criterion for success in this type of arena. The principal may emphasize institutional rules or may emphasize interpersonal, human contact but the bottom line for judging success is stability. Change must be a slow, measured, incremental process where the principal has power figures in the arena discover and own[20] the new directions.

The Unstable Arena

At the other end of the continuum players often act as individuals rather than representatives. Coalitions guide the process of deciding, but these are formed as a result of arena interactions and the issue at stake rather than the result of instructed delegates. The unstable arena emphasizes the decision behavior of players as they compete. The pulling and hauling of the fight often determine the outcome. Over time, better fighters emerge as chiefs and lesser players become Indians.[21] To participate in an unstable arena the principal must understand action, for the arena itself is the result of the bargaining process. Further, *action must be distinguished from intention*. An unstable arena is rife with posturing and false signals from actor behavior. The principal must understand that a smile can mean either a friend or a shark.

The unstable arena is understood as *a game of participation* among central players.

> Games proceed neither at random nor at leisure. Regular channels structure the game's deadlines, force issues to the attention of incredibly busy players. The moves, sequences of moves, and games of "chess" are thus to be explained in terms of the bargaining among players with separate and unequal power over particular pieces, and with separable objectives in distinguishable subgames....[22]

The principal in an unstable arena must cope with the particular rules, pace, structure, and rewards of the game. Rules may stem from formal constraints, conventions, or even culture. They sanction some behaviors (e.g., persuasion, deceit, bluff, threat) while making others inappropriate (or illegal or immoral). The critical ingredient of rules is that *the players themselves define what is appropriate and the rules are particular to the game in question.*

The game is also governed by the pace of play. A major dynamic is to get each other's attention, which varies time in play. The structure of the game usually describes what is meant by a *binding choice.* It may be majority rule; it may be unanimous consensus or something else. When the structure is not clearly specified, two general phenomena occur: the persons who hesitate lose their chance to participate at a point in the process. Second, the persons who are uncertain are overpowered by those who are sure.[23]

Finally, the reward of the game is judged both in immediate wins and losses (payoffs and costs) and in personal obligations incurred to win or attempt to win (long- and short-run costs).

There is no sure formula for "success" by any player in a unstable arena. Coalitions shift issue to issue and those who were chiefs often become Indians (or are eliminated from the arena entirely). In general, the Golden Rule (Do unto others as you would have them do unto you) makes both political and ethical sense. The unstable arena almost guarantees that the others will have their chance and that every player is known, foremost, by his or her track record and style.

A FURTHER WORD ON INSTABILITY

Because this text emphasizes school administration in unstable situations, some further words about control are needed. The basic unit of deciding in coalitions is the triad. There is a systematic tendency for three individuals (or groups of political interest) to split into a combination of two against one. This combination is called a coalition. Although there are eight basic patterns of triads in social groups,[24] three types are most applicable to bargaining in an unstable arena. Figure 3.1 illustrates three types of coalitions in which a principal (and his or her allies) might find himself (themselves). Notice that there is always a hierarchy of power, but the principal is not automatically at the apex.

To maintain control, a principal must bargain to prevent a rebellious coalition. Simmel[25] argues that two equal subordinates are dangerous because they invite the formation of a coalition that replaces the relative strength of the principal with relative weakness. The answer (assuming a principal has won enough in the arena) is for other players to always see each other as slightly unequal. A second strategy is to promote the voluntary A and C relation (C being the weaker of B and C). If C judges that

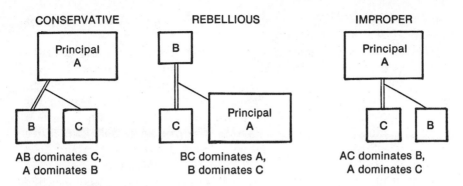

FIGURE 3.1   *Three Member Coalitions*

the rebellious coalition only means replacing *A* as controller with *B*, then *C* may choose voluntarily to stay with the principal (*A*). However, if the option is available and cost acceptable, research indicates that the principal (*A*) should try to form a coalition with the stronger *B*. The *AC* coalition is called improper because it creates an ambiguous relationship between *B* and *C*. Ambiguity and uncertainty between two subordinate players is preferable only if a conservative (*AB*) coalition cannot be formed. The conservative coalition shifts the power dynamics to a one-on-one situation between the principal and the next strongest player. The odds for maintaining control are better one on one than the principal versus a potential coalition.

The final guidance for maintaining control in an unstable arena comes from collective bargaining literature. Perry and Wildman[26] distinguish types of bargaining climates that can describe the local school arena. The most dangerous condition is called *crisis bargaining* that occurs where (1) one or more players are insecure or inexperienced or (2) a gross imbalance of power exists from the past decision making. In crisis bargaining players desire a real test of strength to find out who is the most powerful. The orientation is to win all or lose all right now. A principal can do little to alleviate this kind of situation if other players truly wish a war. The best strategy is to counsel against the waste of political energy, stay on the sidelines during the actual fight, and be a major vehicle for saving the face of losers and picking up the pieces afterwards.

A second climate is called *brinksmanship*. It resembles the crisis bargaining situation except for the crucial difference that players do not desire a real fight. For whatever reason, the climate is one of threat and sabre rattling, *but it is posturing*. The principal's strategy is to recognize the adversary spirit ("We don't have to love each other" and "we agree to disagree") but control the process so actual war does not occur by accident. The basic efforts include shifting attention from short-run to long-term expectations and to substitute psychological victories for great transfers of significant resources.

The third climate, called *utility matching*, is the one preferred in an unstable arena. In this situation, all players recognize that one party's gain does not automatically mean an equal loss for another faction, and that any win also incurs some loss. The members calculate their strategy for play as a *ratio*. In a mature arena it is possible for all players to have a larger win side of their respective ratios. The principal's role is to foster an attitude of tough-minded, mutual respect. Players will retain their suspicions and skepticisms as long as shortage and instability exist. However, the utility-matching climate allows the quasi-adversary, competitive spirit to be channeled into constructive decision making.

STRATEGY PLANNING FOR CONTROL

The information already presented is critical to understanding the arena context of the local school. Once the principal has become familiar with these indicators and feels secure with a general description of the school environment, the information must be channeled into a strategy for maintaining control. Several basic strategy decisions must be made that will establish the principal in a particular arena. *In a stable arena* the best strategies for the principal as player are:

1. to align most decision objectives and purposes to general premises rather than specific issues.
2. to express symbolic loyalty to the concept of unlimited resources and to the fortunate condition of resource abundance in presenting choice options. Do not discuss the dismal future of scarcity but rather present the image of security in resource availability.
3. to couch purposes and proposals in terms of the existing standard operating procedures. If the arena has a large number of true bureaucrats the principal should emphasize the *formal* precedents of the organization's rules and regulations. If the arena has many home guard members the principal should emphasize the *informal* precedents of how decisions are made and resources allocated.
4. to form a decision coalition and alliance with the predominant pyramids of power within the school. In the most stable situation there will be a single pyramid of key actors. In the next most stable situation there will be two or more pyramids differentiated by expertise or specialized interests but general agreements about "our school."
5. to expect and compensate for the natural laws of bureaucratic

politics in all decision proposals. The best strategy to adopt is "the mill grinds slowly but exceedingly fine." Specific decision actions include:

    a. divide local school problems among subunits for resolution, and expect existing patterns of allocation to remain.
    b. provide symbolic rationalizations to justify the problematic search and marginal adjustments that characterize school decisions.

6. to carry out a broker or mediator decision role within the arena. The basic assumption is that the local school is now stable and running well. The basic objective is to provide security and avoid uncertainty.
7. to be ever alert for a transformation of arena stability and be ready to provide a new kind of decision leadership if the choice situation becomes unstable.

The seven premises outline the best strategies for maintaining control in a stable local school arena. The principal does not play an indirect or indecisive role but one guided by the stability of the decision environment. The principal's control relation is a function of alignment and mediation.

The above strategies *do not apply* to the principal who is operating in an unstable decision environment. In fact, just the opposite is true for maintaining control. In an unstable situation there is no automatic allegiance or loyalty to the existing organizational arrangements or to the past. People have little optimism for a rosy future. Most important, the power structure of organizational members lacks stability. In an *unstable arena* the best strategies for the principal player are:

1. to align decision objectives and purposes to specific issues of allocation and control.
2. to emphasize that the luxury of resource abundance is gone and that reality means only the consideration of concrete facts about availability. Discuss scarcity and decline as a necessary consideration in most realistic choice situations.
3. to couch purposes and proposals in terms of needs defined by particular issues and payoffs or consequences to individuals within the organization. If the arena has many disaffected and malcontent players, the principal should emphasize the personal consequences of bad play or dirty tricks in the reactions of other members of the arena (*not* just the principal) and that utility matching is the best guide for everyone. If the arena has a large number of cosmopolitans, the principal should emphasize the particulars of the issue, rewards, and sanctions for individual prestige rather than organizational improvement.

4. to form coalitions and alliances by issue and to not get too closely aligned with any single pyramid of power of arena members. The most significant lesson in an unstable arena is that present wins can turn into future losses (the battle is not the war). The present pyramids are in direct competition because none can gain a general, predominant influence. Until stability occurs the principal should align according to the issue and pay the personal price of the image of being inconsistent.

5. to expect that crisis and emergency will negate many of the natural laws of bureaucratic bargaining. The issue context can override procedural precedent and existing patterns of allocation among haves and have nots. The principal will have many opportunities to decide for the organization (in sharp impasse or extreme uncertainty it will be *demanded*) but be careful. *Any* independent action in an unstable arena incurs costs and obligations no matter how successful the particular decision outcome. Specific actions might include:

   a. being reluctant to assume independent decision making. The best times are after denying the crown several times or if the other members demand a Robin Hood.
   b. not going to the same well too often. In either objectives or actions, predictability and regularity are not treasures if they lead to a static position. The unstable arena demands a *dynamic* equilibrium. Remember the distinction between the balance of the person running versus the balance of the person standing still.

6. to carry out a leader role within the arena. The unstable arena creates a natural power vacuum and the principal will be expected to influence that vacuum in some manner. Influencing is a sensitive balancing act with at least as many traps as benefits. The basic assumption is the arena is *in search of some continuity in how to play* or decide and the principal must play *some* role in leading the search. The basic objective is to provide leadership without being sacrificed in the process.

7. be alert for indications of growing stability within the arena. No system can stay in a state of extreme uncertainty or instability for long and survive. Be ready to shift your decision role as the arena changes.

Thus far we have discussed the basic premises of maintaining control in local school situations that have stable and unstable arenas. We have emphasized the critical need for accurate identification of the particular arena in which the principal finds himself or herself. Once an accurate description is obtained the principal should align his or her decision style to the political configurations of the arena. These concepts can be applied to a familiar problem of governance: conducting a meeting.

PRACTICAL PROBLEMS
OF RUNNING A MEETING

Strategy implementation is essential to establishing effective administrative relationships in a school, and the principal's role in fostering such relationships will be judged most closely in conducting formal meetings. For his or her image the principal must work hard to make such meetings successful. The principal must learn the dynamics of formal meetings, be able to identify which people are contributors and detractors, and understand the role of the status leader in conducting such meetings.

Formal meetings, which proceed with decorum, often possess a hidden agenda. The interests, needs, and values of the people in attendance suggest an active social fabric that must be woven together with care if conflict and distraction are to be avoided. The meeting leader has at his or her command a procedural format, usually a modified version of Robert's Rules of Order, which can be used to guide the flow of the meeting. The degree to which the leader allows discussion and decision making to deviate from these procedures is a matter of judgment on the part of the leader. There is a delicate balance in such formal meetings between constrained behavior and the freedom of meaningful interaction.

One of the first things the principal has to learn is to recognize whether a member of the group is making a contribution or detracting from the purpose of the meeting. The following behaviors can be thought of as contributing to the good of the group:

1. A person brings the discussion back to the point.
2. A person seeks clarification of meaning when the ideas expressed are not clear.
3. A person questions and evaluates ideas expressed in an objective manner.
4. A person challenges reasoning when the soundness of the logic is doubtful.
5. A person introduces a new way of thinking about the topic.
6. A person makes a summary of points previously made.
7. A person underscores points of previous agreement or disagreement.
8. A person tries to resolve conflict or differences of opinion.
9. A person introduces facts or relevant information.
10. A person evaluates the progress of the meeting.

By contrast, the principal should be able to spot those participant behaviors that are detrimental to the conduct of the meeting. Roles that can be thought of as nonproductive or distracting are:

1. A person aggressively expresses disapproval of ideas of others.
2. A person attacks the groups or ideas under consideration that have not had a full hearing.
3. A person tries to reintroduce an idea into the discussion after it has already been rejected.
4. A person tries to assert authority by demanding.
5. A person introduces information to the meeting that is obviously irrelevant to the discussion at hand.
6. A person tries to invoke sympathy by a depreciation of self or his or her position.
7. A person uses stereotypes to cover his or her own biases and prejudices.
8. A person attempts to downgrade the importance of the group's role or function.
9. A person tries to interrupt the group process by speaking tangentially or citing unrelated personal experiences.
10. A person seeks to call attention to himself or herself by excessive talking, using extreme ideas, or displaying unusual behavior.

Sensitivity to such roles will often allow the meeting leader to analyze the flow of the discussion and head off potential distractions to the group's progress.

While conducting a meeting, it is not necessary for a principal to restrict his or her role to that of an impartial guide or passive observer of the process. It is possible for the principal to take steps that will encourage greater group productivity and enhance the leader's image as one who is in command. In any meeting there are six ways a principal can assist the group in attaining productivity: (1) presenting the topic for discussion, (2) initiating the discussion, (3) guiding the discussion, (4) controlling the discussion, (5) preventing side-tracking, and (6) summarizing the discussion.

In presenting the topic to be discussed in the meeting, the principal should suggest the importance of the problem, place the general purpose of the discussion before the group, suggest a logical pathway for the discussion to follow, and define any ambiguous terms to remove misunderstanding. Where possible, the principal should relate the current meeting to previous meetings or other handy reference points in the school system.

In initiating the discussion, the leader provides advanced thinking for the group. Major questions to be answered are identified, and relevant facts and statistics are cited. For purposes of illustration, or to establish a way of thinking about the problem, the principal may want to develop a case study. If an area under discussion is controversial, the principal may even misstate a position to provoke a thoughtful discussion.

The leader's job in guiding the discussion involves keeping the discussion on task, assisting the members in expressing themselves by providing feedback through paraphrasing, and providing the transition from one aspect of the discussion to another. As the leader fulfills this role he or she may use direct questions, illustrations, stories, or leading questions to maintain the flow of interaction.

In controlling the discussion the leader is concerned with the pace of progress and the involvement of the participants in the discussion. The techniques that might be used to keep the discussion moving are purposeful negative statements, highlighting contrasts among the positions of the participants, and regularly calling attention to the time remaining for discussion.

The discussion leader in a meeting can prevent side-tracking in a number of ways. The original question or problems can be restated on a regular basis. The leader can secure a statement from a reliable group member to head off the rambler. The leader can request that side issues be postponed until the main issues are settled.

Finally, the leader summarizes the discussion. This involves a judgment as to when it is best to terminate discussion without appearing to cut off meaningful input. Additionally, the leader should review the major points that have been made in the discussion, being careful to include relevant input from all sides.

Three situations in conducting a group discussion in a meeting are troublesome to many new leaders: (1) the periods of dead silence, (2) the overtalkative member, and (3) the silent member. Any of these three situations, if not handled skillfully, can sabotage an otherwise fruitful discussion and make the leader appear not in control.

A most anxiety-laden moment for someone new to leading large group discussions occurs when there is a complete absence of participation from members of the audience. The natural response to this long awkward silence is to speak in order to fill the conversational vacuum. The leader must refrain from such behavior because, to do so, will build in a dependence for similar action in the future. Silence in any discussion can mean that real thinking is occurring; the discussion leader must make this assumption. Another common impulse is to seek out a single member of the group and prod him or her for a contribution. This, too, is a tactical error for the same reason. A more promising route, once the leader has determined that the silence will be unproductive, is to initiate an encouraging remark such as, "There must be some different points of view here." Failing response, the leader should then return to the process of discussing such as, "Let's see if we can discover what is blocking us."

Another situation that can be ruinous to the image of the meeting leader is the overtalkative group member. Such a person, if permitted, will monopolize discussion and produce anxiety among the group members. The leader must stifle the urge to nonplus such a member because while that person is talking the group is sympathetic to the leader's plight. To attack the member is to invite a swing in anxiety toward the leader. The best strategy, under these conditions, is to intervene after a respectable interval with a comment such as "perhaps we can hear from other members of the group." In the event the dominating member still doesn't get the message, the leader can initiate an evaluation of the process and draw attention to the fact that a way must be found to get input from all members.

A final situation that can be awkward for the leader, and the group as a whole, occurs when a member of a small group is regularly silent. Such silence prevents the group from experiencing self-disclosure and moving the discussion to one of the real issues. The leader should recognize the reluctance of some individuals to be put on the spot or speak out publicly, and not spotlight the person with a request for input. Rather, the leader can watch the person for an opportunity to invite participation when the individual signals he or she is ready. The signal may be fidgeting in the seat or the opening of the mouth, or the beginning of a raised hand. If the member is on the verge of speaking, an encouraging glance or nod may be all that is needed.

In cases where the leader becomes convinced that nonparticipation is an indication of boredom or withdrawal on the part of the individual, it may prove useful to confront the person away from other group members with a challenging question. Whether the group member should be forced into the discussion after the above tactics have failed to elicit a response, is a matter of judgment and discretion determined by the situation and objective of the discussion.

Group meeting leaders can use the time between sessions to ask themselves some evaluative questions about the progress of the discussions. Did all members of the group contribute to the discussion? Was the meeting dominated by the discussion of a few individuals? Did members of the group talk primarily to the leader or to other members of the group during the discussion? Was there any evidence of cliques or special interest groups during the meeting? Such questions may suggest new leader strategies at subsequent sessions.

In conducting faculty meetings the principal should be on guard against behaviors that may retard creative thinking due to regulating discussions in nonproductive ways. Among the most common errors in this respect are:

1. an overemphasis on order throughout the discussion
2. stressing too often the need for data or factual information to be used as evidence
3. placing too much emphasis on the history of the organization or the way things were

4. using coercive techniques to insure participation
5. suggesting, in any way, that mistakes are unacceptable

Finally, leaders of discussion groups and meetings must work to become better listeners. Numerous studies have identified poor listening skills as the biggest impediment to personal communication. Nicholas has identified ten steps that can help the principal become a better listener:

1. While listening, concentrate on finding areas of interest that are useful to you.
2. Judge the content of what is said rather than the delivery.
3. Postpone early judgment about what is being said. Such a posture will allow you to remain analytical if you favor what is being said or keep you from being distracted by calculating embarrassing questions should you disagree with the speaker's message.
4. Focus on the central ideas proposed by the speaker. What is the central idea? What are the supporting planks or statements?
5. Remain flexible in listening. Think of various ways to remember what is being said.
6. Work hard at listening. Try to direct all conscious attention on the presentation being made.
7. Resist distractions from the environment by making adjustments or by greater concentration.
8. Exercise your mind by regularly listening to technical expository material that you haven't had experience with.
9. Keep your own mind open to new ideas by being aware of your own biases and limited experiences.
10. Capitalize on thought speed. Since comprehension speed exceeds speaking speed by about 3:1, the listener must work to maintain concentration. This can be done by anticipating what is to be said, by making mental summaries, by weighing speaker evidence, and by listening between the lines.[27]

In summary, the administrative skills exhibited by a school principal contribute to an overall image of competence and actual maintenance of control. The image of the principal can be enhanced if the process skills of the administrator fit the environment in which he or she works. Because the school environment of the 1980s will call for purposeful behavior and predictability, the principal should seek to project an image of stability as well as competence. In this chapter certain process skills have been identified that may contribute to an image of the ability to work with groups in the conduct of meetings. A final perspective on the issue of maintaining control can be gleaned from the following case story on power politics.

CASE STORY: THE SQUABBLE

It took Jack about two weeks as a new principal at the high school to fully contemplate the seriousness of the power problem among the faculty. At first, everyone was so helpful and cooperative that the basic antagonisms between junior and senior faculty were obscured. When a small group of young teachers came to visit, the strength of their message caught Jack by surprise. The honeymoon had been a brief one at the high school.

Speaking without extensive formalities the assembly of young teachers told Jack that they were tired of being abused by the "old heads" at the school. The department structure at the school fully excluded young teachers from participation in decision making, and the existing department heads constantly patronized younger teachers. In Jack, said the young teachers, they saw hope for change in the governance structure. Failing significant action at reformation, however, the young teachers were committed to work for Jack's removal. Eventually, they stated, they'd get a principal who'd move the old teachers out. The visiting group thought that some concrete action should be visible by the first of November at the latest.

Following the visit from the young teachers Jack cancelled his other appointments and gave his full attention to what he knew was his first serious crisis. While acknowledging the power of the young teachers to "make waves," Jack knew from previous experience that the old guard could make significant trouble for a new principal. A balancing act was called for. The problem was to appear stable to the older faculty while satisfying the needs of the younger faculty to share in school governance.

Jack's first move was to bring this concern to the attention of the department heads. Raising the issue of involvement at the monthly department head meeting, Jack was quickly informed that this was not a new problem. The younger faculty had been pushing for a power realignment for two years and, in fact, listening to the young faculty had cost the last principal his position. If Jack was smart, the department heads informed him, he'd leave this issue alone and get on to important things like instructional improvement and basic administration.

As the month of September faded into October, Jack felt less and less able to negotiate an understanding between the two groups. The older teachers refused to share decision making and the younger faculty continued to press for new department heads. Finally, after a particularly bitter squabble over some resources for a class in the social studies department, Jack hit upon an idea. He would retain the existing department structure, but would parallel it with a series of ad hoc advisory groups. The purpose of these ad hoc groups would be to do advanced thinking for the department heads and to recommend, where it existed, a consensus on issues of concern to all faculty.

Outlining his plan to the faculty during the October meeting, Jack could read the suspicion of both young and older faculty in the faces in front of him. He hoped that the response from the older faculty would be that the new principal was sending the young ones on a goose chase that would sap their energies. Jack hoped that the younger faculty would read his actions as the beginning of a power transfer from the old guard to the younger faculty. As it turned out, Jack's hopes were confirmed as neither side raised serious objections to the ideas of ad hoc study groups.

Jack then presented suggestions for several groups: one to look at resource allocation in the school, one on academic standards, one on new directions for the school, and even one on faculty concerns. Obviously, Jack observed, there were many other possible groups. The groups would study a need area and make recommendations for action to the department heads or principal. Upon making such recommendations, the ad hoc committee would disband. These would not be standing committees, said Jack. The meeting ended with Jack passing out a list of possible ad hoc committees with a deadline for faculty responses for participation. Faculty were encouraged to suggest other committees where needed.

As anticipated, the response to Jack's proposal was heavily determined by whether the faculty member was in or out of the formal power structure. Although both young and older faculty served on each of the committees gaining a sufficient response to merit the formation of an ad hoc group, most groups were dominated by younger faculty. Eventually, ad hoc committees were formed and met on the following topics: (1) school resource allocation (2) student concerns (3) academic standards (4) faculty concerns, and (5) new directions for the high school.

The committees themselves proved to be useful communication vehicles within the school. Even though each committee was dominated by younger faculty, minutes of the meetings were distributed to all faculty and word of discussions was spread in the lounge and informally in the halls. A lot of the initial heat of the younger faculty was thrown into study of problems and gathering data for recommendations. Although it was Jack's intention that the ad hoc groups would bring their recommendations to the monthly department heads meeting, in practice a different procedure evolved.

In terms of student concerns and faculty concerns the committees focused on immediate problems rather than global issues. In practice these groups found it easier to go straight to Jack than to wait for the monthly meeting. The department heads really didn't care to address small matters that were basically calling for administrative actions. The department heads did hear the reports of the Academic Standards Committee and the Resource Allocation Committee, but these concerns were interdepartmental and therefore crossed age boundaries. In particular, one debate over grade inflation in the English department did a great deal to destroy what solidarity there was among department heads.

The new directions committee turned out to be the most interesting group of all because it was through this group that the new power alignments manifested themselves. After one year of study, the New Directions for the High School Committee was able to recommend a different administrative arrangement for the school, which cleared the ad hoc committee in proposal form. Taking a small risk, Jack moved the proposal directly to the general faculty meeting for vote. Being split, the department heads failed to question this obvious usurpation of their previous power.

Case Questions

1. In this case Jack employed several techniques of bureaucratic bargaining. Identify which techniques were used and how they were introduced.
2. How did Jack's ad hoc committee structure affect coalition formation within the faculty?
3. Should Jack have adopted a different decision style in dealing with this situation?
4. If you were a member of this faculty, what moves would you have made in response to those Jack initiated?

NOTES

1. Carl Friedrich, *Man and His Government* (New York: Free Press, 1963). Also see Peter Bachrach and Morton Baratz, "Decisions and Nondecisions," *American Political Science Review* 157 (September 1963): 631–642.
2. See Daniel Lortie, "The Balance of Control and Autonomy in Elementary School Teaching," in *The Semi-Professions*, ed. Amitai Etzioni (New York: Free Press, 1969).
3. David Wiles, "Resource Availability and Policy in Education," *Educational Forum* 39, no. 3, (March 1975): 295–300.
4. Robert Dahl, *Who Governs?* (New Haven: Yale University Press, 1961).
5. Borrowed from Allan Barton's concept of data reduction. See "The Concept of Property Space in Social Research" in *The Language of Social Research*, ed. Paul Lazarsfeld and Morris Rosenberg (New York: Free Press, 1955), pp. 40–53.
6. Term associated with economics but also with a famous article on bureaucratic decision making. See Charles Lindblom, "The Science of Muddling Through," *Public Administration Review* 19 (Spring 1959): 79–88.
7. Often with a fundamental shift from initial allocative decisions of new resources to reallocative decisions of existing resources. See E. E. Schattschneider, *The Semi-Sovereign People* (New York: Holt, Rinehart and Winston, 1960).
8. Wiles, "Resource Availability," p. 298.

9. Ibid. Also see Michael Katz's discussion of types of liberal reformers. See Michael Katz, *Class, Bureaucracy and Schools* (New York: Praeger, 1971).
10. Wiles, "Resource Availability," p. 303.
11. E. M. Schumacher, *Small is Beautiful* (New York: Harper & Row, 1973).
12. See Ivan Illich, "Outwitting the 'Developed' Countries," *New York Review of Books* 13 (June 1972): 20–24.
13. For reviews of the debates see John Walton, "Substance and Artifact: The Current Status of Research on Community Power Structure," *American Journal of Sociology* 71 (Spring 1966): 430–438; Willis Hawley and Fred Wirt, eds., *The Search for Community Power* (Englewood Cliffs, N.J.: Prentice-Hall, 1968).
14. Ralph B. Kimbrough, *Political Power and Educational Decision-Making* (Chicago: Rand McNally, 1964), pp. 83–106.
15. Richard M. Cyert and James G. March, *A Behavioral Theory of the Firm* (Englewood Cliffs, N.J.: Prentice-Hall, 1963), pp. 117–125.
16. Anthony Downs, *Inside Bureaucracy* (Boston: Little, Brown, 1967); and Michael Crosier, *The Bureaucratic Phenomenon* (Chicago: University of Chicago Press, 1964).
17. The basic characteristics of the stable arena are essentially the same descriptors as the Model II paradigm presented by Graham Allison. The unstable arena is described roughly analogous to Allison's Model III. See Graham Allison, *The Essence of Decision* (Boston: Little, Brown, 1971).
18. Ibid., p. 94.
19. Personal interview with big city principal, December, 1978.
20. For "ownership" see Peter Blau, *Exchange and Power in Social Life* (New York: Wiley, 1964).
21. Allison, *The Essence of Decision*, p. 176.
22. Ibid., pp. 162–164.
23. Called the 51–49 principle, meaning the undecided will go along with the majority in a close call.
24. Theodore Caplow, *Two Against One: Coalitions in Triads* (Englewood Cliffs, N.J.: Prentice-Hall, 1968).
25. Georg Simmel, *The Sociology of George Simmel*, trans. Kurt Wolff (Glencoe: Free Press, 1950).
26. Charles Perry and Wesley Wildman, *The Impact of Negotiations in Public Education* (Washington: Charles Jones, 1971).
27. Ralph Nicholas, "Listening as a 10-Part Skill," *Nation's Business* 36 (September, 1975).

CHAPTER 4

Making Changes

For many years school administrators have been counseled to exert leadership and move their school environment in a positive direction. Many administrators have translated these exhortations as a mandate to make changes. The concept of planned change has been muddied by the halcyon days of the 1960s that fostered beliefs that successful change was primarily a function of clarity of purpose and effort expended. Further, that change meant doing something *new*. Today, administrators recognize that systematic change does not occur in automatic conformance to the 1960 assumptions. For example, it is entirely possible that the change effort that has crystal clear objectives will flounder alongside the change effort that has a mushy set of expected outcomes. It is possible that individuals can "sweat blood" to make changes occur and still fail. Finally, change itself often means refinement of existing practices rather than the creation of some new product. We can only speculate why educators were so prone to believe in the 1960s interpretation of planned change. Perhaps the resources that guide competition (and publicizing of educational change effort) emphasized the rules of rational planning and creating something new. In any case, the results of evaluating 1960 change efforts for success are sobering and destroyed many of the ideological assumptions. In the 1970s (and 1980s) *making changes* has undertaken new meanings for who, how, what, when, and where the phenomenon occurs. Rational planning processes have been replaced by political practices. Creating something new has been transformed into refining something already in place. The fundamental shifts of meaning about change in this decade *do not* negate the proactive role of principal as a change agent. The concept of making changes still relates to moving the school organization in a specified direction in a purposive manner. The decision role still involves allocating and reallocating critical resources to give hoped for change the best chance of occurring. What has changed (for the best) are some of the overblown assumptions that a particular action will lead to a certain outcome. Administrators are less pretentious about how people become convinced to change or what is a winner strategy from a planning perspective. In a perverse way, the famine of the 1970s saved educators by crashing abstract prescriptions against the realities of political life. We can now extract the real messages about the change phenomena and construct an honest strategy for the principal as change agent.

WHAT THE LITERATURE
SAYS ABOUT CHANGE

It has become a popular academic pastime to try to document when and what events triggered the demise of the quasi-sacred [1] nature of public education. A common landmark is the Russian launch of Sputnik, which signalled (with much more psychological impact than technical reality) that education in the United States was second best. Another popular event was the study of schooling effects conducted by Dr. James Coleman in 1966 for the U.S. Congress.[2] What initially was to be a study of the compensatory effect of federal funding through the Elementary and Secondary Educational Act (Title I) became known by popular interpretation as the study that popped the bubble. Coleman reported that schooling, in relation to home and personal characteristics of the student, made no statistically significant difference in pupil achievement. The bubble that burst was the ability of public education to stay insulated from harsh scrutiny by citizens who exhibited a growing negative feeling about the schools' product.

In the specific area of planned change there were two other events[3] that can be identified with the demise of some popular misconceptions. One was the study of planned change reported by the Rand Corporation in 1975 [4] and another was the report on planned variation released by the Brookings Institution in 1975.[5] Both studies were attempts to discover whether federally subsidized planned change or systematic intervention efforts had any lasting effects on the educational practices of local school districts. Both studies reported that efforts had, to date, made no statistically significant changes in the actual operation of schools. The myth-destroying impact of these findings was related to the credibility given to independent research corporations to conduct educational evaluations in the mid-1970s. The days of the giants (meaning individual spokespersons like James Conant) had been replaced by the corporation as the ultimate legitimizer of what education was about. School system personnel or university professors may be suspected of a vested interest in research results, but the image of the research corporation (especially those who had previously focused outside education) was above politics.

The Rand Corporation and Brookings findings challenged the most cherished assumptions of what planned change meant. It became legitimate to rediscover that people like Seymour Sarason[6] had been challenging the basic notions for some time. Educators were particularly interested in

(1) the realistic expectations of success for local school change effort, (2) the actual dynamics of the change process, and (3) the most facilitating role that a principal could try in changing a school practice.

In terms of realistic expectations for success, both reports emphasized that people are not prone to try new things or change what seems to be working now or, most important, negate their own professional training and personal claim for expertise. Although not controlled for in either corporate study, it could be added that people are particularly inclined *not* to change during the first stages of growing scarcity. If anything, the first touch of curtailment will trigger efforts to refine and improve the current operation. Individuals and organizations have to be in fairly dire straits before brave-new-world change seems appealing.[7]

A second major finding concerned the mechanisms for making people change. Public education has been enamoured of the assumption that classic rationality or reason is the core of change since the turn of the century.[8] There are two basic variations. One is the rational problem-solving approach, identified in administration as scientific management. The second approach is labeled the organizational development (O.D.) approach, which traces its historical lineage to the human relations movement of the 1930s. Although scientific management emphasizes institutional procedures and organizational development emphasizes person dynamics as the focus,[9] both implicitly assume the same rational process about how decision making occurs (and, inferentially, what steps planning for change should emphasize). The formula is so common and accepted today that many educators may have trouble thinking outside the parameters. To make a rational decision or change a practice a person or members of a local school should (1) define the problem, (2) list alternatives, and (3) make a choice of the best alternative by calculating the relative costs and benefits of each option. That this assumed logic of rational persuasion does not "fit" with the earlier discussions of deciding in an arena was borne out by the Rand (and Brookings) findings. The term *partisan mutual adjustment* was invented to emphasize that the process assumed for scientific management and organizational development was *not* the way change occurs in schools. People do not reason together *and automatically change*, either because of the logic of some higher order of institutional process of deciding or because they feel empathy and exhibit authentic behaviors toward one another. Actual changes in real practice are sustained only when *partisans* make mutual adjustments. Partisans have a vested political interest. Mutual adjustment is the outcome of political exchange within the arena. There is no neat formula of rational decision process that underlies political trading.

The third basic finding of the Rand and Brookings studies relates to the appropriate role of the principal as change agent. Under the discussion of intervention strategies, the role of principal as facilitator of change efforts became clear. A reason for failure in federally subsidized planned change efforts was the lack of ownership that those affected by the change proposal felt (even if they were involved in the process of deciding). The implicit message was the huge gap between talking and doing or between formulating a change proposal and its actual implementation. The concern for rationality in formulation forgot the irrational world of payoff and face-saving that governs implementation. Those who were the most forgetful were the process experts, planners, or change agents who guided the local school decisions. If the expert was an outsider, he or she normally wore the label consultant; if an insider, the label was often principal. To be a change agent many principals felt they had to give up their instincts and experience with real-life decision making and adopt some artificial process. The adoption may have made the principal more verbose and have a better expert image but it did little to help facilitate effective change. To be effective, the principal must be a politician.

After Rand and Brookings, it became popular to deride planning expertise and change efforts. Unfortunately, we live with the backlash today and it threatens to negate some important lessons learned about how and why people change. The excesses of past enthusiasm and pretention does not take away from the valuable, practical understandings that a principal can incorporate in being a realistic change agent. The only cost from the past is that the planned change language should not be used. Practitioners are generally fed up with discussions of both input-output analysis and sensitivity training. Today, the best strategy seems to attempt systematic change efforts that can be couched as an extension of normal operations.

LESSONS ABOUT CHANGE

If the above discussion created a pessimistic picture about the change phenomena the following section should share a more optimistic light. There are eight major lessons learned through the study of change, which can be of direct help to the principal. Some of the lessons are general understandings and some are specific to the role of the administrator.

General Lessons

One of the most fundamental lessons of organizational change is that it occurs in stages and that different members of the school participate in different stages. A change effort is never an all-or-nothing attempt but a concentration on those who have the best chance of being persuaded to change. Figure 4.1 presents a classic illustration[10] of those affected by a change proposal. The key individuals for concentrated effort are the in-

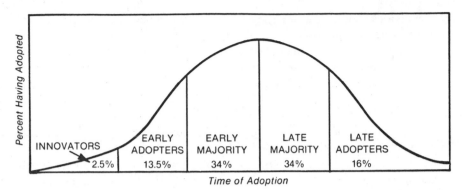

FIGURE 4.1   *Stages of Adoption*

Source. Reprinted by permission from *Adoption of New Ideas and Practices* by Herbert F. Lionberger © 1961 by The Iowa State University Press, Ames, Iowa 50010.

novators, the early adopters, and the early majority. As will be discussed later, the innovators tend to be the most creative members in the school, but they are also isolates and have little power in the arena. They are important because they will implement an idea and if successful, other members will give grudging respect that (at least) the idea works. The early adopters are important because they are the initial group of arena players who will try something new—usually if the price is right (some extra rewards or compensation attached). If the early adopters have a positive experience, the crucial demonstration by respected members will be achieved. The early majority are important because they are the key power figures of the arena. They are usually labeled *progressive*, but only because more rewards than sanctions seem to happen with a moving-target strategy of progressivism. The early majority will be convinced only by the success of the early adopters. Their crucial political role is to provide legitimization.

The principal should not invest resources in late majority or late adopters groups. The tipping point is 51–49 and the momentum of the three other groups should cause the rest of the process of acceptance to occur.

The second message is demonstration. The key to persuasion is showing actual results rather than talking about possibilities. The vehicles in a planned change effort are the pilot study or the experiment. This type of demonstration is most acceptable if the principal can convince the wait-and-see members of the school that few resources were used to carry out the experiment (none is even better) and that negative finding will stop future change efforts in this direction.

Another lesson of change is the necessity of a true feeling of ownership by those involved in implementation. The principal who introduces a change idea should plan for the demise of that personal association. Here is a problem of ego that all principals should face directly. All people want recognition. How important is it that the public know a new idea is the principal's? The best political strategy says to transfer ownership, but psychological sacrifice is something else that each principal must work out alone. Remember the symbolic distinction between the hero and the villain or fool rests with the same fine line of ego need.

The fourth lesson about change is that natural, dynamic patterns occur over time.[11] There are three basic patterns. All organizations are in some state of evolution from growth, to stability, to decline. The 1980s will probably be an era of overall decline for public education. However, there will be gross differences within education and each principal should map the pattern for his or her particular school. The second natural pattern relates to the staggered process of evolution. Change moves through a series of jerks and sharp transformations. (Although it is often interpreted later as a smooth, gradual process.[12]) Lowi[13] notes that reform goes through a blip of temporary departure from established patterns, then a return to the established and only then a final lasting (structural) change. This means that organizational change must expect temporary alteration before institutional change and an intermediate period of seeming failure. Finally, the pattern of change resembles a spiral [14] rather than a static circle. There are many statements that "there is nothing new under the sun" and that education just rediscovers old practices time and time again.[15] However there is a critical difference between a cycle as a circle and as a spiral. In a retrenchment era, change as refinement means relooking at previous practices but not necessarily adopting them without modification. Educators don't replicate the good old days *exactly*, because the world is different, but they may resemble earlier positions on a different (hopefully higher) plane.

A fifth lesson is that the innovations of most organizations are the result of borrowing rather than original invention.[16] This lesson has relevance to a later discussion of the creative isolate in the school. All people borrow; this fact may be a critical bridge in making a loner feel part of the organization.

A sixth message is that the process of systematic change is usually preceded by a period of unfreezing, which develops a need for change and establishes the relationship for changing within the arena.[17] Experts suggest the use of diagnosis tools and process consultant to help unfreeze a school situation.[18] We believe the particulars of the schools environment determine the best techniques for unfreezing an arena. For example, schools that experimented in T-Group[19] training during the 1960s and 1970s had considerable variation in the success of this type of diagnosis-intervention specialist technique.

The final two lessons deal with change under conditions of threat or fear. The first is that all systems will initially ignore, then resist, and finally adapt to the minimum extent possible any perceived stress that threatens the status quo. This phenomenon was discussed in Chapter 2 on taking charge and it is also applicable to making changes. Finally, the graph of possible reactions of a system to a threatening change resembles an inverted *u* when plotting decision actions to the extent of threat.[20] Study of groups under stress reveals that there is a focus upon the source of threat and an expected adaptive response (ignore, resist, adapt to the source) *only to a point*. At the apex (of what finally diagrams as an inverted *u*) a new phenomena called group think[21] emerges. Group think is also called psychological huddle for its key characteristic is the pre-occupation of group members to face the threat together *regardless* of the specific adaptive response taken. It is no longer a decision issue of what is right or even what is smart, but rather, "Do we all agree?" Expert knowledge of what occurs beyond group think is sketchy. One side argues that a decision system enters a type of catatonic state. Another side argues that the decision body will run amuck in some last unpredictable act of self-preservation. While both are interesting theories, such speculations of reaction to stress are beyond this discussion. For our purposes, the relation of fear or threat to making changes should stay within the outer boundaries of what is politically manageable within the school arena.

Thus far eight general lessons about the change dynamic have been considered. These messages form the cornerstone of a principal's effort in politicized planning of change. In addition, three specific lessons help the principal.

Specific Lessons

Beyond the general messages about change in local schools there are specific lessons that can be given. Seymour Sarason[22] wrote a landmark text that addressed the role of principal in change efforts. Although Sarason's text has been questioned as being too greatly oriented to the change issues of resource expansion (by compensatory subsidies) and civil right turmoils of the late 1960s, he makes several valid points for our discussion here. First, the loner role of teachers (and teacher turned administrator) is related to arena[23] decision making. Teachers are not used to or expected to make *educational* decisions as groups. The school with self-contained classrooms and traditional teaching styles is most likely to have teachers who expect to make fundamental curricular and instructional decisions alone, as these decisions will affect *their* children and *their* classroom environment. Group or arena decision making are for school-wide or administrative decisions. If issues of actual classroom behavior must be discussed in the arena, the basic rule of thumb is to raise the abstraction level so that personalities become blurred *or* use the arena forum to scapegoat a bad guy. Sarason might argue that the normal tradition[24] of teaching makes *classroom issues* the most difficult for arena decisions *and the least likely for true planned change success.* (Decisions that actually affect what occurs in the classroom are the most important "pots" in the school type of poker.)

Another specific lesson about planned change relates to timing and taking charge (Chapter 2). Chapter 2 emphasized symbolism and principal image as major arena concerns. Although the relation to the honeymoon phenomenon and weak or strong predecessor was mentioned, the *behavioral* expectations of a new principal was down played. For the principal who wishes to make sweeping changes during the early days of his or her tenure, Sarason offers the following thoughts:

> From the time of appointment until the formal opening of the school the principal spends almost all of his time in what can only be called housekeeping matters: ordering books, supplies, and furniture, assigning rooms, arranging schedules, negotiating the transfer of students from other schools, interviewing and selecting prospective personnel, making up bus schedules...the complexity of housekeeping is more than he imagined... *the major goal—a goal determined by others but which he fully accepts and in relationship to which he has increasing anxiety—opening the school on time and in good order...up until the opening of the school the principal is not concerned* with such issues as what life in a classroom should be, how teachers will be related to decisions and planning about educational values and goals, the role of parents and neighborhood-community resources, the handling of problem children, the purposes of evaluation, and other issues that bear directly on the educational experience of all those who have or should have a vested interest in a school. In fact, up until the opening of school there is precious little discussion of children or education.[25]

The message of timing suggests that the type of problems a principal will be initially concerned with will not relate to life in the classroom. Consequently, the initial track record of planned change efforts by a principal should probably have a housekeeping flavor. Bluntly, the basic reputation of decision leader or change agent will *not* be built on classroom concerns or wins on the fundamental issues of actual curricular or instructional practice. To undertake the *core* issues of the local school (issues that directly affect the education of children) the principal must demonstrate previous success as change agent in safer realms. *The timing of administrative concerns affected by the larger school system* makes a natural vehicle to focus initial local school arena decision making away from the core issues of change.

A final lesson about the principal's role in planned change is the tendency to look upward in considering the impact of specific internal change beyond the boundaries of the local school. Later chapters are devoted to the detailed implications of a school setting in the larger political environment. Sarason points out that the principal's view of the system in a change situation is a calculation of personal risk (possible loss of power, assessment of educational worth) and the possibility of a legal question.[26] Thus a planned change effort is least likely to be initiated where the principal perceives high personal risk or legal challenge.[27]

Summary

In summary, some general and specific things can be said about making changes that should help the principal:

1. Change, both in who might consider a new way and who will actually implement, does *not* involve everyone. Find the 5 to 15 percent and invest your efforts there.

2. The most effective counter to the resistance of a skeptical show-me attitude is to do so. Use the demonstration of the pilot or experimental test to replace personal pleas or pronouncements.

3. Unless an actual feeling of ownership is developed for those responsible for implementation, forget any real change. The true battle is over what must be given up for achieving an ownership commitment—*not* the rational elaboration created to justify a particular change decision.

4. Change occurs in natural patterns over time. In change efforts, take into count (a) the patterns of growth, stability, and decline, (b) the pattern of temporary reform, a return to the established, then lasting structural reform, and (c) the cyclical nature of the spiral.

5. Most innovation is the result of borrowing rather than original invention.

6. Systematic change efforts usually initiate a preliminary unfreezing process before a specific intervention attempt.

7. Time constraints and resource scarcities are related to the susceptibility of people to try something new and perceptions of threat.

8. Change under threat or fear resembles an inverted *U*. Medium level threat or fear will promote conservative tendencies treating change as refinement of existing practices. Extreme fear or threat will cause unpredictable response and a tendency toward group think.

The principal should consider these lessons about the change phenomenon in any systematic effort that he or she might attempt. The specific mechanisms that guide planning for purposive change will be discussed next.

THE CONTROL OF CHANGE

The type of change desired and experienced in the 1980 to 2000 period will differ considerably from the type of change that has characterized American education in the past. Rather than the relentless pursuit of novelty, change in the future in public schools will address stability. In the past, most efforts at change found in schools were focused on the introduction of new ideas, concepts, and practices that were intended to disrupt or even replace existing practices. Change was a mandate, often equated with progress and growth, that manifested itself in the form of novel ideas, experimental programs, and the demonstration of new techniques. The objective of such planned change was instability—to promote a condition for new forms of education. As such, the change efforts of the past two decades have been rife with false starts and change for change's sake. Those who hesitated to change lost their chance to participate and were replaced by those who were more certain.

In contrast, change efforts in the future in public schools will be directed toward increasing the degrees of stability. With a mandate for goal clarity, wise use of resources, and accountability, only the foolish will pursue greater diversity. Change in the 1980s and 1990s will be directed by the protection of interests and existing rewards and sanctions rather than expansion. The control of resources, not new ideas, will be the prime mover of change. Those change efforts that are initiated by administrators will seek to disperse workable ideas, standardize efficient practices, develop cost-effective techniques, and contribute to systems goals. The need for stability will govern the change process; there will be few, if any, new sandcastles.

The administrator of the 1980s who understands the change process and the human behavior associated with change will be skilled in using governance mechanisms. In particular, an understanding of the lessons of change will allow the administrator to develop strategies and construct change planning that will be successful. Such resistance can be viewed in terms of both social norms in organizations and individual predispositions to change.

The norms found in any organization will always reflect the individual habits of the personnel that make up the organization. Such norms are nothing more than the customary or expected ways of behaving. These norms make it possible for members of the organization to work together. Because of such norms, each member knows what can be expected of others. Any behaviors outside of established norms is disruptive and thereby resisted.

Goodwin Watson posited the following observations on the reception of change in formal organizations based on the early findings of the Cooperative Project for Educational Development (COPED):

1. Resistance will be less if administrators, teachers, board members, and community leaders feel that the project is their own—not one devised and operated by outsiders.
2. Resistance will be less if the project clearly has wholehearted support from top officials of the system.
3. Resistance will be less if participants see the change as reducing rather than increasing their present burdens.
4. Resistance will be less if the project accords with values and ideals that have long been acknowledged by participants.
5. Resistance will be less if the program offers the kind of new experience that interests participants.
6. Resistance will be less if participants feel that their autonomy and their security is not threatened.
7. Resistance will be less if participants have joined in diagnostic efforts leading them to agree on the basic problem and to feel its importance.
8. Resistance will be less if the project is adopted by consensual group decision.
9. Resistance will be reduced if proponents are able to empathize with opponents to recognize valid objections, and take steps to relieve unnecessary fears.
10. Resistance will be reduced if it is recognized that innovations are likely to be misunderstood and misinterpreted, and if provision is made for feedback of perceptions of the project and for further clarification as needed.
11. Resistance will be reduced if participants experience acceptance, support, trust, and confidence in their relations with one another.
12. Resistance will be reduced if the project is kept open to revision and reconsideration if experience indicates that changes would be desirable.
13. Readiness for change gradually becomes a characteristic of certain individuals, groups, organizations, and civilizations.[28]

Taking the Watson points for measuring the resistance to change, Wiles has constructed an Educational Innovations Probability Chart (EIPC) for administrators to use to assess their organization. (See Table 4.1.) Shading in the most appropriate description of existing conditions

TABLE 4.1 *Educational Innovations Probability Chart*

	Higher Risk →			→ Lower Risk	
Source of Innovation	Superimposed from outside	Outside agent brought in	Developed internally with aid	External idea modified	Locally conceived, developed, implemented
Impact of Innovation	Challenges sacrosanct beliefs	Calls for major value shifts	Requires substantial change	Modifies existing values or programs	Does not substantially alter existing values, beliefs or programs
Official Support	Official leaders active opposition	Officials on record as opposing	Officials uncommitted	Officials voice support of change	Enthusiastically supported by the official leaders
Planning of Innovation	Completely external	Most planning external	Planning processes balanced	Most of planning done locally	All planning for change done on local site
Means of Adoption	By superiors	By local leaders	By Reps	By most of the clients	By group consensus
History of Change	History of failures	No accurate records	Some success with innovation	A history of successful innovations	Known as school where things regularly succeed
Possibility of Revision	No turning back	Final evaluation before committee	Periodic evaluations	Possible to abandon at conclusion	Possible to abort the effort at any time

Higher Risk ← → Lower Risk

	Higher Risk				Lower Risk
Role of Teachers	Largely bypassed	Minor role	Regular role in implementing	Heavy role in implementation	Primary actor in the classroom effort
Teacher Expectation	Fatalistic	Feel little chance	Willing to give a try	Confident of success	Wildly enthusiastic about chance of success
Work Load Measure	Substantially increased	Heavier but rewarding	Slightly increased	Unchanged	Work load lessened by the innovation
Threat Measure	Definitely threatens some clients	Probably threatening to some	Mild threat resulting from the change	Very remote threat to some	Does not threaten the security or autonomy
Community Factor	Hostile to innovations	Suspicious and uninformed	Indifferent	Ready for a change	Wholeheartedly supports the school

Shade the response in each category which most accurately reflects the condition surrounding the implementation of the middle school. If the "profile" of your school is predominately in the high risk side of the matrix, substantial work must be done to prepare your school for change.

Source: From Jon Wiles, *Planning Guidelines for Middle School Education.* Copyright © 1976 by Kendall/Hunt Publishing Co., p. 30. Reprinted with permission of the publisher.

allows the administrator to profile his or her situation. Once the profile is established, those areas in greatest need of preparation can be attended to.[29]

In addition to organizational considerations that impede change, there are many personal reasons why individuals do not accept change. Resistance to change is a natural tendency found in all people. To filter change through the prisms of perception and experience helps individuals cope with the overwhelming number of stimuli encountered daily as well as to bring order and predictability to existing patterns of the world. Some perfectly logical reasons why individuals might resist change are:

1. Fear—the individual has had a previous experience with the change that was unpleasant, or the individual possesses a distorted knowledge about the change, or the individual fears failure in attempting the change.
2. Logical conservatism—the individual has learned from similar experience that such change is undesirable, or the individual is unable to see how the change will benefit him or her in light of his or her information about the change.
3. Previous obligations—the individual sees this change or growth opportunity in conflict with previous obligations or understandings.
4. High risk—the individual assesses that such change may have a price in terms of lost prestige, status, possession, or so forth that does not warrant the risk of trying.
5. Lack of identification—the individual may not be able to see that the change or experience has anything to do with his or her needs.
6. Awareness level—the individual may not be able to consider the change or experience because habit or tradition prevents the full analysis of the situation.

Armed with an understanding of resistance to change, the school administrator can begin to hypothesize how change might be promoted and the ways in which he or she can increase the potentials for desired changes. When such observations are put in an ordered form, they become the basis of a theory of changing that will guide administrative action. As Eye, Netzer, and Krey point out:

> Theory evolves from, or crystallizes the verbalization of, basic assumptions, principles, observations, and notions that are held about a particular phenomenon or area of activity. When these are collated in an orderly manner so that they constitute a constellation of supporting ideas and evidence, the theory is identified. On the basis of theory, a model can be developed which will illustrate the theoretical concepts. This allows the practitioner not only to verbalize organization of ideas, but also a design for his plan of action.[30]

Addressing the need for theory building from a research perspective, the COPED project cited earlier had these prescriptions for someone interested in promoting change in a school environment:

1. Clarify expectations of the parties involved regarding the purposes of the program, the probable time schedule, the amount of effort (dollars and time) likely to be required, roles and relationships of organization members, methods of collecting data for diagnosis and assessment, and the use to be made of the data.
2. Collect information from system members, usually through interviews or questionnaires. The data will be used to aid diagnosis and planning.
3. Use information obtained to formulate statements about how goals, attitudes, and beliefs in different groups of the system agree with or are discrepant from one another and what problems most urgently need a solution.
4. Using the information from point 3 above, examine current operations, work on problems shown in the data, and improve problem-solving effectiveness.
5. Carry out plans derived from point 4 above.
6. Set up structures and procedures to institutionalize and support continuing self-renewal processes.[31]

Obviously, the COPED model of change just presented attempts to promote institutional change as a rational, problem-solving process that involves those people affected by the change. Whether this model, or other less democratic models are applicable depends upon the environment in which the administrator is located. The important point, in terms of change in schools, is for principals to telegraph their intentions when addressing politicized change. The use of external change agents, block-busting strategies, or seeing change as something to sneak past others appear to have a diminished applicability for the 1980s. Such actions can only promote greater instability in the arena that, after all things have settled out, will mean some winners and some losers. The school principal who promotes instability through change efforts will have only pyrrhic victories.

School administrators should use a form of mapping to reveal intended changes in school programs. Such mapping is nothing more than verbal descriptions of change, placed on continuums, and an indication of status quo and intended conditions. From such a blueprint, other people in the school can understand the nature of intended changes and the specific goals and objectives used to promote change.

In Table 4.2 a plan for converting a junior high school to a middle school is mapped out.[32] Major areas of concern, such as school environment, participant roles, instructional arrangements, and administrative

TABLE 4.2

	Present Condition	Awareness Stage	Experimentation Stage	Adoption Stage	Desired Condition
	Stage 1	Stage 2	Stage 3	Stage 4	Stage 5
The School Philosophy	Either no formal statement or a written document on file in the school office.	School staff share beliefs, look for consensus, restate philosophy and objectives in terms of expected, behavior.	Staff begins use of goals as guide to evaluating school practices. Begin to involve students and community in planning.	Philosophy and goals used to shape the program. Formal mechanism established to monitor program and decision making.	Philosophy a living document. Guides daily decisions. The program a tool for achieving desired educational ends.
THE LEARNING ENVIRONMENT					
Use of the Building	Only uniform instructional spaces. Little use of the building spaces for educational purposes.	Some deviation from traditional space utilization (classroom learning center). Possibly a complete demonstration class for bright ideas.	Limited building conversion (knock out walls). Begin to identify unused spaces. Planning for large learning spaces.	Development of a comprehensive plan for use of grounds and building. Total remodeling of spaces.	Tailor-made learning environment—all spaces used to educate. Building facilitates the learning intention.
Use of Materials	Classrooms are dominated by a grade-level text. Library with a limited offering. Used as a study hall for large groups.	Use of multilevel texts within classroom. Materials selected after an analysis of student achievement levels. Supplemental resources made available to students.	Diverse materials developed for the students. Resource centers established. Cross-discipline selection of materials. More multimedia used. Some independent study.	Materials purchasing policies realigned. Common learning areas established as resource centers. More self-directed study built in.	Diversified materials. Something for each student. Integrated subject materials. Portable curriculum units (on carts). Heavy multimedia. Active learning centers.

Use of Community	Little or no access to school. Information about programs scanty. Trust low.	Some school program ties to community. Token access via PTA and media. School perceived as island in neighborhood.	Preliminary uses of community as learning environment. Identification of nearby resources. Use of building for community functions.	Regular interchange between school and community. Systematic communication. A network of services and resources established.	School programs outwardly oriented. Community seen as a teaching resource. Systematic ties with services and resources around school.

INSTRUCTIONAL ORGANIZATION

Staffing Patterns	Building teachers isolated in self-contained classrooms. Little or no lateral communication or planning present.	Limited sharing of resources. Some division of labor and small-scale cooperation in teaching. Informal communication about student progress.	Regular cooperative planning sessions. Some curricular integration via themes. Students rotate through subject areas. Problems of cooperation identified.	Interdepartmental organization. Use of common planning time. Administrative support such as in scheduling. Use of philosophy as curricular decision-making criteria.	Teaching staff a "team" working toward common ends. Staff patterns reflect instructional intentions. Administration in support of curricular design. Coursework integrated for students.
Teaching Strategy	Some variety but lecture and teacher-dominated Q-A session the norm. Homework used to promote day-to-day continuity.	Observation of other teaching models. Skill development via workshops. An identification of staff strengths and weaknesses. Some new patterns.	Building level experiments by willing staff members. "Modeling" of ideas. On-site consultant help made available for skill development.	School day divided according to the teaching strategy employed. Faculty evaluation of the effectiveness of new ways after a trial period.	Great variety of methods used in teaching, uses of media, dealing with students. The curricular plans determine strategy.

TABLE 4.2 (Continued)

	Present Condition	Awareness Stage	Experimentation Stage	Adoption Stage	Desired Condition
	Stage 1	Stage 2	Stage 3	Stage 4	Stage 5
Staff Development	Staff development is global, rarely used to attack local needs and problems. Occurs as needed.	Staff identifies in-service needs and priorities. Philosophy assists in this process. Local staff skills and strengths are recognized.	Staff development re-aligned to serve needs of teachers. Opportunities for personal growth are made available.	Formal procedures for directing staff development to needs established. Staff development seen as problem-solving mechanism.	Staff development an on-going process using available resources. An attempt to close theory-practice gaps.

ADMINISTRATIVE CONDITIONS

	Present Condition	Awareness Stage	Experimentation Stage	Adoption Stage	Desired Condition
	Stage 1	Stage 2	Stage 3	Stage 4	Stage 5
Organization of Students	Uniform patterns. One teacher, 30 students in six rows of five in each row in each period of each school day.	Understanding that organization of students should match curricular intentions. Some initial variation of group sizes in classroom.	Limited organization to facilitate the grouping of the students. Begin use of aides and parents to increase organizational flexibility.	Full administrative support for a reorganization of students. Building restructured where necessary. An increase in planning for effectiveness.	Group sizes vary according to the activity planned. Full support given to eliminate any problem areas.
Report of Student Progress	"Progress" is defined narrowly. Letter grades or simple numerals represent student learning in the subject areas.	Recognition of broader growth goals for students. Use of philosophy to evaluate the existing practices.	Experimentation with supplemental reporting procedures. Involvement of student and parents in the process.	Development of a diverse and comprehensive reporting procedure for student progress.	Descriptive medium used to monitor individual student progress. Broadly focused evaluation. Team of teacher, student, and parents involved.

Rules and Regulations	High degree of regimentation. Many rules, most inherited over the years. The emphasis on the enforcement and on control.	Staff and students identify essential rules. Regulations matched against the school philosophy.	Rules and regulations streamlined. Used as a teaching device about life outside of school. Increased student self-control.	Greater use of student and staff input into the regulation of the school environment. Rewards built in for desirable performance.	Moving toward minimal regulation and an increased student self-control. Regulations a positive teaching device.
Discipline	Reactive pattern ranging from verbal admonishment to padding and expulsion. Reoccurring offenders.	Staff analysis of school policies. Shift of emphasis to causes of the problems. Some brainstorming of possible solutions.	Establishment of a hierarchy of discipline activity. Begin implementing preventive strategies.	Design of curriculum programs to deter discipline problems. High intensity program for regular offenders.	Program of the school eliminates most sources of discipline problems. The procedure for residual problems clear to all.

ROLES OF PARTICIPANTS

Student Roles	Passive recipient of knowledge. Instruction is geared to average student. Reactive communication with the teacher.	Investigation of new student roles by teacher. Limited hierarchy of trust established in the classroom. Needs and interests of student investigated.	Ground rules for increased student independence set. Student involvement in planning. Role of student connected to philosophy of the school.	Periodic staff review of student roles. Roles linked to school-wide rules and regulations. Philosophy guides role possibilities.	Students involved in planning and conducting the program. Increased independence *and* responsibility. Use of "contracts" to maintain new understandings.
Teacher Roles	Defined by the subjects taught. Perceived as the source of all knowledge. Other roles peripheral.	Perceiving roles suggested by the philosophy. Roles accepted at verbal level. Limited experimentation with new roles.	Investigation of new roles—trying on new relationship. Goal setting for individual teacher. Skill development through in-service.	Administrative reorganization for role support. A sharpened planning and action skills needed to serve the student according to the philosophy.	Teacher role is defined by student needs. Teacher the organizer of the learning activities. Teacher talents used more effectively.

TABLE 4.2 (Continued)

	Present Condition	Awareness Stage	Experimentation Stage	Adoption Stage	Desired Condition
	Stage 1	Stage 2	Stage 3	Stage 4	Stage 5
Principal Roles	Solely responsible for school operation. The "boss." Enforcer of all rules. The linkage to all outside information and resources.	Awareness of role limitations. An awareness of real leadership potential. A setting of role priorities.	Limited sharing of decision making in area of curriculum. Limited joint planning with the faculty. Review of existing policy according to the philosophy.	Role perception changes to manager of resources. Emphasis on development (active) rather than on order (static). Increase in curriculum leadership functions.	An instructional leader. Administrative acts support the curriculum program. Philosophy guiding decision making. Built-in monitoring system for evaluating building level progress.

Source: from Jon Wiles, *Planning Guidelines for Middle School Education.* Copyright © 1976 by Kendall/Hunt Publishing Company, pp. 36–39. Reprinted with permission of the publisher.

conditions are described in terms of stages of development. Stage 1 is an attempt to describe in a few words the realities of the present conditions. Stage 2 reflects an awareness of the direction of possible changes and possibly some tinkering with the status quo. Stage 3 is generally an experimentation stage during which the desired changes are tested. Stage 4 represents an adoption stage during which the change is institutionalized or supported by administrative resources. Stage 5 is a brief description of the ideal or desired condition of the change being pursued.

The advantages of such telegraphing of intent in promoting educational changes far outweigh the disadvantages, especially when stability is a desired condition. Such purposeful mapping of change provides a master blueprint for comprehensive change. By using a stages-of-development format, existing discrepancies, inconsistencies, and severe problem areas can be identified and confronted. Finally, if such descriptions are described behaviorally and placed in a management system, such a plan can serve as the framework for comprehensive evaluation. Above all, by spotlighting the intended changes to be promoted, the administrator structures a medium for communication about the changes that *need* to be made. Again, the process may outweigh the product in terms of importance.

Because change in the future will be directed toward increasing stability in public school environments, as opposed to promoting novelty, the principal should act as openly as possible in addressing and controlling change. Developing a theory of changing, and communicating that theory to all who may be affected will reduce the possibility of surprise and disruption in the school environment. Process consistency and predictability will prove far more rewarding to the aspiring principal than the achievement of token successes in controlling change within the political arena.

CREATING AN INNOVATIVE ATMOSPHERE

The above discussion emphasized specific, systematic activities that a principal might try in making changes. There is also a more diffuse, general concept of change that considers the principal in a less systematic, indirect role—the principal as a general facilitator who fosters change by promoting general school atmospheres of creativity and innovation (see Chapter 3). This topic is usually avoided in specific discussions of change because of the tendency to get absorbed in fuzzy concepts of *good morale* and *open climate*. The operating meanings of morale and climate are a function of the particular school arena and offer little help in the general concepts of *structure* and *consideration* except to create a *general* image.

Halpin and Croft argue that a good leader has a good mix and is high on the following:

1. *Initiating structure* refers to the leader's behavior in delineating the relationship between himself or herself and the members of his or her workgroup, and in endeavoring to establish well-defined patterns of organization, channels of communication, and methods of procedure.
2. *Consideration* refers to behavior indicative of friendship, mutual trust, respect, and warmth in the relationship between the leader and the members of his or her staff.[33]

While it is hard to disagree with such pronouncements if used for image, these statements offer little guidance for actual decision behavior in a real life situation.

It may be that the activities of a principal to create an innovative atmosphere (apart from the other activities of maintaining control or working for planned change) may rest with the protection of the creative individual. In an earlier chapter, the ambivalent type of school member was identified as a teacher described as creative or a person who wants to be left out of extracurricular activities. Earlier in this chapter the innovators were identified as the 2.5 percent who try new ideas first. The characteristics of innovators are given as "young, cosmopolite, relatively high in education and income, exert opinion leadership and (emphasis added) *likely to be viewed as deviants by their peers and by themselves.*" [34]

Finally, the creative innovator has been described in terms of distinctive mental and personality traits.

They rate high on conceptual fluency and flexibility, respond to stimuli in original and atypical ways, and enjoy complex problems. They are likely to be stubborn about their opinions, somewhat lonely, impulsive, and resistant to authority. In other words, they are almost the antithesis of conventional organization men.[35]

Regardless of the label, the creative school organization would seem to have people who are characterized by words like deviant, lonely, stubborn, and impulsive, which infers that other members of the school may have a great distaste for the creative person and perceive such an individual as an organizational liability. Because of their tendency to work alone, the innovators are probably not key members of the political arena, which makes them susceptible to scapegoating. The first level of principal protection is that of advocate in the arena. If the school is in a condition of scarcity and threat then the survival of the strongest may be a prevailing theme. The innovative isolate runs the risk of being expendable or cited by others as the cause of current troubles. In most cases neither is true and the protective skill of the principal involves shifting the bargaining process to the real issues and away from the most expedient scapegoat.

The second level of principal protection involves the presentation and implementation of the innovator's ideas. The autonomy of the creative person may produce exciting ideas and improvements but the cost of the autonomy is the increased suspicion of the innovator's peers. The problem is most pronounced when a brilliant idea needs a massive team effort to implement it. If the principal cannot convince the isolate to change roles (i.e., to protect his or her idea) then he or she may have to become the spokesperson.

In the final analysis, the protection of any individual or object always involves some bargaining costs to the principal and must be weighed against the good of the rest of the school. The balance is tipped when one person's rights or special status destroy the larger social organization. The principal must attempt to make the isolate understand that reality and not to cross the final boundaries of political acceptance. Beyond the final line the principal is only protecting a fool and is not fostering an innovative atmosphere.

PRACTICAL QUESTIONS
FOR PRINCIPAL ACTION

The broad conceptual bases that undergird consideration of taking charge, maintaining control, and making changes can be outlined as a series of practical questions for the principal in the local school. To be an intelligent and effective political participant, the principal must know his or her style of operating and the mix of that style with the local school environment. Critical questions of style include:

1. Am I to emphasize symbolic appeal or concrete actions in management?
2. Am I to be perceived as proactive or status quo in relation to the arena?
3. Am I to act as a team player or an individual in issues of governance?
4. Am I to emphasize the rationality of the organization position and the rationality of management expertise or my political, interactive skills as an arena player?

Critical questions of mix with the environment include:

1. Do I match with the locals or the cosmopolitans?
2. Do I match with a short-run, problem-oriented arena or a long-range, goal-oriented arena?

3. Do I match with an episodic, crisis-oriented decision context or a routine, noncrisis type of context?

These and other questions of general style and mix present the principal a political picture as administrator. The person who can answer such questions and seek to change or reinforce the particulars of the politicized answers has a great advantage over other members in the local school environment. Political understanding is the critical ingredient to successful decision making and school administration.

Consider the application of the ideas found in this chapter by reading the following case story.

CASE STORY: ELLEN'S DREAM

Ellen is a principal in one of the older elementary schools in the district. The school is characterized by a stable student population, low teacher turnover, and strong parent support. Teachers and the more active parents work closely together, and are often involved socially outside of school. Even though Ellen has been serving as principal for three years, many people in the community still consider her a newcomer.

With the exception of the totally self-contained kindergarten and first grades, all grades are ability grouped for reading and math instruction. Other subjects are taught in heterogeneously grouped homerooms. All teachers are required to complete individual profile records of students indicating achievement of basic skills, but the records are maintained by individual teachers, not in a central location. Thus, teachers of reading and math rarely know of a student's progress in homeroom subjects and vice versa.

Noting this problem, Ellen has often advocated returning to self-contained classrooms where there would be greater flexibility in scheduling and student movement. Certainly, record keeping and student prescription would be more effective under such a set-up. The faculty, however, has not responded in a positive manner to such overtures. Test results indicate that students are acquiring the basic skills in reading and math measured by the district and state tests. Further, most of the active parents support the teachers and the existing instructional program.

Ellen feels that she must persuade her teachers to establish self-contained classrooms in all grades of the school, even though she anticipates resistance. Over a period of several months she takes the following steps:

1. Meeting with grade chairpersons, Ellen inquires about the effects of increased record-keeping requirements and the time teachers

are spending on drill activities. She also inquires whether having students change classes interferes with parent conferences.

2. Ellen schedules a summer inservice workshop for her teachers on the management of self-contained classrooms. Major topic areas to be covered by the workshop include building learning centers, flexible grouping of students, and methods of diagnosing skill needs of students. The format at the workshop will be simulation of a self-contained classroom.

3. Ellen arranges for district curriculum specialists and salespeople from publishing companies to assemble and demonstrate materials for heterogeneously grouped classrooms. Emphasis of the materials is on the relationship between skill building and reinforcing activities.

4. Ellen initiates a study group among receptive teachers to discuss the operation of the self-contained elementary classroom. The group focuses on the strengths of flexible grouping in self-contained classrooms.

5. Ellen issues a memo to inform her teaching staff that next year, she will arrange for special teachers (federal programs, gifted and talented, etc.) to work with target students in self-contained classrooms as much as possible. This will reduce out-of-class movement and the waste of important learning time.

6. Finally, at the beginning of the new school year, Ellen sends a letter to all parents projecting a move to self-contained classrooms for all grades. She also asks, in the letter, for parent volunteers to work in the self-contained rooms.

Reactions from the teaching staff at the school were mixed. Primary teachers in grades two and three wholeheartedly supported the proposed change, citing the problems students had in adjusting to several teachers. Teachers in the intermediate grades were vocal in protesting such a move to the old ways. They pointed out that it would be wrong to alter a program that was producing results. Some teachers at the intermediate level even suggested that there was a need to further departmentalize. Parents, too, were mixed in their reaction to Ellen's dream. In general, primary student parents supported the change, but intermediate student parents thought that returning to self-contained classrooms would penalize high-achievement students. Both the primary and intermediate parents were disappointed that Ellen had waited until the beginning of the new school year to inform them of a major organizational change in the school.

Case Questions

1. How would you describe Ellen's effort to change her school in terms of those things learned about change during the past two decades.

2. Using the grid found in Table 4.1, analyze this case from the information given. In which areas should Ellen concentrate her attention if she is to increase the chances of success in this effort?

3. Develop a continuum of options that Ellen might offer to teachers and parents for action should her plan become hopelessly bogged down.

4. If Ellen were to allow the intermediate teachers to continue with ability-grouped classes taught by separate teachers, how could she explain the dual organizational pattern operating in her school?

5. What can be observed about the timing of this effort to change the school? About the ownership of this effort to change the school?

NOTES

1. Laurence Iannaccone, *Politics in Education* (New York: Center for Applied Research in Education, 1967). Iannaccone popularized the religious connotations of educational governance by terms such as the "polite priestcraft" and "rites and vows of passage."
2. James Coleman, *Equality of Educational Opportunity* (Washington, D.C.: U.S. Government Printing Office, 1966).
3. Of course, many other significant events are identified as contributing to the general transformation of the quasi-sacred character of public education. For example, the Civil Rights Act of 1964 and the initial absolute decline of school-aged children in 1971.
4. Paul Berman and Milbrey McLaughlin, *Federal Programs Supporting Educational Change*, vols. 1–5 (Santa Monica: Rand Corporation, 1975).
5. Alice Rivlin and Michael Timpane, eds., *Planned Variation in Education* (Washington, D.C.: The Brookings Institution, 1975).
6. Seymour B. Sarason, *The Culture of the School and the Problem of Change* (Boston: Allyn and Bacon, 1971). This book is recommended as "basic" reading for all practicing principals, especially pp. 110–150.
7. For extended discussion of the psychological orientation of individuals, small groups and institutions toward conservation see Phillip Slater, *The Pursuit of Loneliness* (Boston: Beacon Press, 1970).
8. See Raymond Callahan, *Education and the Cult of Efficiency* (Chicago: University of Chicago Press, 1962).
9. Also the scientific orientation is concerned with what is while O.D. emphasizes what ought. See Chris Argyris, "Some Limits to 'Rational Man' Organizational Theory," *Public Administrative Review*, May/June 1973, pp. 253–267.
10. Herbert Lionberger, *Adoption of New Ideas and Practices* (Ames: Iowa State Press, 1960), pp. 3–23.
11. The hedge is in the time definition of *future*. For a comprehensive discussion of this topic, see Matthew Miles, ed., *Innovation in Education* (New York: Teachers College Press, 1964).
12. For such an interpretation see Alan Filley and Robert House, *Managerial Process and Organizational Behavior* (Chicago: Scott, Foresman, 1969).
13. Theodore Lowi, *At the Pleasure of the Mayor* (New York: Free Press, 1964). Especially Chapter 8.

14. William I. Thompson, *Evil and World Order* (New York: Harper & Row, 1976). Some educators may find this book too "far out" but the distinction between cycle as spiral and cycle as circle is well made.
15. For example, Michael Katz, "The Present Moment in Educational Reform," *Harvard Educational Review* 41 (August 1971): 342–359.
16. James March and Herbert Simon, *Organizations* (New York: Wiley, 1958), p. 188.
17. Ronald Lippitt, Jeane Watson, and Bruce Westley, *The Dynamics of Planned Change* (New York: Harcourt Brace and World, 1958), p. 130. Unfreezing is part of a five-stage change process that also involves moving and refreezing.
18. Specific recommendations include the use of a survey and an external consultant; see Robert Owens, *Organizational Behavior in Schools* (Englewood Cliffs, N.J.: Prentice-Hall, 1970), pp. 154–158, 161–166.
19. For example, Harold Leavitt, "Applied Organizational Change in Industry" in *Handbook of Organization,* ed. James March (Skokie: Rand McNally, 1965), p. 1155.
20. Irving Janis, "Group Identification under Conditions of External Danger," *British Journal of Medical Psychology* 26 (1963): 230–242.
21. Ibid. Also Alexander George, "Adaptation to Stress in Political Decision Making," in *Coping and Adaptation*, ed. A. George et al. (New York: Basic Books, 1974), pp. 175–234.
22. Sarason, *The Culture of the School.*
23. Ibid., discussed as the teacher in "work" or planning groups.
24. Ibid., called "behavioral regularities," such as, teachers teach as they were taught in how questions are asked of students.
25. Ibid., p. 116. Reprinted by permission.
26. Ibid., pp. 135–141.
27. The possible exception to this statement is the principal posturing in a group servant hero role or Robin Hood type of villain role rather than having a real expectation of major change.
28. Goodwin Watson, ed., *Concepts for Social Change* (Washington, D.C.: National Training Laboratories, National Education Association, 1967), p. 22.
29. Jon Wiles, *Planning Guidelines for Middle School Education* (Dubuque: Kendall/Hunt, 1976), p. 30.
30. Glen Eye, Lanore Netzer, and Robert Krey, *Supervision of Instruction* (New York: Harper & Row, 1964), p. 48.
31. Watson, *Concepts for Social Change*, pp. 83–84.
32. Jon Wiles, "Developmental Staging—In Pursuit of Comprehensive Curriculum Planning," *Middle School Journal* 6, no. 1 (Spring 1975): 6–7.
33. Andrew Halpin and Donald Croft, *The Organizational Climate of Schools* (Chicago: University of Chicago Press, 1963).
34. Owens, *op. cit.*, 159.
35. Theodore Caplow, *Two Against One: Coalitions in Triads* (Englewood Cliffs, N.J.: Prentice-Hall, 1968), p. 200.

CHAPTER 5

Boards of Education
and Central Administration

The relationship of the central office or board of education to the local school is political within an organizational context. Regardless of the *educational* relationship or intent, these system-wide actors can, and often do, affect local school decision making. By introducing new dynamics with the local school arena, the central office and board affect the political interests of the principal, in terms of both governance and control. They can raise new concerns about what is legitimate, what is the distribution of resources, and what is the nature of competition. The effect of the central office and the board of education on the local school relates to both the composition of the arena and the alteration of "regular" play and bargaining.

THE BOUNDARY

At the core of concern about the board of education or central office is the question of appropriate governance of the local school center. This issue of decision making is couched in many terms and reflects basic issues found in all large, complex organizations: What is the sum? What are the parts? And how do they relate? Common terms used to describe the issues include centralization and decentralization or autonomy and coordination. From a decision standpoint, the key word is *boundary*.[1] The boundary is that point of differentiation that separates the system (or arena) from its environment. Although most texts consider the community the environment of the school system, this definition begs the crucial, internal differentiation of the local school center from its larger organizational environment. The boundary *within* the school organization environment is confused because the local school is simultaneously a part of the big system and a separate decision entity. This definition of boundary is more than a matter of interpretation and semantics. At one time educators could discuss a centralized school system or describe a local school center that had much decision autonomy *and assume that various indicators of governance were pointing to (essentially) the same organizational distinctions.* One of the fallouts of the last two decades is that an agreement about a single set of indicators has disappeared in many school situations. Today, educators discuss the school system and arena boundary recognizing that many decision meanings and interpretations exist. A basic role of the principal is to identify the multiple decision boundaries in his or her local school situation. The politics of the principalship concerns how to cope with multiple and shifting decision boundaries that affect the local school poker playing.

Obviously, the traditional interpretation of school system made the local school center a part, under the control of the central office and board of education. From a legal standpoint of the district to the state, other interpretations of the local school made little sense. From a philosophic position concerning authority, the same big-system picture was assumed. However, this assumption of local school governance role is *not* true for all school systems. Those systems buffeted by the political turbulence of the 1960s and 1970s have undergone a fundamental transformation in the decision making of local school centers. *Three factors contributed to the partial separation of the local center from the larger district system* (in all likelihood, an informal, political separation but a distinct governance separation in any case). First, in the 1960s, many principals were a focus of controversy over community control. While Ocean Hill-Brownsville[2] became a popularized expression of how parents and local community leaders could gain control of local school decision making, the challenge was occurring (in less volatile forms) all over the United States. In many cases, the governance message from the larger school system to the principal in the embattled local center was crystal clear: "It's your problem, handle it." The central office, superintendent, and board of education became reluctantly involved only when there was no other alternative. Often a common signal for the shift in decision loci was the firing or transfer of some hapless principal. Some of the kinder expressions for this sacrifice were *poor leadership* or *couldn't relate to changing times.*[3]

A second condition emphasized in the 1960s was the growth of master contract stipulations that limited the autonomy of the principal in the local school. Principals were caught between having full responsibility for the school center as line officers, yet constrained responsibility in many administrative areas due to contractual stipulations (negotiated between the teacher federation and local board of education).

The third and final condition, which became most evident in the 1970s, was the reaction to organizational bigness, which was brought on by growing scarcity and accountability.[4] Many school systems had centralized their control and governance mechanisms in the name of economic and educational efficiencies. "Bigger means better" was the cornerstone of decision rationality in budget, personnel curriculum, and facilities. Centralized decision making was also rationalized as critical to carrying out social mandates, such as desegregation.[5] The 1970s have witnessed a general disenchantment with growth models and macro system decision making. Some places that invested heavily in building elaborate transportation nets or huge comprehensive facilities found the harsh realities of *diseconomy* of scale when gasoline and heating fuels became sparse. Some school systems that had provided centrally coordinated curricular opportunities found that savings became costs when empty classrooms and lack of students became important. Finally, even some ardent desegregation advocates began to discover the values of magnet schools as an option to expand client opportunities through voluntary choice following much logistical concern about the busing option.

From the political perspective of the principalship, these conditions *served to reemphasize the local school center as a critical decision system.* Although this fundamental shift in educational governance is almost lost in the popular focus upon district versus state (and federal) control issues,[6] we feel it is a major and significant change for the 1980s. In school systems that have experienced any or all of the three conditions, there is a distinct decision boundary *between* the local center and the rest of the educational environment. This text is designed for principals who are forced to pay symbolic lip service to the total system but live with the political reality that the local school has again become a center of crucial decision action.

HOW TO DEAL WITH THE BOUNDARY

A politically effective principal must be able to identify the decision boundary of the local school arena. The boundary determines the shape of competition for scarce resources and the rules for playing. The correct identification can lead to such practical understandings as when the decision making must appear to be system-wide while actual choice is within the center. The bottom line of boundary identification rests with three questions:

1. How much upward looking occurs in making crucial local school decisions?
2. How much threat of the override or veto exists?
3. How much system support is guaranteed as a resource for the principal in local school bargaining?

To answer these questions the principal should use the following discussion to guide a personal assessment of his or her local board of education and central office.

Boards of Education

There are six issues that help define the political relation of a board of education to the local school center:

1. Who inhabits the board?
2. How does the board operate in relation to the central administration?
3. How does the board operate in relation to teacher and classified personnel federations?
4. What is the board's relation to state agencies, especially the Department of Education?
5. What has been the board's decision role in highly controversial issues?
6. What is the board's history of direct involvement in local school issues?

Despite the empassioned expressions of desires to serve all the people, which are heard in many official and unofficial pronouncements, boards are rarely, if ever, truly representative (in the assumption of one person, one vote) of the population of the local district they serve. Particularly when compared to the larger community in the United States, the composition of boards of education overrepresents certain political, economic, and social classes. Board members are most likely to be "upper middle class, WASP, and business oriented."[7] Clearly, boards must be thought of as elite mechanisms whose incumbents are a political interest group.[8] One way to determine the nature of particular political interest is to understand the processes of recruitment and selection of board members in a certain community.[9]

Perhaps the most important filter is the degree to which school board incumbents "sponsor" new recruits. As Eulau notes, "a procession of like-minded men through office is equally as effective in stabilizing policies as is low turnover."[10] In appointive situations the like-minded filter depends on the value orientation of those with power to appoint.

The distinction between recruits and candidates depends upon the ambition and anticipation of the select individuals. In reality, the individuals who survive the other political filters upon the selection process are usually very much alike. It is not surprising that school board elections are traditionally characterized by low voter turnout and lack of concrete educational issues for voters to distinguish among the candidates.[11]

In quiet or nonconflict districts, the primary indicators of board incumbency would be knowledge of efforts to perpetuate like-mindedness (whether through election or appointment). The principal needs to understand the informal pyramid(s) of community power that exist and the relation to the board as a governance mechanism. *If school matters are important to the community yet few run for office and those that do run compete by a low profile, popularity contest this does not indicate a state of no politics.* It does indicate the need for the principal to understand informal recruitment and selection as the mechanism of a special, quiet type of politics. (See Chapter 6 on noncompetitive power structures.)

In conflict districts, basic interest group theory will give indicators of board incumbency. Conflict boards usually mean a decision split in the membership voting (the label of the split can be called *liberal/conservative,* but usually means little). The principal should first determine the strength of the political majority by tracing their control over crucial votes and their consistency to hold to particular policy positions. Assuming a stable majority can be identified,[12] three indicators of clout determine political membership. First, how many points of access[13] to raise political controversy does the majority control? In the board mechanism, points of access are related to:

1. community values
2. procedures and institutions
3. defeat and modification of actual issue
4. interpretation for implementation and enforcement.[14]

Each barrier if controlled, determines access.

A second indicator is the capacity of the ruling majority to expand and/or limit the scope of conflict.[15] The third indicator of clout is the extent to which the rulers present the *layer-cake image* of school governance (chain of command) while understanding and operating within its *marble-cake realities.*[16] These indicators will give the principal a rough measure of the political sophistication of the ruling members and the possible relation of the board to school system decision making[17] *without* being sidetracked by philosophic expressions or lofty pronouncements.

Another basic question about boards of education is the relationship to central administration. Since the mid-1960s boards have been charged with being little more than rubber stamps or agencies of legitimization for administration (especially in large school systems.)[18] A major study in the 1970s[19] found that boards were controlled by administrators, but the question is still open. Boyd [20] correctly points out that *the question of control is particular to the local district.* Although central administration control will be discussed later, it is obvious that the relation of the local school decision boundary is affected by the board-central administration power situation. Generally, a board controlled by the central administration will be less likely to directly affect local school decisions than one that is not. Even if this premise fails, the controlled-board situation offers the local school principal more options to stop excessive board member interference by appealing to central administration sources for mediation.

The board's relation to teacher and classified personnel interest groups can be inferred from master contracts. It is a mistake to make a control judgment based upon public rhetoric and posturing. The contractual stipulations tell the outcome of results of bargaining. The principal should pay particular attention to the relation of actual resource agreements and constraints on real operations versus the psychological victory type of decision.[21] A second judgment should be made on the negotiating style of the board in relation to the federation. If the board completely farmed out their advocacy role to external consultants they *may* lack control of crucial choice making. Another indicator of style is the degree that the board and federation negotiate with grudging mutual respect versus immature shouts and insults. In general, the more quiet and businesslike (imitate big labor and big management) the process, the more in control of itself is the board of education.

The fourth question of the school board's relation to a local school's decision boundary concerns state and federal connections, which is far from detailed assessment of the political effect on a local school arena. However, the principal can make a rough judgment based on the number and type of rewards and sanctions a particular district receives. Some districts are perceived as lighthouses of the state, receiving many grants and subsidies from state, regional, and federal agencies, which indicate a strong board of education or, at least, a board that represents a strong district.

The fifth question concerns the history of the board in relation to controversial issues. Did the board or central administration take the initiative to handle major issues, such as a desegregation effort, or a teacher strike, or an operating levy? If the board handled the hot issue, was it their choice or were they forced into it?[22] Finally, was the hot issue cooled satisfactorily?

The sixth and final question is the most important in determining the local school boundary vis-à-vis the board of education. *If there is a recent history of direct involvement by individual board members in local school practices, the self-contained arena is in trouble.* Direct involvement usually means an override capacity by those who can solicit board member interest or, at best, a preoccupation with the possibility of such an override. The symbolic nature of public education will rarely allow a local school administrator to win in a head to head battle with a board member (regardless of how deviant the role a particular member might play to the rest of the board). If there is direct, *unwanted* involvement the principal should grin and bear it and possibly try to make the board member *a regular* in the local school arena. At first glance this strategy seems radical, but it follows the time honored tradition of overloading the system (if you can't resist by withholding, then smother).

In summary, six basic questions allow a principal to assess the strength of the local school decision boundary in relation to the board of education. The seeming we-versus-they tone of the discussion reflects the predicted "what is" of political control in the 1980s rather than a normative discussion of "what ought to be." The issues boil down to one essential question: is the local school arena off limits to specific intervention by the board of education? If the answer is yes, the boundary (for good or for evil) is secure on this front. If the answer is no, a larger arena and different assumptions of boundary are called for.

Central Office

As much as school administrators like to be identified as coming from the same club, the issues of autonomy and control differentiate the local school from the central office. The principal can gain a rough judgment of boundary by answering four questions:

1. What is the nature of the central office regime?
2. What key individuals in the central office are your greatest source of support?
3. What is the decision situation of the superintendent?
4. To what extent are principals politically organized?

Kimbrough defines central office regimes as variations of the pure bureaucracy model of organizations where the "rationally prescribed plan and the irrational manifestations of informed organizations are twisted into a particular system mix." [23] He identifies four types of regimes: the paternalistic, the bureaucratic, the confederated, and the pluralistic. The paternalistic regime emphasizes the father figure role of the superintendent in governance. Formal rules of authority and decision making are replaced by personal charisma and interactions based on loyalty. The family harmony of this regime is guaranteed by the hard-soft monkey combination. The superintendent's image of nice guy is maintained by hatchet men in the central office who play the villains (usually the business administrator). Kimbrough points out that the superintendent is a captive of this type of regime as its leader. He or she has delegated the clout to gain the image. The critical issue of local school boundary rests with the relationship of the villains or hatchet men to the principal.

Another type of regime emphasizes the bureaucratic proliferation of fixed rules, regulations, and standard operating procedures. The emphasis on routinization of policy fosters administrative dependence upon the structure of the institution and a reverence for the hierarchy of authority. The local school boundary is a function of how the chain of command is defined operationally. Autonomy can be gained, but the watchword is *CYA* (cover your donkey) with paperwork so that the appearance of a centralized orientation is always presented.

A third type of regime resembles a confederation of feudal lords. If the lords are local school principals the local school boundaries are politically recognized as the source of real power. However, it is just as likely that the confederation describes the central office arrangement of area and functional superintendents. The confederation may have occurred because of the demands of citizens, some reaction to a previous consolidation effort, or the product of how assistant and associate superintendents divide the pie. In any case, the local school boundary relates to the interpersonal connections to the various lords and the political issues in question.

The final regime emphasizes a high degree of rank-and-file participation in major decisions throughout the system. (At least the *feeling* of pluralism exists). There is much public expression of democracy and commitment to a core of ideas in this regime. Constructive criticism and dissent are accepted as a way of life in major governance decisions. No single person or group is felt to control the destiny of the schools.

Obviously, the four regimes require different strategies and tactics for a principal in the local school center. The paternalistic and bureaucratic regimes demand systemwide control and the confederated regime may require centralization if focused with the second level superintendents and supervisors. The pluralistic regime offers the best chance to maintain local school autonomy and stay consistent with system-wide sentiments. The other types of regimes need to appear to depart from actual decision operations.

The second central office question follows directly from considering types of political regimes. *The key to a successful central office relation is the identification of key individuals. The principal must know the interpreters and brokers and attempt to gain their support (or at least not make them the enemy).* The central office actors provide the advance warnings, tell the crucial details that give meaning to many central office required actions (Often the memo or letter itself makes no sense by design!) and the political support to stave off hard challenges by detractors. The same strategies that helped the principal gain and maintain local school control are applicable—*with one crucial addition.* The principal should always emphasize the superordinate relation of the central office person. Whether deserved or not, central administration personnel perceive themselves in a superior position of control. This image will be maintained, by extreme effort if necessary, regardless of political realities. The principal cannot gain by attacking the symbol that means so much; it is the cornerstone of gaining central administration alliance.

The third question of central office relation concerns the Superintendent of Schools. Traditionally, the most powerful actor in the professional structure, the superintendency has paid the price in the 1960s and 1970s. Today, administrators live with the reality of "Chiefs under Fire" [24] and a survival time ranging from 18 months in big cities to a national average of less than four years in all school systems. Two popular roles for superintendents today are the statesperson with a national reputation or the leader of a business oriented management team. (The third role in the paternalistic system is decreasing in political credibility.) Either of the popular roles increases the probability the superintendent will not take a major responsibility for local school decisions. The important message for principals is that the "top of the system" may not represent the political potential for boundary maintenance that it once did.

The final factor to consider in judging the relation of the central office is the principal's organization. In some systems the principals have banded together to help shape their political destinies. Any member of such a principal's organization should use it to help define local school decision boundaries. However, in many school systems today local school principals continue to remain the lost tribe in school politics. In this case, the principal will have to go it alone.

In summary, four questions concerning the central office relation to a local school arena help round out the general guidance for a principal's assessment of decision boundary. With the basic identification completed, this discussion turns to specific strategies for maintaining the local school boundary to its school system environment.

STRATEGIES

At first glance it may seem strange to suggest operating strategies designed for federal agencies dealing with Congress as the best guides for local schools to use to cope with the educational environment. What is to follow is most appropriate for local schools that have some decision boundary and resemble the quasi-independent relations of the federal agency to a larger governance system. For the administrator in a school system that sends the following three informal messages, the strategies suggested by Aaron Wildavsky[25] are most appropriate. The informal messages are:

1. Don't challenge us publically.
2. Don't get in trouble.
3. Whatever you want we probably don't have.

Wildavsky argues there are two general strategies to follow in an organization that gives the above messages. One strategy (ubiquitous) is designed to create a generally favorable image with the board and central office. The second strategy (contingent) is designed to (1) guard against cuts or (2) increase size of resources with old programs, or (3) increase size of resources with new programs.

The Image Strategy

When a principal creates a generally favorable image he or she has the ability to have his or her local school identified from all other schools in the system (and himself or herself from all other principals) in a positive light. The general guidelines include:

- find, serve, and expand your clientele (students, parents, etc.)
- concentrate on individual constituents (emphasize the personal)
- create the image *divided we stand, united we fall* (one school versus the rest)
- don't admit to giving in to pressure
- understand spending and cutting moods

The general guidelines for creating an image lead to specific strategies that can help to gain a board's and/or central office's confidence. The specific strategies for image making include:

- be what they think *they* are (e.g., if they are progressive, be progressive)
- play it straight (be above board)
- develop sense of integrity for all actions
- understand give and take
- pay special attention to working with subcommittees (the board) and key staff (administration)

The third part of a strategy to create a favorable image deals with guidelines for securing local school resources, once confidence has been secured. This concerns the way the heading (by board or central administration) about a specific proposal should occur:

1. have a rehearsal (guess the tough questions)
2. avoid surprises (gain inside information if possible)
3. have "a plant" (if possible, someone sympathetic to frame the right questions)
4. paint a portrait (set request in general framework)
5. know the budget (the bottom line will be questions of cost)
6. play the game (sometimes only defeat is possible)

The Contingent Strategy

Beyond the strategies of creating a favorable local school image there are three decision situations when the principal needs further guidance. The contingent strategy is employed to (1) guard against cuts in present resources, (2) increase the present resources on the basis of what is now going on, and (3) increase resources by arguing for new programs. The conditions require different emphasis and the defense against cuts seems to be the order of the day for many administrators in the 1980s. Wildavsky offers six different arguments that might be used against local school program cuts:

1. offer to cut the most popular program
2. present cut options as all or nothing
3. argue you are squeezed to the wall
4. alter the form but not the substance of the present conditions
5. shift the blame (if cuts are based upon failures)
6. argue that the board or central office must choose cuts

Obviously, the particular political relations determine if any or all of these strategies will do any good. *The basic rationale is to defend existing resources by strengthening the perception of negative consequences related to possible cuts.* However, the principal must also temper defense strategies against the earlier message of image. When the cutting mood is in full swing there may be no satisfactory defense. In these situations, the savvy principal is one who lives to fight another day.

On a more optimistic note, there are also contingent strategies for expanding the local school resources. When a principal plans to increase resources by arguing from the existing programs his or her basic strategy is to inch ahead. This strategy is facilitated by the following suggestions:

1. argue the increase is old stuff and just part of the base
2. show some slight shifting, don't stand pat
3. use the advantage of rounding figures upward
4. transfer items so no one increase seems out of line
5. emphasize maintenance rather than buying something new

The final strategy guideline occurs when the principal is attempting to increase the local school resources by arguing for new programs (the most difficult case). Some arguments include:

· start with the wedge—if the camel's nose is accepted, the body might follow

- argue "just for now"
- present arguments in percentages or ratios to total so that increase seems small
- relate to a long-range goal
- argue increase as "if this, then that"
- argue as part of workload
- "it will pay for itself, long-run profit"
- tie to crisis

THE LANGUAGE OF UPWARD COMMUNICATION

The principal's perspective concerning the identification of board and central office politics has been discussed, and the particular issue of negotiating the boundary under conditions of scarcity has been addressed. Still remaining is the question of what *language* is appropriate for negotiating *up the hierarchy*. Regardless of personality and political relations with key individuals, the principal acts within the formal organization. In most school systems the appropriate formal language to present demands and negotiate decisions is systems planning.

When planning language is considered from the arena perspective much of the mysticism of planning expertise and the rhetoric of rational decision making dissolve. The planning process or systems approach[26] is little more than a special set of rules by which a particular brand of poker can be played for dealing with those on top. Those people who have a particular investment in planning argue that the rules create a superior decision process and, consequently, a better product. While true for mechanistic problems this argument is debatable in human problems and in unstable decision contexts.[27] From a political standpoint, the value of planning per se is found in the common language it promotes among players and the limits placed upon decision making for particular options. Planning does make players consider legitimate issues of choice and it has high symbolic value in promoting a feeling of being logical, but it does not automatically make the arena better.

The relationship of systems analysis to decision making is explained:

> It consists of an assumed, if preliminary, objective; the derivation of alternative paths towards achieving this objective, which may itself change as the options are enumerated; the estimation of performance and cost/effectiveness measures to ensure that the chosen objective is being met by an efficient use of inputs in relation to outputs; and finally a closing of the circle through feedback mechanisms that review actual performance in the light of objective.[28]

In theory, the process is continuous and repetitive, with an ongoing reevaluation of alternatives, objectives, and results. In the real life of large organizations the reevaluation and readjustment process bogs down once a decision is made and resources implemented.[29]

The basic question of systematic planning or the systems approach is how do costs relate to benefits for each choice alternative. This question is focused in setting goals or objectives, choosing strategies, and setting specific tactics. Figure 5.1 schematically illustrates the planning process.

The process can be used for several practical purposes. In goal setting, the process demands that specific indicators be identified. An indicator must be identifiable in concrete form and be able to assess progress toward achieving a goal. The principal who is involved in this stage of the process makes sure that choice over goal indicators reflect (1) conditions of suc-

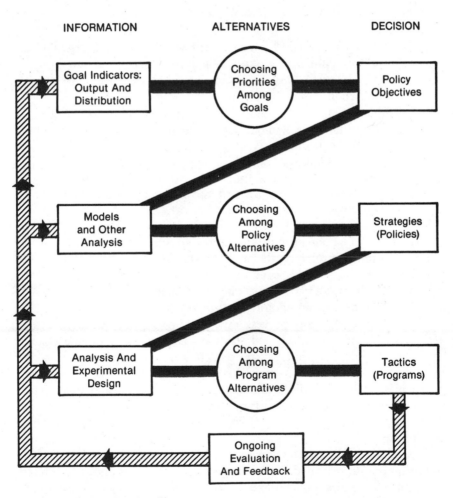

FIGURE 5.1   *The Planning Process*

cess not a judgment of good or bad change and (2) a measure of real "what is" results, not the *shoulds* or *oughts* of self-fulfilling prescriptions. Planners argue the indicators should be quantifiable for statistical analysis, but this argument is a two-edged political sword. Many principals have been outstripped when the special language of planning becomes statistics. Each administrator should attempt to use the indicators that he or she can discuss most cogently and monitor most effectively.

Strategy selection usually introduces feasibility issues into the choice process. The meaning of feasible is also a political concern no matter how the planning language about efficiency or effectiveness presents the case. The principal should guide the feasibility consideration of various change alternatives to issues of finances, socialization, and technological possibility. The impact of resources availability and the state of mind of educators on change possibilities has already been discussed. Caplow[30] offers the following guidance in the consideration of technological change:

1. Adopt a technological improvement when it offers a large and un-mistakable reduction of costs or gain of efficacy, or both.
2. Reject a technological improvement when its costs or its efficacy are uncertain.
3. Adopt a technological improvement if it can be introduced on an experimental basis without serious jeopardy to the organizational program in case of failure.
4. Reject a technological improvement that exposes the organization to disaster in certain contingencies such as the disappearance of a supplier or the displacement of the proposed new technology by a still more advanced technology.

In times of abundance people seem to turn to technology as the panacea. In times of scarcity, the principal should insure that those affected consider such issues as the value of multimedia equipment without electricity and so forth. The true meanings of efficiency and effectiveness in strategy selection depend upon these types of practical questions.

Finally, the planning process raises questions of specific tactics or activities to carry out a selected strategy. Depending upon the change, this stage provides the principal an excellent reason to raise concerns about incumbents of the school or emphasize scarce conditions. The best-planned goal and strategy will die without appropriate tactics, and this focuses the questions of the school's strengths and weaknesses. Can principals deliver what they want to do? If so, who, how, what, when, and where will it happen.[31]

In summary, the systems approach to a change effort is most politically valuable because it provides a language to talk upward and, if mastered, gives particular rules to play poker with. The language should be matched to the realities of a certain change proposal as it goes through three stages of consideration: goal setting, strategy consideration, and the selection of tactics. As a player, the principal can use the language of the planning process to guarantee consideration of the change being sought. Like all elements of the arena, there is no guarantee of success through such maneuvering. However, even the failure of the principal's desired change does not render the planning process useless. Its value could be presented as a way to foster some order and understanding to the arena of the local school, which the language creates itself. Bluntly, systematic planning has some value as a way to communicate about decision making that is above and beyond the specific results of the change effort.

CASE STORY: NEGOTIATING REDUCTIONS

The following case story shows a practical example of bargaining about the local school's interest and establishing a political boundary using systems language.

An unsettled feeling came over Sylvia as the Superintendent continued his budget report to all administrators. So this was what a conservative school board meant. They were really serious about cutting 15 percent of the local school district budget by next year. Never had any of the administrators thought that a basic budget could mean this. Sylvia leaned forward to catch the Superintendent's summation. . . .

> . . . and so I'm asking for the assistance and cooperation of each of you in meeting this contingency. You will be asked to assess your drop in enrollment since last year and adjust your staff patterns accordingly. . . .

The following week Sylvia received the much-dreaded envelope from the district office that indicated what the fair share would be at her junior high school. The figure, $49,000, was roughly equivalent to four personnel lines any way you cut it. Four teaching positions lost when they were already at over 1:21 in teacher/student ratio. Each building principal had two months to indicate which teaching positions would be eliminated for the coming school year.

A week later Sylvia was at the district office for her appointment with the Assistant Superintendent for Business. She went armed with what she considered a number of logical arguments why she couldn't eliminate any positions at this point. First, she had a small school compared with other intermediate schools in the district. Any cut in staff would necessarily affect the curriculum available to students. Further, the enrollment drop in her attendance area had to be a temporary phenomena . . . probably caused by the closing of that small machine manufacturing plant over on Jefferson. Finally, she reminded the gentleman that her school had not been one to make lavish financial demands on the district in the past. Her junior high had a good record of giving.

While the conference did not improve her school's position for the reduction in force mandate, Sylvia did find out what she couldn't do to meet the required savings. First, she could not use equipment or operations money to make the $49,000 payoff. Since approximately 85 percent of her school budget was in salaries, the board felt that use of other monies at this time would erode the base (fixed items like operating capital for materials, etc.) in the eyes of the new board. If she could get along without $49,000 in equipment this year, the board would reason that she could also get along without it the following year.

Second, the board was quite emphatic that some programs were not to be disturbed during this cut. They did not, for instance, want any principal scapegoating sports programs at this time. Nor could any teacher in basic areas (not defined) be removed. The principals were to use professional judgment and do the job for which they were being paid.

Finally, the board had specifically requested that principals not meet with one another to discuss these reductions. Each principal was to eliminate the positions least necessary for the operation of his or her school.

Sylvia returned from her meeting with the Assistant Superintendent fully depressed. She could not juggle figures to average enrollment years. She could not argue her decline as a temporary solution. She could not use comparative data in arguing for a critical mass needed to operate her school given its small size. She could not go after those sacred cows grazing in the educational pasture such as the junior high football league, the strings ensemble, or the junior theatre program. She could not even look to special appropriations for remedial or gifted programs as a target. No, it would be the base faculty positions that would be targeted for reduction.

Sylvia remembered reading about two approaches to this situation. In another city nearby, one principal had simply hired a team of consultants to come in and point the finger. Such an analysis and decision-making technique, while often superficial, left the impression of objectivity. The other technique she had read about was to fire everyone (termination notices), write new job descriptions, and hire back all but four of her people. That technique had been widely used in California after Proposition 13. Neither of these approaches was really Sylvia's style.

Sylvia finally decided on going to a modified zero-based budget approach with her faculty. Using program as a focus, Sylvia asked department heads to identify those programs (1) most critical, (2) necessary, and (3) useful. Each of these categories were to be linked with personnel teaching in the program and dollars expended on those personnel. In the meantime, Sylvia began compiling data on how many students were enrolled in certain classes and what those classes cost in terms of equipment, consumable materials, and other support dollars.

The first attempt at such analysis, given that the "word was on the land," was not highly successful. Nearly every position came back as critical, with the exception of one department which was feuding with each other. Noting mentally that it all rolls down hill, Sylvia sent the forms back to the department heads with a stronger mandate to discriminate. Finally, after conferring with each department head individually, Sylvia was able to get two discernable categories: critical and necessary. Reviewing the necessary group, there appeared to be two positions that could be eliminated without terrible problems for the curriculum. One position was in social studies and the other was the second business education position. Beyond these two positions, there was nothing that could be eliminated without really tearing into course offerings.

Following a week of contemplation Sylvia knew that she must try once more to get relief from the reduction in force mandate. She finally decided on a move that had served her well in the past, and invited a member of the school board who had children at her school to lunch. While at lunch Sylvia described to the board member the problems she was having. Sylvia was careful to have a photographer at the school who took numerous pictures of the board member in the lunchroom and especially in the art and music rooms. She thanked the board member for hearing her out as she left the school.

A week later, a special article in the local newspaper featured Sylvia's school and its fine arts programs. With the article was a picture of a member of the local school board during a visit inspecting the art and music areas. The caption under the picture read: "Local Board Member Supports Arts Program." Sylvia clipped the article and sent to to the board member with a short note indicating that these programs would probably be eliminated if her small junior high school had to find any more than $25,000 for the reduction effort. Sylvia noted that she thought such reductions should be related to the size of the school and that two positions would surely be her fair share.

Case Questions

1. In this case Sylvia tried several ways to deal with the reduction demands. Did she overlook some promising possibilities for resolution?
2. What were some specific contingency strategies that Sylvia might have used to sway the Assistant Superintendent for Business?
3. Should Sylvia have contacted other principals in an attempt to find a solution even though she was instructed not to do so?
4. What risks did Sylvia take in inviting a school board member into her school under these conditions? Was she setting a desirable precedent?

5. If a principal goes "public" with a case, such as the newspaper technique used by Sylvia, what happens to boundaries and arena stability?

6. Can you suggest another strategy or technique that might be used to deal with this situation?

CHAPTER SUMMARY

Relationships with boards of education and the central administration are political and defined by the organizational context. In the 1980s the local school center will be the critical decision system in public schools. Principals must, therefore, identify and define the boundary that pinpoints the demarcation of local school concerns from system (environment) concerns.

The boundary determines the *shape* of competition for scarce resources and the rules for playing in the arena. Patterns of upward communication, the threat of decision veto, and system-level support are all indicators of the real boundary for decision making.

Six basic questions are provided that a principal may use to assess the strength of the local school decision boundary as it relates to the board of education. In determining central office strength, the principal should identify key individuals as the most effective means of assessing the interface. Finally, strategies for the principal are suggested and a case story presented for analysis and reflection.

NOTES

1. David Easton, *A Framework For Political Analysis* (Englewood Cliffs, N.J.: Prentice-Hall, 1965), especially discussion of *Gatekeeping*.
2. M. Fantini, M. Gittell, and R. Magat, *Community Control and the Urban School* (New York: Praeger, 1970); Maurice Berube and M. Gittell, *Confrontation at Ocean Hill-Brownsville* (New York: Praeger, 1971).
3. David Wiles, "Community Participation Demands and Local School Response in the Urban Environment," *Education and Urban Society* 6 (August 1974): 451–467.
4. Jonathan Sher and Rachel Thompkins, "The Myth of Rural School and District Consolidation," *Educational Forum*, November 1976–January 1977, pp. 95–107, 137–153. Highly recommended for a general understanding of the bigness issue.
5. W. Grant, "Community Control vs. School Integration: The Detroit Case," *Public Interest* 24 (Summer 1971): 62–79.
6. Iannaccone makes the extreme statement "every policy of any importance is determined at the state level." See Laurence Iannaccone, *Education Policy Systems* (Ft. Lauderdale: NOVA Press, 1975), p. 97.
7. A 1962 U.S. survey found over 60 percent of all board members were either

in business or rendered professional services. This finding has been confirmed in more recent studies by the National School Boards Association.

8. Robert Salisbury argues that boards perpetuate the *myth of the unitary community* to keep the image of pluralism in an elite structure. The myth is based upon the assumption that a nonpolitical board should not recognize representation differences to insure equal, objective treatment of all children. He further notes there is nothing so unequal as the equal treatment of unequals. See Robert Salisbury "School and Politics in the Big City," *Harvard Educational Review* 37 (Summer 1967): 342–359.

9. Kenneth Prewitt, *The Recruitment of Political Leaders* (Indianapolis: Bobbs Merrill, 1970).

10. Heinz Eulau, *Micro-Macro Political Analysis* (Chicago: Aldine, 1969), p. 316.

11. See, for example, Peter J. Cistone, "Municipal Political Structure and Role Allocation in Educational Decision Making: An Exploration of One Linkage," *Urban Education* 6 (July/October 1971): 147–165; Neal Gross, *Who Runs Our Schools?* (New York: Wiley, 1958); Laurence Iannaccone and Frank W. Lutz, *Politics, Power and Policy: The Governing of Local School Districts* (Columbus, Ohio: Charles E. Merrill, 1970). The Iannaccone and Lutz effort is especially helpful in assessing change of boards over time.

12. There is the special case where original coalitions have dissolved and no one can tell who wants what (and may not want to know!). The best strategy for the principal is to study undercover and watch out for central administration efforts to shift the heat downward. See Theodore Lowi's discussion of the "iron law of decadence," in Theodore Lowi, *The Politics of Disorder* (New York: Basic Books, 1974).

13. David Truman, *The Governmental Process* (New York: Alfred A. Knopf, 1951).

14. Peter Bachrach and Morton Baratz, *Power and Poverty* (New York: Oxford University Press, 1970), pp. 58–62.

15. E. E. Schattschneider, *The Semi-Sovereign People* (New York: Holt, Rinehart and Winston, 1960). However, he also notes that those who perceive themselves to be losing always try to expand the scope of conflict, while those winning try to limit the scope. A related term, "Wallop," refers to the capacity to generate multiple access *and* strength (if the issue is to convince some other agency). See Morton Grodzin, *The American System* (Chicago: Rand McNally, 1966).

16. Morton Grodzin, *The American System* (Chicago: Rand McNally, 1966).

17. David Minar, "The Community Basis of Conflict in School System Politics," *American Sociological Review* 31 (December 1966): 822–835.

18. Norman Kerr, "The School Board As An Agency of Legitimization," *Sociology of Education* (B 8, 1964): 34–59; David Wiles and Houston Conley, "School Boards: Policy Making Relevance," *Teachers College Record* 75 (February 1974): 309–318.

19. Harman Zeigler and Kent Jennings, *Governing American Schools* (Scituate, Mass.: Duxbury Press, 1974).

20. William Boyd, "The Public, The Professionals and Educational Policy Making: Who Governs?" *Teachers College Record* 77 (May 1977): 539–577.

21. Charles Perry and Wesley Wildman, *The Impact of Negotiations in Public Education* (Worthington: Charles Jones, 1971).

22. A particular indicator of administrator strength is the ability to transfer no-win issues to the board for resolution.

23. Ralph Kimbrough, *Administering Elementary Schools* (New York: Macmillan, 1966), p. 52.
24. Larry Cuban, *School Chiefs Under Fire* (Chicago: University of Chicago Press, 1975).
25. Aaron Wildavsky, *The Politics of the Budgetary Process*, 3rd ed. (Boston: Little, Brown, 1979), pp. 63–126.
26. Although systematic planning and systems analysis are used interchangeably in this discussion there is some debate whether one is the subset of the other. For a discussion of general application see David Easton, *A Systems Analysis of Political Life* (New York: Wiley, 1965).
27. For example, urban planning has not solved the alienation of the city ghetto and military planning did not win the hearts and minds of the Vietnamese. See Phillip Slater, *The Pursuit of Loneliness* (Boston: Beacon Press, 1970).
28. Economic Council of Canada, *Design for Decision* (Ottawa: Information Canada, 1971), p. 28.
29. This is a partial reason for cost overruns and why zero-base budgeting in large bureaucracies is often a joke. It becomes impossible to go back to square one. See Aaron Wildavsky, *The Politics of the Budgetary Process*, 3rd ed. (Boston: Little, Brown, 1979).
30. Theodore Caplow, *How to Run Any Organization* (Hinsdale, Ill.: Dryden Press, 1976), p. 195.
31. The fourth stage of feedback is usually included at this point. Planning will be discussed in the realm of policy formulation, and the monitoring and evaluative part of the systems cycle will be included in later discussions of actual implementation.

CHAPTER 6

Parents, Community Groups and Students

People other than educators are also politically involved in local school matters and form a second boundary issue for arena concerns. These people can be loosely identified as the community. From the principal's perspective, the community can be divided into three sets of actors. These groups are, in order of *political* importance to the local school center: the parents, the organized interest groups within the attendance area, and the students. Many educators will sharply question this generalization about order of importance and cite specific examples where students or interest groups outside a particular attendance area dominated political attention. We argue for the primacy of parents as the key boundary actors of the community for the following reasons:

1. Principals can successfully mobilize parent support to withstand challenges of attendance area interest groups. Put another way, a principal can identify parents as *the* interest group with direct interest in the education of their children, which supersedes the political legitimacy of other groups who represent the community.

2. In nonneighborhood school situations where students are drawn to a location from a larger system-wide jurisdiction, parents may become the only sustaining link with community interests.

3. Most issues that involve organized interests with influences beyond the attendance area are negotiated at the school system level of school governance. A local school may be identified as an *example* of a particular problem, but the actual dynamics of politics that resolve issues are usually a system-wide phenomenon.

4. The overt external political expression of student unrest in the late 1960s has gone inward. Today, students have a greater potential to be political actors inside a particular school arena than boundary links that represent a larger community interest.

These reasons lead us to conclude that the 1980s principal should concentrate on affecting the parents within the immediate school boundary. The lessons learned from dealing with parents as an interest group should have merit in considering strategies to approach nonparent groups. Although the personality relationship between parents and their children is tenuous in some situations, we assume a sustained political relationship. This is especially true in situations where the principal can point out the consequences (legal and political) of a parent's taking responsibility for his or her child.[1]

THE PARENTS

Perhaps the first issue a principal should be concerned with is the historically negative way in which educators have treated parents and other community members. Part of the quasi-sacred insulation of public schools relates to the fact that educators were generally immune from direct, critical scrutiny by the very people who contributed clients (children) to the institution.[2] It seems fair to expect some general retention of that insulation today, no matter how open the local school or how much present realities may have altered past arrangements. Professional expertise and formal role continue to place a type of hierarchical barrier and promote an implicit superordinate-subordinate relationship between the parent and the administrator. While this arrangement seems appropriate for some functions, it seems unnecessary and unproductive for other relations. A critical task for the principal is to make the different and shifting communication roles of the arena clear to the parent. Remember that many parents have only experienced school as a student and, quite possibly, see only a passive role as natural. In many cases, they retain a parental image of the principal that blocks effective two-way communication.

Recognizing the impact of this previous experience by parents, the principal can counteract its negative effect by emphasizing a new day. Our advice is that it's a losing proposition to give the impression that parents are to contribute their child for educational processing or to suggest that they are not to scrutinize school practices. Boundary identification and maintenance depends upon open recognition of give and take and, more important, that student achievement seems related to parental support. Since 1966 when James Coleman first studied the impact of federally subsidized compensatory learning efforts[3] one research message has come through clearly: *the home and community account for much of the variation in pupil achievement.* The parent is the most direct link to the home *and for that reason alone must be considered a partner in helping their child become educated.* This seems to be a political reality, not philosophic sentiment. The purpose of the school is to educate the child and a major contributor (perhaps *the* contributor) to achieving that purpose needs to be included *within* the school arena when possible.

A second negative image should also be confronted openly—the past uses of organizational mechanisms to manipulate parents. Robert Dahl [4] notes that some schools have attempted to create a democratic ritual as a means for principals to gain and retain an image of popular support. The past misuse of special parent-oriented associations to achieve the ritual has created a present skepticism in bodies such as the PTA. Dahl captures the most negative impression of this misuse:

> Ostensibly, of course, the Parent-Teachers Association is a democratic organization....brought into being and sustained by joint interests. In practice the P.T.A. is usually an instrument of the school administrator....it is a rare P.T.A. that ever opposes the wishes of a principal and *its mere existence helps give a certain legitimacy*....a P.T.A. is also useful to head off or settle conflicts between parents and the school....P.T.A. meetings create an atmosphere of friendliness and conviviality that blunts criticism....the experienced principal or teacher learns from P.T.A. meetings who are the most interested parents and who the "trouble-makers" might be....[5]

A third contributor to blocks between parents and educators is the past practice of treating school-community relations as some function best served by a Madison Avenue promotion agency. In this situation the personal element and direct, concrete contact between educators and parents are deliberately replaced by glossy abstractions about the good of the kids and pedantic advice, such as "visit a school, attend a board meeting, tour areas where new schools have been built in recent years." [6]

These general impressions may only augment specific negative experiences parents may have encountered concerning their child or themselves as school-aged children. The principal should not be surprised by a parent's initial suspicion or even open hostility. We believe the parent is an essential actor in the school enterprise and the principal should make every effort to convince the parent of such a reality.

The problem for the principal reduces from *if* the parent should be within the decision boundary of the local school, to *how* should the parent be involved. The most important lesson to come out of collective negotiations is that people do not just get into making substantive decisions. In fact, the track record shows that those who attempt to start making real decisions immediately often end in impasse. These lessons are as appropriate for two individuals as they are for two organized groups. The "dance" may look different but the "stepping on toes" seems to occur in both cases. What is needed *is specific understanding of procedural rules for deciding before trying to make a decision.* Decide how to decide with your parents (this message holds for the principal's contact with any community interest). Because parents have the most direct investment, they as both individuals or a group are most likely to argue and decide on emotional grounds. From a political perspective, this style of play is as good as any other except that it violates the normal, hard practicality of most local school arenas. In some cases, its novelty may make a parent a winner in a heated controversy. Most likely, the emotional parent(s) will be ignored or "ganged up" only by the "reasonable" players. This unfortunate circumstance can be avoided. Parents have an important decision role in the local school arena if procedural rules are established and agreed upon beforehand.

The most basic understanding to be reached is whether a parent is included in the arena to be informed by the other players, to advise the real players, or to actually be a player. Obviously, this understanding calls for differentiation of specific issues where a role would be appropriate. This understanding is hard to achieve but it is the cornerstone of real parental involvement. The principal should devote his or her effort as a major player to bringing the understanding about (e.g., devote inservice training to an actual demonstration of the consequences of not achieving understanding). Sometimes the parental decision role is decided for the principal by other authorities. For example, Title I funds mandated *advisory* boards[7] but the Individualized Educational Practice (IEP) portion of handicapped legislation (PL 94-142)[8] mandates parental *approval* of training specifics for their child. This distinction may be useful in getting other arena players to understand the possibility of a variety of issue-specific parent decision roles.

The second basic concern is to gain parental understanding of their actual decision role in relation to the other players (assuming their involvement is beyond being informed or advising). The parents need to understand the poker rules of play. The principal should be especially aware of the sensitivity surrounding this parental awareness. The school arena may well be seen as an alien, threatening place where the parent often expects professional jargon and hostility to dominate. The rules of play should be explained *in conjunction with* special emphasis on making the parents know they are a valued, significant, and welcome addition to the arena. Specific questions to be resolved before actual parental involvement include: When is majority rule appropriate? What are professional issues where the parent does not exercise a vote? What are parental issues where the parent players have veto power? What do the parents expect the decision role of the principal to be?

The third concern to be determined *before* parents are involved in deciding particular issues is the relation of the individual players to the larger constituency of parents. First, do parents represent others or act on their own when deciding? Second, do the parent players decide as instructed delegates or vote their own conscience?

If the three concerns of arena involvement are addressed openly, parents can become valuable members of the local school arena. The following suggestions for working with groups of parents also have applicability to other constituents.

WORKING WITH GROUPS

While interpersonal relationships in organizations occur in dyads on the one hand and large populations on the other, much communication by administrators will be in groups (such as parent committees). As such, promoting effective small-group communication is one of the most important process skills an administrator can possess, and is an area where the administrative skills will be most closely scrutinized.

Groups can be described as two or more people who interact for a common purpose. As groups pursue objectives their behavior is affected by a number of variables including the background of the group, the participation patterns of the group, the goals of the group, institutional standards that affect the group, procedures affecting the group, and the atmosphere or climate affecting the group. Administrators can control most of these variables using their interpersonal and decision skills.

Groups perform many tasks that are important to the development of school programs and the overall image of administrative effectiveness. Among those tasks are:

- initiating activities such as suggesting new ideas, defining problems, proposing solutions, developing materials, and initiating communication
- coordinating activities such as pulling ideas together and relating the activities of various subgroups within the school
- summarizing activities such as pooling related data and restating suggestions after discussions
- testing activities such as examining the feasibility of ideas and making preevaluation decisions about activities

Research on group work is extensive and provides for the administrator a number of observations that can guide interaction with groups. Wiles and Bondi[9] summarize some of the findings about what it takes for a group to be effective in its proceedings:

> If a group is to be productive, the individuals in the group must first become a group in the psychological sense by acquiring a feeling of group belongingness. This feeling is the product of individual members accepting what they feel to be a central purpose.
>
> If a group is to be productive, its members must have a common definition of the undertaking in which they are to engage.
>
> If a group is to be productive, it must have a task of some real consequence to perform.
>
> If a group is to be productive, its members must feel that something will actually come of what they are expected to do; said

differently, its members must not feel that what they are to do is simply busywork.

If a group is to be productive, the dissatisfaction of its members with the aspects of the status quo to which the group's undertaking relates must outweigh in their minds whatever threats to their comfort they perceive in the performance of this undertaking.

If a group is to be productive, its members must not be expected or required to attempt undertakings which are beyond their respective capabilities or which are so easy for the individuals in question to perform that they feel no sense of real accomplishment.

If a group is to be productive, decisions as to work, planning, assignment, and scheduling must be made, whenever possible, on a shared basis within the group, and through the method of consensus rather than of majority vote; in instances in which these decisions either have already been made by exterior authority or in which they must be made by the group leader alone, the basis for the decisions must be clearly explained to all members of the group.

If a group is to be productive, each member of the group must clearly understand what he is expected to do and why, accept his role, and feel himself responsible to the group for its accomplishment.

If a group is to be productive, its members must communicate in a common language.

If a group is to be productive, its members must be guided by task-pertinent values which they share in common.

If a group is to be productive, it is usually necessary for its members to be in frequent face-to-face association with one another.

If a group is to be productive, its members must have a common (though not necessarily talked about) agreement as to their respective statuses within the group.

If a group is to be productive, each of its members must gain a feeling of individual importance from his personal contributions in performing the work of the group.

If a group is to be effective, the distribution of credit for its accomplishments must be seen as equitable by its members.

If a group is to be productive, it must keep on the beam and not spend time on inconsequential or irrelevant matters.

If a group is to be productive, the way it goes about its work must be seen by its members as contributing to the fulfillment of their respective tissue and social-psychological needs, and, by extension, of those of their dependents (if any) as well.

If a group is to be productive, the status leader must make the actual leadership group centered, with the leadership role passing freely from member to member.

If a group is to be productive, the task it is to perform must be consistent with the purposes of other groups to which its members belong.

If a group is to be productive, the satisfactions its members expect to experience from accomplishing the group's tasks must outweigh in their minds the satisfactions they gain from their membership in the group per se.

Especially when working with parents in groups on student concerns at the school the principal should regularly check his or her performance standards by assessing group member satisfaction. The group evaluation form in Table 6.1 suggests the type of considerations such evaluation might address.

The form offers some simple direction to the arena processes without being so specific that members feel threatened. People who are unfamiliar or uncertain of the actual dynamics of decision making may use a simple evaluation form (Table 6.1) to diagnose group communication processes without being manipulated by a complex assessment form. Bluntly, such a simple form may generate less real data but it also allows everyone to be the expert interpreter of the process. From a political standpoint in dealing with parents or other community groups, simplicity seems to be more honest and effective as a way to improve group interactions.

COMMUNITY INTEREST GROUPS

The ideas of parents acting as representatives of a particular constituency (the parents) raises another arena boundary issue. Interest groups from the community have played a direct decision role in local school affairs for many years. Some of the more publicized are the community-control movement in large cities of the late 1960s[10] and the Charleston, West Virginia "godless" textbook controversy of the mid 1970s.[11] At the less publicized level, local schools throughout the nation face particular interest group demands to help decide everything from hiring a new coach, changing a school nickname, or altering a particular curriculum.

To help understand the boundary issue for the *local school*, the principal should first determine the extent to which interest groups focus on educational issues at the school *center* level. Knowledge of the general power structure(s)[12] in the attendance area and a tracing of how past issues were resolved *should tell whether the attendance area is a natural political boundary*. If the climate is to kick major local school issues up

TABLE 6.1   *Group Evaluation Form*

A: GOALS

Poor   1   2   3   4   5   6   7   8   9   10   *Good*

| Confused; diverse; conflicting; indifferent; little interest. | Clear to all; shared by all; all care about the goals, feel involved. |

B: PARTICIPATION

Poor   1   2   3   4   5   6   7   8   9   10   *Good*

| Few dominate; some passive; some not listened to; several talk at once or interrupt. | All get in; all are really listened to. |

C: FEELINGS

Poor   1   2   3   4   5   6   7   8   9   10   *Good*

| Unexpected; ignored or criticized. | Freely expressed; empathic responses. |

D: DIAGNOSIS OF GROUP PROBLEMS

Poor   1   2   3   4   5   6   7   8   9   10   *Good*

| Jump directly to remedial proposals; treat symptoms rather than basic causes. | When problems arise the situation is carefully diagnosed before action is proposed; remedies attack basic causes. |

E: LEADERSHIP

Poor   1   2   3   4   5   6   7   8   9   10   *Good*

| Group needs for leadership not met; group depends too much on single person or on a few persons. | As needs for leadership arise, various members meet them ("distributed leadership"); anyone feels free to volunteer as he sees a group need. |

F: DECISIONS

Poor   1   2   3   4   5   6   7   8   9   10   *Good*

| Needed decisions don't get made; decision made by part of group; others uncommitted. | Consensus sought and tested; deviates appreciated and used to improve decision; decisions when made are fully supported. |

G: TRUST

Poor 1 2 3 4 5 6 7 8 9 10 *Good*

Members distrust one an-
other; are polite, careful,
closed, guarded; they listen superficially but in-
wardly reject what others
say; are afraid to criticize
or to be criticized.

Members trust one an-
other; they reveal to
group what they would
be reluctant to expose to
others; they respect and
use the responses they
get; they can freely ex-
press negative reactions
without fearing reprisal.

H: CREATIVITY AND GROWTH

Poor 1 2 3 4 5 6 7 8 9 10 *Good*

Members and group in a
rut; operate routinely;
persons stereotyped and
rigid in their roles; no
progress.

Group flexible, seeks new
and better ways; individ-
uals changing and grow-
ing; creative; individually
supported.

Source: From Jon Wiles and Joseph Bondi, *Supervision: A Guide to Practice* (Charles E. Merrill Publishing Company, 1980) pp. 155–57. Used by permission of the publisher.

to system-wide arenas, the principal should *not* try to involve nonparent interest groups. The local school arena will only become a place for a priori posturing to build a case for getting into the big leagues. In this case, the principal should make symbolic gestures of concern and facilitate the transfer to the larger arenas.

Assuming certain interest groups are identified that confine their concerns to the local school center, the second issue of involvement is to judge why certain people may wish to influence school decision mak-ing. Many popular schemes to classify interest group demands are exactly *wrong*. One example is to judge left and right or progressive and con-servative as a *continuum*. A landmark expression of this fallacy in an article by Michael Katz[13] discusses which groups are likely to push the schools for reform (of any type). He challenges the continuum model by listing five different groups of reformers: middle class liberals, radical romantics, middle class conservatives, ultra conservatives, and the poor. Some or all of these groups may be found in a particular attendance area.

One of the interest groups attempting to influence local school deci-sions is the upper and/or middle class *liberal*. The liberal position is cen-tered on an optimistic faith in the schools as they exist today, an environ-mentalist view of causes for school failure, and a strong elitist position for class oriented control. At the beginning of the late 1960s reform movement, the liberal focused his or her efforts on the improvement of urban schools and ending *de facto* segregation. Katz points to the emphasis on heredity and environment in the ultimate rationale for school problems as the direct cause of liberal frustration. Pointing to terms such as cultural deprivation and compensatory effort Katz states:

> The racism inherent in the liberal's position is subtle .... its genteel wrapping covers its animus; the general tone is pity for the deprived slum child .... who lacks respect for education. This attitude strenuously avoids condemning the child and places blame on the background. It views the job of the schools as massively compensatory .... its sponsors consistently have failed to see that it is condescending and patronizing, or offensive, to the poor themselves. Two ways in which (this position) is insidious; .... it teaches the child to regard his parents and home with an emotion, ranging between pity and contempt. Second, it removes responsibility for educational failure from the teacher and the school.... [14]

The dilemma of the reform oriented liberal is centered in the question of control. Katz points to governance arrangements that raise the dilemma. First, paternalistic voluntarism where a disinterested and wise body of nonpolitical citizens exercise control. The basic message is one elite class must *civilize* another less elite class. On the other side of the coin is democratic localism that centers control in the people and is based upon a faith in their governing ability and legitimacy as a course of change. A third felt value is a faith in bureaucratic technology. Control is vested in carefully structured systems of schooling and sophisticated technological innovations to improve content and procedures, however, middle class liberals also espouse the concept of democratic localism as the rationalization to promote paternal voluntarism. The liberal faith in the present school system demands no allegiance to true democratic localism, or control would shift to parents and result in a fundamental structural change in professional control relations.

A second interest group that might be found in the local school attendance area is the *radical romantics*. The romantics have common interests in centering control of education in the hands of the people and abolishing the present schooling institution. Schools, rather than educating people, institutionalize them to accept the current society:

> Many students, especially those who are poor, intuitively know what the schools do for them. They school them to confuse process and substance. Once these become blurred a new logic is assumed. The more treatment there is the better are the results; or escalation leads to success. The pupil is thereby schooled to confuse teaching with learning, grade advancement with education, a diploma with competence and fluency with the ability to say something new. His imagination is schooled to accept service in place of value, medical treatment is mistaken for health care, social work for the improvement of community life, police protection for safety, military poise for national security, the rat race for productive work. [15]

The romantic believes individual learning happens without manipulation of others. Instruction in schools hampers participation by making a person identify personal cognitive growth with elaborate planning and manipulation.[16] The radical perspective assumes people are good, free, creative, curious, and loving. Teaching is a nurturing act, based upon loving, personal respect, and not a trading of the purely intellectual relationship. All romantic radicals are antibureaucratic and deeply suspicious of technology and other mechanisms of centralizing control relations. They agree with Myrdal that conflict in present United States society is caused by deeply socialized values and institutional arrangements.[17]

Many 1960s administrators mistakenly assumed that the challengers from "the left" were unified, that the middle class liberal and radical romantic formed political coalitions to fight the present schooling arrangement. However, the essential issues of control and belief in the present composition of public schools force irreconcilable wedges between the two groups. The radicals are deeply contemptuous of the progressive liberal who they judge a sellout to present society. Goodman shows the radical contempt in charging that progressive training has become easy adjustment to life, when *life* means people's taking their roles in the organized system:

> The doctrines of progressive education that have made headway in the public schools are precisely learning to get along with people, tolerance, and "real life problems" such as auto driving and social dancing. They are not those that pertain to passionately testing the environment rather than "adjusting" to it.[18]

Consequently, the romantic argues that the dominant class controls the value system and promotes the progressive education needed to substantiate their position. Under these circumstances, the 1980s evolution of schools simply means further sophistication of past control features. For example, 1980s schools discourage overt force in corporal punishment and prefer to rely on advanced socialization techniques such as behavior modification. When revolution is called for, the radicals charge, those who opt for progressivism offer no hope as political alliances.

A third interest group often found in the local school attendance area is the middle class conservatives. This group represents the true believers of the American school system, and the intensity of their faith is the basis for the political challenge. Calling upon the Protestant work ethic of a fair day's work and the ideals of industrial mass production, the conservative critic attacks the schools upon questions of products and efficiency. In Katz's perception of the community interest groups the middle class conservative is wedded to insipid bureaucracy. The conservative class elitism is stated openly and, perhaps, most vociferously by those who have most recently escaped the lower class distinction. Banfield and Wilson are purported to illustrate the conservative class mentality:

> A lower class person cannot as a rule be given much training because he will not accept it. He lives for the moment and learning to perform a task is a way of providing for the future. If the training process is accompanied by immediate rewards to the trainee, if it is fun, or if he is paid while learning, the lower class person may accept training. But even if he does, his earning power will not be much increased because his class outlook and style of life will generally make him an unreliable and otherwise undesirable employee. Besides, the ability to perform tasks (that is, to do what he has been trained to do) is seldom a very rare or valuable commodity. He would increase his earning power if he became educated (as opposed to trained). To have a high degree of both general education and the traits of character mentioned above is rare and valuable. Unfortunately, however, the lower class person acquires in childhood an outlook of style of life antithetical to education.[19]

Many educators have heard variations of this argument, particularly in comparison of vocational to academic program performance at both citizen and professional meetings.

The middle class conservative challenge occurs when faith in the educational profession wavers. When the attacks come, they are normally couched in fiscal or curricular arguments but the underlying problem is an event that caused a loss of faith in the professional, such as Sputnik. To many people, the Russians' achievement indicated the United States' technological *inferiority*. This type of psychological argument can take the form of curricular attacks on progressive education and accommodations to civil rights minorities that are seen as degrading academic standards. Professionals seeking to shore up conservative confidences in the 1980s by accountability and technological innovation may find that 1970s taxpayer's revolts or 1960s attacks on sex education pale in comparison to the future criticisms of the public schools. The middle class conservative is most concerned that the school's product can find access into the societal occupational structure. The classic argument goes: When vocational jobs do not exist for inner city products, the conservative is concerned *but* when suburban high school academic preparation, (coupled with university training) fails to secure the good job, he or she is incensed. Academic preparation programs may improve in quality and still be judged an abject failure if there is no job payoff.

When the tipping point of public school failure is reached and the conservative belief structure is shattered, a fourth interest group is formed: the *ultra conservative*. The ultra conservative constituent rejects the current system of public schools for a variety of social, political, or economic reasons. Touting arguments for social contract,[20] classic theory of competition, and assumptions of individual choice, the extreme interest groups of the ultra conservative constituency call for the end of the present compulsory schooling institution: The ultra conservative's concept of control would be what could be called corporate voluntarism. As most of them have a vested interest in the present United States societal structure, the resolution of public schools calls for surgical removal and replacement with private schools designed to retain favored positions.

Thus far, the four groups of school challengers from the community in the local school attendance area represent elites. *The administrator should be aware that the basis of societal support for the present institutional arrangement rests with the beliefs of the middle class liberals and conservatives.* Although the support is qualified in terms of needed improvements, the support is generally sustained by the belief in final salvation and/or fear of the consequences of other alternatives to the public schools.

The 1980s educator's relationship rests with liberal modifications for improving social effectiveness criteria, on one hand, and conservative modifications according to efficiency standards on the other. In both cases, reform still means institutional modifications, but not abolishment of the whole system.

The radical romantics and ultra conservatives both call for the disintegration of the public schools and their professional job structure. The 1980s educator should recognize that relationships with the extremist challenger will be dominated by prescriptive assumptions about the nature of man, society, learning, and control that are antithetical to schooling assumptions. Ideological goals and reconciliation with present reality are, by definition, impossible. Reasoned elaboration and consensus building *cannot* occur so that schools and extremist groups both recognize political gain that is consistent with their ultimate objectives.

A final interest group is the *nonelites*, variously named the poor, the disadvantaged, or the ghetto dweller in the literature. This group is judged as worthless, a necessary evil, a prick to social conscience, and the inheritors of the earth by the four elite groups discussed previously. For this reason *the poor are incompatible, as a true ally, with any of the other four elite challengers.* It has been shown that liberal, reform-oriented political life does not accommodate itself to contemporary disadvantaged groups searching for self-identity and cohesion.[21] The poor argue for the return of the openly political, ward based, ethnic machine[22] that could be quite consistent with the bargaining assumptions of an open school arena.

The radical romantics, although consistent with nonelite control demands of democratic localism, generally make a poor political ally for any other interest group because of their failure to deal with operational strategies and tactics appropriate to carrying off the necessary change from present conditions. Radicals who offer concrete suggestions for change, such as Freire's program for adult literacy,[23] run a race with the mounting frustration of the nonelite that may look to other forms of self-help (such as power through the barrel of a gun). Some people argue that past attempts to help the poor have only reinforced the potential of violence[24] by those educated in public schools.

The middle class and ultra conservative view the nonelites as opponents that form in effect, a second society. *For one reason or another, it would seem that the five interest groups have little chance of forming any united coalitions against the local schools.*

Hopefully, this extended example makes the point of superficial left-right designations of interest groups and provides a scheme to classify groups wanting to participate in a local school arena. Obviously, the middle liberal or conservative make potential players because of their underlying commitment to public schooling. Quite as obvious, radical romantics and ultra conservatives are poor players because they fail to give credibility to the arena in the first place. The poor or nonelite are more a collection of individuals than an organized interest. To consider their involvement as a group is a misnomer unless there is a concentrated effort at organization; the principal should probably consider their participation on a person by person basis.

Once various interest groups in the attendance area are identified, the principal should approach the inclusion of particular players in much the same way he or she includes specific parents.

THE STUDENTS

Many texts about the principalship ignore the students in a discussion of local governance or control.[25] Students are implicitly related to the decision-making dynamics. As the markers who cross the boundary of the community to the school, they are the clients about which processing decisions are made. Their political relationship to schooling is less one of involvement in deciding than the trigger to start others deciding (e.g., the percent of dropouts or the graduate that cannot read). From this perspective, the principal is assumed to have a legal, structural relationship with students vis-à-vis the making of crucial decisions. Political concern centers on the authority to control pupils in punishment (especially corporal), suspension/exclusion, and sanctioning behaviors off school property. A standard textbook response is to list various due process issues and outline organizational mechanisms of fair hearing and opportunity for grievance.

Student needs in the 1960s and early 1970s received a great deal of attention in the form of alternative schools. Advocates of student rights wrote about the institutional nature of the school, the irrelevance of the curriculum, and the oppressive overtone of the educative process. In the

1980s, those concerns are still present and the needs of students are largely unmet. As conditions for educating deteriorate in the 1980s, due to diminishing resources and increasing expectations for performance, the student will remain the primary client. It can be expected that student power will make itself felt again in the 1980s as pressures on them to perform are increased.

The principal can reduce the possibility of student problems to the degree that he or she gains information about the students and initiates programs to serve them. Many schools fail to gather the type of information that allows an adequate response. School programs cannot be built around the results of achievement test scores or graduation criteria, for these ends do not reveal the social and emotional factors that affect school motivation and school achievement. Instead, the principal must propose assessments that indicate the levels of student understanding and the ways in which such understandings are constructed; in short, the type of information that will allow the construction of adequate learning theory.

Sources of information about students that are not usually utilized in planning school programs are:

- interest surveys
- informal, anthropological observations
- time samplings of student behavior
- student anecdotal records
- sociometric analysis of learning environments
- cumulative records analysis
- parent and pupil conferences

Sources like these will provide the principal with subjective and impressionistic data that can supplement the more formal school records already available. More important, such data can sensitize the principal to the immediate needs and perceptions of the student.

In particular, the principal in the 1980s will need to provide for the culturally diverse student. During the 1970s school leaders learned that being culturally or ethnically different did not mean that the student was deficient or inferior. During the 1980s there will be increased pressure for schools to accommodate such diversity in their programs. Rather than *responding* to such pressure, the principal can *initiate* program reviews and curriculum development that will prove satisfying to these students. The Association for Supervision and Curriculum Development Commission on Multicultural Education has suggested that all educational content and processes be examined for evidence of realistic treatment of cultural pluralism. They offer the following recommendations to educational planners:[26]

1. Examine text materials for evidence of racism, classism, sexism, and realistic treatment of cultural pluralism in American society.

2. Develop new curricula for all levels of schooling—curricula that enhance and promote cultural diversity.

3. Provide opportunities to learn about and interact with a variety of ethnic groups and cultural experiences.

4. Include the study of concepts from the humanistic and behavioral sciences, which are applicable for understanding human behavior.

5. Organize curricula around universal human concerns, which transcend usual subject-matter disciplines; bring multicultural perspectives to bear in the study of such issues.

6. Broaden the kinds of inquiry used in the schools to incorporate and facilitate the learning of more humanistic modes of inquiry.

7. Create school environments that radiate cultural diversity.

8. Maximize the school as a multicultural setting, with the idea of utilizing the positive contributions of all groups to accomplish common tasks and not just to reduce deficiencies for the deprived.

9. Recognize and utilize bilingualism as a positive contribution to the communication process, and include bilingual programs of instruction to monolingual children.

10. Examine rules, norms, and procedures of students and staff with the purpose of facilitating the development of learning strategies and techniques that do not penalize and stigmatize diversity, but rather encourage and prize it.

11. Institute a system of shared governance in the schools, in which all groups can enter equally in the learning and practice of democratic procedures.

12. Organize time, space, personnel, and resources to facilitate the maximum probability and flexibility of alternative experiences for all youngsters.

13. Institute staffing patterns (involving both instructional and noninstructional positions) that reflect our culturally pluralistic and multiracial society.

14. Design and implement inservice programs to improve staff ability to successfully implement multicultural education.

These are important aspects of dealing with students in the role of the principal but they do not address the issue of school governance directly. Can students make a case to be political players in the local school arena? Yes, but to make a case does not mean a reasoned elaboration of need but a political presentation of consequences of noninvolvement that gives them a chair at the poker table. Situations exist where students can and do make a political case (the walkout) and that is why it becomes a governance issue to consider in the principalship. However, it would seem to be a less visible issue in the early 1980s than the late 1960s. For this reason we placed students third on the list of community boundary actors. The important lesson is that students may have a great deal of political influence in particular school situations. Consequently, the principal should not ignore their potential to be players or treat their existence as some by-product of the real action.

Perhaps the greatest political consideration of students is their transient nature in relation to the local school arena. No matter how powerful a particular individual, coalition, or class of students, the time of involvement in the arena is short. At best the time of possible student involvement is four to five years.

The realities are that it takes time to mobilize power, that the junior and senior grades are the ones with greatest dropout rates, and that the schools most likely to have political demands for student involvement are often the ones with highest mobility patterns. These factors contribute to the *nova* perception of student players by some teachers and principals. Student interest in playing is seen as a huge solarburst of power/ego that can fry an administrator with its short-term political intensity, but fades quickly. The cynical strategy is to wait the student out (have their day in the sun? ouch!) and let one step forward become two steps back. Proponents of this interpretation point to the difference between SNCC (Student Nonviolent Coordination Committee)[27] of the 1960s and the student government assembly of today.

The second political consideration about students is style. Today, the political expression that exists seems to have gone underground and works within the establishment frame of deciding.[28] Since the *Tinker Case*[29] (student right of expression) students have used the mechanism of the courts as a political avenue to resolve school control issues. In local schools, students in real power will probably be related to the formal mechanism of governance. There may well be an informal power structure but it is doubtful that such a structure exists apart from the formal mechanism (as was often the case in the 1960s and early 1970s). The principal should try to identify the students that link pupil power structures to formal mechanisms of school government. These students are most likely to be arena players and those with the best chance of developing a utility-matching strategy for play.

A third and final consideration of students as potential arena players must be noted. Much has been made of the susceptibility of young minds to political socialization so that trust is *created* for dominant authorities. With positive wrappings, this idea may translate to teaching respect while a negative interpretation may envision Hitler's youth corps. In either case, what educators actually know about the creation of political trust in children is often *far less* than what they pronounce.[30] The principal should be skeptical of any plan that creates the idea of a single-school solution to building student trust in authority.

CASE STORY: THE BALANCING ACT

Bill James is a native son. Not only did he grow up in the town where he is a principal, but Bill James actually attended high school in the building that is now Oaks Elementary. As a local boy, Bill has spent twenty years in the district, the last eight of which have been in the role of principal. Bill's wife also teaches in the district, and their home is just three blocks from the school. Oldtimers in the community like Bill James, and a number of parents in Bill's school were once students there.

Until fifteen years ago, when the school was integrated by black students, the school was a neighborhood school drawing students from an area less than three miles from the school. Nine years ago, a large Spanish-speaking population, attracted by new industry, moved into the district. Hispanic and black students are bussed to and from school while white students, who live in the immediate area, walk to school or ride with parents.

Bill is one principal who has selected his faculty carefully. Bill emphasizes a family atmosphere at the school, and convinces the faculty to accept his ideas through the concept of family responsibility. Teachers work long hours in the building because it is expected. Bill often counsels faculty members on personal matters. He protects his faculty from things that he perceives as threatening. The children of the teachers at the school refer to Bill James as Uncle Bill.

To cultivate a family atmosphere, Bill does small things to draw the faculty together. On teacher inservice days he may purchase steaks from the coke fund for a luncheon. A yearly Christmas party is held at Bill's house for faculty families. Bill is a teacher's friend forever, as long as the teacher is loyal to the school family unit.

When changes must be made in school procedures or policy, Bill has little trouble getting the faculty to go along. No one would let Bill down! However, working with parent and community groups has been a different story for Bill, especially since the school enlarged its attendance boundaries to accept students from outside the neighborhood.

A number of organized interest groups exist within the attendance area of the school. Parent groups that are organized are the PTA and the Parent Advisory Council. The PTA poses no real problem for Bill because he serves on the nominating committee and his choice is always the one selected as PTA President. The Parent Advisory Council, however, is a different matter. Mandated by state and federal directives, the group represents a cross-section of racial and ethnic groups in the school. Since the amount of outside funds in the district is considerable, the Superintendent wants the Parent Advisory Council to function smoothly. Since the PAC is appointed by the Superintendent, Bill has less influence with this group.

Recently, a large subdivision was built in the attendance area of the school. The expensive homes have attracted young, upper middle class professional and business people with young families. Most of the people in the subdivision still work in the city, thirty miles away, where they once lived. Although it is too early for these parents to infiltrate the PTA, they attend such meetings in force. They are more heavily involved with the PAC.

By going directly to the Superintendent and threatening political action against the Board, several of these new citizens have gained an appointment on the Parent Advisory Council. These parents are demanding a greater access to the curriculum for all students, especially their own children, and favor more parent involvement in the determining of what is taught in the school.

Other organized interest groups that exist within the attendance area of the school include the Oaks Civic Club, a local branch of the National Association for the Advancement of Colored People (NAACP), the Hispanic Caucus, and a Parents for Decency group. The latter group, organized by the wife of a conservative state political leader, has recently demanded that over 100 books be removed from the Oaks Elementary school library.

The issues that these respective groups are pursuing are beginning to become unmanageable. Beside the library, the groups are concerned about frills in the curriculum, the cultural relevance of classroom activity, the need for bilingual instruction, and a host of more immediate concerns. Thus far, Bill James has managed to avoid implementing their suggestions. By working through his safe PTA group, Bill continues to do what is right for his school. Yet, Bill James realizes that the times are changing. Like it or not, he must soon begin to make some sort of accommodation with the parent and citizen groups in his attendance area.

Case Questions

1. How can the parents of minority students and new students become more active players in this arena?

2. What steps should Bill James take to improve communications with the Parent Advisory Council?

3. What are some guidelines that Bill might follow in making his interaction with community interest groups more productive?

4. Using the five types of reform groups identified in the chapter, how would you classify the following: PTA, PAC, NAACP, and Parents for Decency?

CHAPTER SUMMARY

In summary, parents, community interest groups, and students represent boundary issues for the local school center that are somewhat different from the hierarchical relations described in Chapter 5. The principal must take an active, positive role to promote constituency involvement in the school arena. Using knowledge of group interaction and the particular characteristics of each constituency type, the administrator can expand the professional arena to include important viewpoints. As the 1980s evolve, this type of involvement may become a core feature of the essential stability necessary to conduct a productive local school program.

NOTES

1. This is especially true for parents of exceptional children and their formal responsibility to act in concert with educators to provide an appropriate school experience.
2. Raymond Callahan, *Education and the Cult of Efficiency* (Chicago: University of Chicago Press, 1962).
3. James Coleman, *Equality of Education Opportunity* (Washington, D.C.: U.S. Government Printing Office, 1966).
4. Robert Dahl, *Who Governs?* (New Haven: Yale University Press, 1964).
5. *Ibid*, p. 158. Seymour Sarason describes the normal conduct of a PTA meeting as a visitor from outer space might see it, "at night, big people sit quietly in orderly rows while one big person stands in front and talks most...during the day little people sit in the orderly rows..." *The Culture of the School and the Problem of Change* (Boston: Allyn and Bacon, 1971), p. 63.
6. Joseph Pois, *The School Board Crisis* (Chicago: Educational Methods, 1964), p. 93.
7. Milbrey McLaughlin, "Implementation of ESEA Title I: Problems of Compliance," *Teacher College Record* 77, no. 3 (February 1976): 397–415.
8. Richard Weatherley and Michael Lipsky, "Street-Level Bureaucrats and Institutional Innovation: Implementing Special Education Reform," *Harvard Educational Review* 47, no. 3 (May 1977): 171–197.
9. Jon Wiles and Joseph Bondi, *Curriculum Development: A Guide to Practice* (Columbus, Ohio: Charles E. Merrill, 1979), pp. 95–96.
10. Marilyn Gittell and G. Berebe, *Confrontation at Ocean Hill-Brownsville Conference* (New York: Praeger, 1971).
11. *New York Times*, Reports of the Kanawha County "Textbook Wars" were published on Jan. 31, 1974, p. 12; Oct. 23, 1974, p. 30; Oct. 24, 1974, p. 41; Dec. 11, 1974, p. 22; Feb. 16, 1975, p. 26.

12. A rough typology of power structure in classification of the community interest groups can be drawn from the same scheme presented in Chapter 4 for faculty classification. A second area for inference is the recruitment and selection of board members discussed in Chapter 5.
13. Michael Katz, "The Present Moment in Educational Reform," *Harvard Educational Review* 41, no. 3 (August 1971): 342–359.
14. *Ibid.*, Footnote 1, page 343.
15. This dilemma is pointed out in Patrick Moynihan, *Maximum Feasible Misunderstanding* (New York: Free Press, 1969).
16. Ivan Illich, *Deschooling Society* (New York: Harper & Row, 1971), p. 1.
17. Gunnar Myrdal, *The American Dilemma* (New York: Harper, 1944).
18. Paul Goodman, *Compulsory Miseducation* (New York: Horizon, 1964). Also see Paulo Friere, *Pedogogy of the Oppressed* (New York: Herder, 1972).
19. Edward Banfield and James Wilson, *City Politics* (Cambridge: Harvard University Press, 1963), p. 37.
20. John Locke, *An Essay Concerning Human Understanding*, Books 1 and 2 (Oxford: Clarendon Press, 1924).
21. Ronald Corwin, *A Sociology of Education* (New York: Appleton-Century-Crofts, 1965).
22. Larry Iannaccone and David Wiles, "The Changing Politics of Urban Education," *Education and Urban Society* 6, 4 (May 1971), pp. 255–264.
23. Paulo Friere, *Cultural Action for Freedom.* Monograph 1, Harvard Center for Development and Social Change, 1970.
24. Quoted in Moynihan, *Maximum Feasible Misunderstanding*, p. 41.
25. For example, Ralph Kimbrough, *Administering Elementary Schools* (New York: Macmillan, 1968), pp. 285–288.
26. Association for Supervision and Curriculum Development, "Encouraging Multicultural Education," *Educational Leadership* 34 (January 1977): p. 29.
27. For example of actual activities see Peter Bachrach and Morton Baratz, *Power and Poverty* (New York: Oxford Press, 1970), pp. 76–78.
28. Overt confrontation seems to be replaced by sophisticated cooperation by smart student players. For discussion of the distinction of styles see Jerome Skolnick, *The Politics of Protest* (New York: Free Press, 1969).
29. *Tinker v. Des Moines Independent School Dist.* 393 U.S. 503 (1969).
30. See David Easton and Jack Dennis, *Children in the Political System* (New York: McGraw-Hill, 1969); M. Kent Jennings and Richard Niemi, *The Political Character of Adolescence* (Princeton: University Press, 1974); Robert Hess and Judith Torney, *The Development of Political Attitudes in Children* (Garden City: Doubleday, 1967). Perhaps the best source relating to perception of authority is Fred Greenstein, *Children and Politics* rev. ed. (New Haven: Yale University Press, 1969), especially pp. 43–52.

CHAPTER 7

Budget Politics

The importance of budget issues in the local school arena cannot be overstated. Some administrators would argue it is the only game in town. Wildavsky states,

> Human nature is never more evident than when people are struggling to gain a larger share of funds or to apportion what they have among myriad elements.... if politics is regarded in part as conflict over whose preferences will prevail in the determination of ... policy, *the budget records the outcome of the struggle* (emphasis added).[1]

Caplow argues that the first political survival task of anyone taking charge of a new organization is to find and get control of the pursestrings.[2] Within this admittedly important area of budget lies a curious educational phenomenon. Many educators feel this area is not a concern of teachers or even administrators at the local school level. Budget is seen as something to do with the board of education and levy passage, or something the business manager at the control office is responsible for. The principal should recognize the implications of the assumption that budget matters are alien to local school center decision making. Unless the principal's basic strategy is to let potential actors be eliminated from the local school arena by perpetuation of this image, he or she must recognize and combat such noninvolvement in a purposeful manner.

The politics of the budget involves careful planning and leadership on the part of the principal. Because of the special language that has surrounded budget concerns, the principal must understand the language used in budget decisions. In other words, there is a critical job of translating abstract budget concepts into practical meanings *before* particular budget issues are decided. A second political problem is getting arena players to understand that the local school budget involves three different types of decision contexts, each with a different type of political expression: the budget politics involving the local school and central office, the politics of local school budget allocations, and the politics of internal accounting. The third basic political problem is to decide whether the special language of systematic planning designed to facilitate budget decisions (specifically, Program-Planning-Budgeting System) has any real value for the local school arena.

THE SPECIAL RELATIONSHIP

It is important to emphasize that the principalship has a special relationship to the meaning of budget in a school system.[3] First, it is commonly assumed that less than 5 percent of the total operating budget is *not* committed or decidable in the sense that monies can be moved around. Second, there are at least two budget processes in operation that affect the principal differently. One is the preparation of the district budget and the political language necessary for a local school to appear logical in relation to the total school system. The second process is the management of the local school internal budget once the district budget has been adopted and monies implemented. The third contributor to the special relationship of budget is that many of the major political fights will not center on dollars per se but funded positions. The particular problem for the principal and local school center is that funded positions are, in many places, an issue of district level collective negotiation. Thus, the political aspect of the budget that is most identified with running a local school is often the decision area removed from direct local school concern. We now turn to the political issues of district level budgetary politics.

THE SYSTEMATIC LANGUAGE OF BUDGET

As noted earlier, being able to use the appropriate language is a powerful political advantage. The special relationship of a principal to district budget matters makes mastery of a special language mandatory to present a local school's needs in an effective manner. A major system of thinking about the budget, which will retain its legitimacy during the 1980s (although its name may change), is Program Planning Budgeting System (PPBS).

Since the 1960s and the *Great Society*[4] much of public education has been enamoured of the idea of relating budget to program in some coordinated system of decision making. Before discussing a most popular example of this thinking, PPBS, a general review of the decision meanings of the budget is needed. One set of meanings concerns the use of budget in governance. In a general way budgets can be identified by emphasis on *inputs* or *processes* or *outputs*.[5] An input emphasis relates to budget as a *control* mechanism. For example, a line-item format to check specific levels of expenditures is an input-oriented budget whose basic purpose is control.

A process-oriented budget has a basic governance concern for *management*. Procedures and activities are emphasized to mean concerns of how to organize for specific tasks or how goals are translated into particular projects.

An output-oriented budget has primary concern for *planning*. The focus is to cost out consequences of various programs by relating expenditures to achievements. The principal should realize that the types of budget emphasis are rarely articulated in relation to governance and control issues. The political value is in making governance sense about particular local school impact when someone talks of input or outputs as budget terms.

The second decision meaning that has to be reemphasized before discussing PPBS is the reality of large, complex bureaucracy. Budgeting is governed in part by the larger choice dynamics of quasi resolution of conflict (factoring an issue to subunits), uncertainty avoidance, and satisficing, which was discussed in detail earlier (see Chapter 5). Thus the rational *plan* for comprehensive budgeting may not reflect the bureaucratic realities. For example, outputs may be rationalized, but the capacity to deliver may be a different proposition.[6]

Utilization of PPBS in schools depends upon how oriented a particular school system is to thinking in terms of *systematic analysis*, emphasis on *output*, and commitment to the *planning process*. Those who argue for PPBS in education argue that it contributes to the analytical framework for planning, reduction of decision uncertainty and the promotion of precision, sequential order, and logical procedures. Hartley,[7] a proponent, states several advantages if PPBS is adopted by schools:

1. Objectives of school system are related to programs. Objectives encompass competing educational philosophies, and allow diversity in curricular offerings, teaching methodologies, and school designs.
2. Programs explicitly stated.
3. Components of each program differentiated; inputs categorized according to output program.
4. Alternatives established; enhances program review and revision.
5. Evaluation at specific intervals.
6. Long-range planning for each program.
7. Decentralization of budget decisions, because each program is a relatively autonomous power center.
8. Cost/benefit analysis used more; a more sophisticated method for costing.
9. A new organizational structure results, which incorporates plan-

ning, management control and operational control. Overall structural design created which promotes use of systems analysis.

10. More use of education data processing encouraged.

11. Resource allocation based on program priorities.

PPBS (Program Planning Budgeting System) has some distinct meanings for governance and control beyond the rational plan for budgeting. Those who criticize PPBS point to the tendency to centralize government that accompanies the implementation of this approach.[8] A second concern is the special, technical language that places control in hands of planners. Many practicing administrators believe that the real impact of PPBS is to create a new breed of decision-making experts who dominate what is considered rational choice.

In a major symposum conducted by Phi Delta Kappa,[9] two major speakers presented diametrically opposing views of what could be the PPBS planner's decision role. Mr. Eide, Minister of Education in Norway, felt reconciliation was possible when faced with the basic question:

Is it conceivable that a planning unit *can ever cease to be felt as a threat to other administrative units,* unless it become completely ineffective? The planning unit should have only a service function... It should restrict its activities to explicit formulation of essential choices, leaving priority choices to the policy makers.[10]

An excerpt captures the flavor.

Mr. Beasley:...I think you are politically naive to feel that the planning unit can be insulated, and sooner or later its work will be identified either to its credit or discredit.

Mr. Eide: Our experience is that the public doesn't say anything because the planning unit's work is part of the total.

Mr. Beasley: Still they are going to attack the (chief administrator) and say "where did you get this information?" And he will say "from the planning unit."

Mr. Eide: The (administrator) is responsible for this. If we make an error he has the responsibility.[11]

The distinction between the planning role in a centralized educational system (such as Norway) and the interpretation of a decentralized federal role is startling. Daniere discussed three aspects of executive planning. The following excerpts capture the flavor of this planner's interpretation of role in working with politicians.

Many of the decisions intended to affect others must therefore be made between the statement of a threat and its eventual enforcement

....executive planning must deal with two major areas of decision; preparation of budget or proposal and additional actions to secure favorable legislation. The other actions consist primarily of information and persuasion, but include bargains and threats as well.[12]

The seemingly abstract controversy over whether planning per se is recognized as overtly political has direct implications for the administrator who is attempting to structure decision making in his or her local school. Three basic questions should be answered. First, is PPBS planning to be confined to monitoring present agreement or also used to predict future possibilities and choices? Second, is PPBS planning seen as a role separate from administration or a set of skills to be utilized by administrators? Third, is the planning function considered a centralized or decentralized situation? It seems that much planning is perceived as a separate role that is centralized and oriented toward delineating future choices. While this method is consistent with the systematic analysis rationale, it directly raises the dominant political issue: the effect of planner expertise as a policy actor. The fact that some planners are growing aware of their political potential is evident in recent literature. Long states,

> *The question is not whether planning will reflect politics but whose politics will it reflect.* What values and whose values will it reflect? When the greasy, grimy hands of politics are laid on planning because it means votes, *the subject and its practitioners have come of age....* the fearful would do well to join Ophelia in a nunnery.[13]

In summary, PPBS has several specific implications for the type of budget politics that could take place in a local school arena. Its use implies both a meaning of planning expertise and central office relationship that could alter the normal rules of play within the arena dramatically. The principal should determine if those promoting this system are primarily (1) interested in its symbolic appearance of rational choice or believe PPBS to be an actual guide to deciding and (2) believe PPBS implementation is an appropriate *local school* function (i.e., expertise now exists, we need only a new language).

PRESENTING THE LOCAL SCHOOL CONDITION

The beginning point of any budget planning and organization in a local school is the assessment of needs. Such assessments seek to determine what the school is to accomplish through its programming. Unlike school surveys and accreditation studies, the needs assessment is a flexible procedure, useful only to those directly involved in planning and implementing the school program. The scope of the assessment and the dimensions of the school program assessed should be determined by general priorities of the faculty, parents, and students. The payoff of such an effort is to provide critical data that will indicate where those involved in providing the program should spend their time and energy. The needs assessment will identify any gaps between established aims and actual conditions.

The most useful design for a school doing its first major internal assessment is a general one that attempts to lay a foundation for later, and more detailed, data. Below the reader will find an outline for a general needs assessment:

1. General information
   a. location of the school and district
   b. demographic characteristics of the immediate area
   c. natural resources of the region
   d. commercial and industrial data
   e. income level of area residents and parents
   f. special social and economic considerations

2. General population considerations
   a. population growth patterns
   b. age and race of population
   c. educational level of parents and community
   d. projected population of school vicinity

3. School population characteristics (ages 3–19)
   a. school enrollment by grade level
   b. birthrate trends in the school district
   c. in-migration and out-migration patterns of neighborhood
   d. race/sex/religious composition of the neighborhood
   e. years of school completed by persons over 25 years of age in the district attendance area
   f. studies of school dropouts and graduates

4. Programs and course offerings in the school
   a. organization of the school program
   b. programming concept and rationale
   c. course offerings—present and planned
   d. special program needs

5. Professional staff patterns
   a. number and distribution of staff
   b. training and experience level of staff
   c. awareness of trends and developments in education
   d. attitudes toward change

6. Instructional patterns and strategies
   a. philosophical focus of instructional program
   b. observational and perceptual instructional data
   c. assessment of instructional strategies in use

d. instructional materials in use
e. decision making and planning processes
f. grouping for instruction
g. classroom management techniques
h. grading and placement of pupils
i. student independence measures
j. evaluation of instructional effectiveness

7. Student data

a. student experiences
b. student achievement
c. student self-esteem

8. Facilities

a. assessment of existing facilities and sites
b. special facilities
c. utilization of existing facilities
d. projected facility needs

9. Summary of data

Even a preliminary needs assessment can reveal areas that need intensive program development and monies allocated. It may be found, for instance, that the community in which the school is located has special needs or expectations for the school. It may be found that the course offerings available to students reflect a population that existed twenty-five years earlier. It may be found that grading policies or the pattern of student retention at the school is a problem area. The relationship between student self-esteem and achievement may be revealed to be important. The point is, none of these things can really be known or proven without hard data gathered through an extensive needs assessment. The principal can hardly be a program leader if he or she isn't aware of the problems and able to support contentions with data!

In communicating the results of the findings of the needs assessments to others, the principal must choose a medium that will be understood. Most board members or central office personnel do not have the time or motivation to wade through a 300 page report to discover problems. Nor will most teachers in the local school have access to all data being secured in a needs assessment. The principal is in a unique position to select data, show its interrelatedness, and project it in ways that point to both problems and solutions. The control of such information represents both a source of power and authority to the school principal. Principals should use graphs and tabulated summaries to communicate with constituents about the needs of the school. View, for instance, the power of the graphs in Table 7.1, Table 7.2, and Table 7.3 in identifying the needs of one southern school.

These tabulated summaries graphically show the needs of this school. The school has a problem with school dropouts, although this school is

TABLE 7.1   *Projected Grade Level Enrollment for 1981–1982*

Age	3	4	5	6	7	8	9	10	
Enrollment	98	108	112	104	111	125	118	131	
Age	11	12	13	14	15	16	17	18	19
Enrollment	123	116	108	96	85	70	69	18	4

only slightly above the natural average in this area. The dropout problem can be suspected to relate to extremely poor reading achievement. It is also likely, in the coming years, that this particular school will have a steady enrollment pattern and a declining average daily attendance figure unless a corrective reading program is initiated by the building principal. Armed with these figures, the principal can make a convincing case to the superintendent, teachers, or parents for the initiation of a new program.

Figure 7.1 shows a schema for developing a continuous system of needs assessment in a school or school district. This schema might be thought of as part of a larger management system that can be employed to promote a systematic effort at program development. Figure 7.2 outlines what such a management system might look like in its totality. Note that the suggested management system uses reports or working documents to keep track of the status of committee work or advisory committees. Such reports are indispensable to continuity since committee membership will be constantly changing and principal assignments may change. Over time, such reports will document the efforts of the principal to bring about orderly change and, hence, serve as a personal evaluation record for the individual principal.

The needs assessment, then, allows the principal to order and control problem solving and program development in the building. It serves as a means of putting the principal on top of immediate and anticipated needs, as well as allowing him or her to do realistic long-range planning for program improvement. Such information, once gathered, will also enable the

TABLE 7.2   *Student Attrition Record*

Year	Number Dropouts	Number Over 16	Annual Dropout %
1976–77	38	263	14.4
1977–78	41	251	16.3
1978–79	44	244	18.2
1979–80	32	241	13.2

TABLE 7.3   *Student Reading Achievement Scale*

Grade Level	Number of Students By Grade Level							
	2	3	4	5	6	8	11	Total
14.0–14.9								
13.0–13.9							6	6
12.0–12.9							8	8
11.0–11.9						4	7	11
10.0–10.9						6	15	21
9.0– 9.9						8	17	25
8.0– 8.9					5	3	13	21
7.0– 7.9				1	7	10	12	30
6.0– 6.9			2	3	4	9	26	44
5.0– 5.9		3	22	17	20	28	9	99
4.0– 4.9	3	7	30	55	21	20	2	138
3.0– 3.9	16	41	20	21	33	8	–	139
2.0– 2.9	65	32	7	11	7	–	–	122
1.0– 1.9	–	2	1	–	–	–	–	3
Totals	84	75	82	108	97	96	115	667

principal to be convincingly knowledgeable about his or her school program.

MANAGEMENT OF THE INTERNAL BUDGET

It has been noted that the politics of a local school's allocated budget may differ from the political processes of the district budget consideration. A fundamental role of the principal is to communicate such distinction and make local school budget decisions politically realistic.

The principal may expect that a local school facing conditions of

138

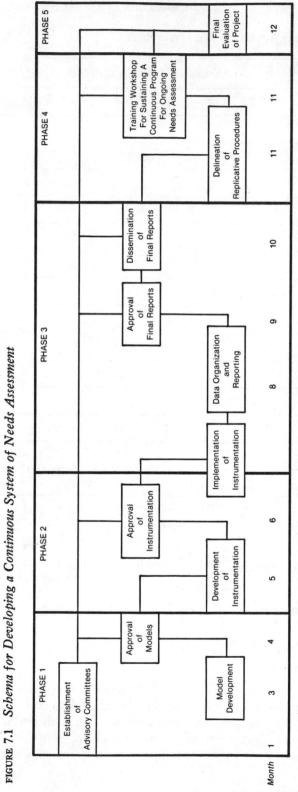

FIGURE 7.1 *Schema for Developing a Continuous System of Needs Assessment*

Source: Jon Wiles and Joseph Bondi, *Supervision: A Guide to Practice*, Charles E. Merrill Publishing Company, 1980, p. 163. Used by permission.

FIGURE 7.2 *Management System*

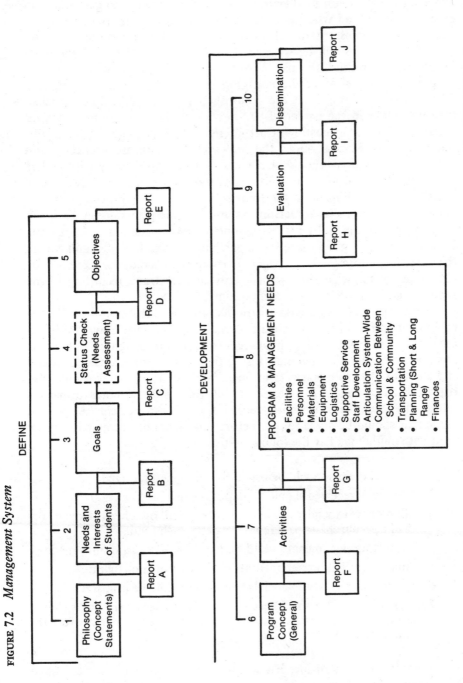

Source: Jon Wiles and Joseph Bondi, *Curriculum Development: A Guide to Practice*. Charles E. Merrill Publishing Company, 1979, p. 349. Used by permission.

scarcity will be dominated by decisions about budget matters. Dollars provide the most overt marker to trace the patterns of who gets and who gives, who wins and who loses within the local school arena. If the arena is politically sophisticated and used to concrete realities the focus on dollars or positions will be welcomed as practical and facilitate the play. If, on the other hand, the participants of a particular arena are used to bargaining in the abstract and engaging in a lot of symbolic trading, the focus on dollars may upset the established rules of play. The principal may be caught in the bearer-of-bad-news role that is sometimes further translated into a scapegoating effort ("He or she is not fighting for us up-stairs."). If a principal senses the indicators of a future preoccupation with budget, the arena should be sensitized to dealing directly with dollars before fundamental allocation and reallocation issues surface. A few dollar decisions should be made in the local school arena. In this case, the out-comes of such decisions are less important than the growing familiarity in bargaining with the dollar marker. Along with the general familiarity, the principal should begin to have arena participants couch their arguments in the special language of the budget. Participants should, for example, be able to argue for what they want and what they trade according to the account classifications of the district budget.

In scarcity-oriented arenas, many decision areas that are normally the exclusive purview of the principal become issues for bargaining. One such area is the internal accounting procedures for a local school budget. If this is the case, the principal must insure that arena participants understand and abide by desirable practices in financial accounting. They should also realize that the principal's interest in this area concerns both formal re-sponsibility *and* the real consequences for mismanagement. A general guide that should be agreed upon before any issues of accountability are dealt with might look like the following list.

1. Official receipts should be issued for all money received.
2. All money received should be deposited in a bank.
3. All money expended should be expended by check, except for small cash purchases paid from the petty cash fund.
4. Supporting documents should be kept for all expenditures made.
5. Bank reconciliation statements should be made each month.
6. Monthly and yearly financial statements should be prepared.
7. An audit should be made each year, and copies of the audit should be filed with persons having administrative authority for the school.[14]

A general process of internal accounting should also be agreed upon beforehand. The process could approximate the flow chart in Figure 7.3.[15]

A normal reaction of many principals is to draw the line and declare

FIGURE 7.3   *The Flow of Internal Accounting*

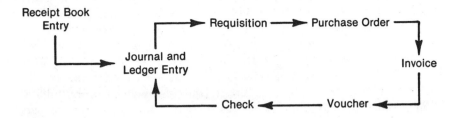

that no one can meddle in internal accounting except administrators. This point should be rethought. Accounting with participation *can* be manageable. In fact, it could solve one of the principal's biggest headaches: faculty and others who deal with dollars as though there were no reason to account for expenditures. In other words, if teachers, secretaries, or students wish to engage in structured, watch-dog activities, this state of mind might be creatively extended to a philosophy of personal accounting with a little effort by the principal.

GENERAL STRATEGIES

Over time, a principal can blend the budget considerations of local school and district allocations toward a general improvement of the arena's decision-making process. Budget issues provide the same focus on scarcity and choosing between desired values as other types of choice. The general strategies and points of critical decisions presented below should have a general applicability toward achieving a mature political arena.

Before making any effort to influence an arena consideration of a budget issue, the principal must make three personal assessments of the existing state of affairs. First, where would the local school be placed on a continuum of feast to famine? As mentioned earlier, the 1980s may be an era of famine for many school and school districts throughout the nation, but that does not mean that all units will be poor. Obviously, a school in true famine will approach the politics of the budget differently from a school in a feast. It is the principal's responsibility to understand *and communicate to the arena* the true condition of resource availability. The posture of hoarding (pretending famine in real feast) has lost its viability in the 1980s. As the school system continues to shrink (dollars, students, faculty positions) and stabilize (no new hires) educators learn more about one another. A common assumption of this text is that *the best chance of decision success rests with the principal's capacity to play fair within the local school arena.* This implies that an attempt to establish an exclusive decision domain—either by "my legal authority" or hoarding resources—has less chance of success. One thing is sure, the principal *cannot* play both strategies simultaneously. The political costs of being discovered as a hoarder in an above-the-board arena would be equivalent to the impact on player trust when a poker player is discovered cheating.

Related to judging feast and famine is the principal's judgment of the extent to which previous budget decisions at the school have reflected the politics of distribution or redistribution. As discussed earlier, the politics of allocating new resources is different from the politics of reshuffling existing resources. The principal needs a sense of what other arena players expect when they talk of making budget decisions about allocation.

The third preplanning judgment that needs to be made concerns the pattern of allocation that, historically, has characterized the particular local school. Although there are departments or program areas (as well as individuals) that can be identified as haves and others that can be identified as have nots, there is also a lack of a universal criterion that can automatically identify a have. Some of the departments with the largest number of faculty are have nots. In some situations, subject areas that have been around the longest represent the most disadvantaged in terms of resources available. The principal should understand the particular composition of haves and have nots before entering into budgetary politics.

Assuming the three understandings just outlined, the first decision task of the principal is to secure practical agreements in five areas affecting the meaning of budget.

Ours

The word *budget* seems to collect multiple meanings about the level of deciding as quickly as any in the educator's vocabulary (maybe curriculum . . .). This chapter began by noting that many educators perceive the budget to be a central office matter. The other side of the coin is the issue of *ours* for those players who do feel part of budget decisions. The first budget agreement to be reached within the arena is what is the exclusive concern of the central office, what is a budget decision involving the whole school (i.e., appropriate for arena consideration), and what is the exclusive purview of subunits of the school. For example, a cosmopolitan teacher secures some external resources. Is this a budget issue for the arena or something apart? If these types of understanding are not reached beforehand the discussion often becomes heated as players try to decide who *needs* additional resources. Does a successful cosmopolitan have the same resource need as his or her local colleague that made no extra personal effort to secure outside resources? This is the stuff of budget politics, and the fact that there are no automatic right answers does not absolve the necessity of particular understandings about *ours*.

Equality versus Equity

It has become popular to note that there is nothing so unequal as the equal treatment of unequals. In all decision situations there is some stratification of haves and have nots. In some schools, the inequalities of particular distributions have decades of history behind them. The meaning of equity implies something other than equal distribution by seeking a retribution or compensation to the have nots. To this point, have and have not players usually have general agreement. The critical political issue revolves around how to achieve equity or letting the have nots catch up in an era of scarcity. In times of abundance, equity means letting the haves keep their current, favorable conditions and focus *new* resources on the have nots. However, in scarcity, equity means haves must contribute *from* their favored condition so that have nots can catch up. Unless this distinction is clarified beforehand much of the budget decision making will be little more than elaborate fabrication within the arena. The principal will not win any popularity contest by raising this most fundamental principle, but it is the only way to avert the inevitable impasse should it not be raised.[16]

Grassroots versus Topdown

A third basic agreement that should be reached is how the budget is formed and how resource needs/demands are to be identified. The popular democratic expression is a grassroots focus because the firing line is the only place where real needs can be known. Without arguing the point of real knowledge, the problem with grassroots applications in an era of scarcity is that needs exceed availability in almost all cases. The cruelty of raising *unrealistic* expectations then leads to skepticism and cynicism about democratic involvement per se. On the other hand, scarcity has been used (in isolated cases) to rationalize a power grab. The topdown approach argues that only a centralized perspective (the big picture) allows an impartial, objective identification of needs. As in most things, the truth probably rests between the extremes. The players of the local school arena might decide whether some combination of grassroots and topdown approach is possible (i.e., centralized general priorities and local interpretations within) for the resource realities of a particular school. In any case, the issue of approach to the identification of needs should be decided upon.

Incremental versus Zero-Based

A fourth understanding to be reached in the arena is whether budget decision making is an incremental building process or a zero-base proposition. Incremental implies that a percent of a school's resources, once distributed, are fixed and cannot be realistically reallocated. Students of large organizations argue that *95 percent or more* of a stable institution's budget is fixed by prior distribution, and actual budget decision making affects only the marginal 5 percent (maximum) that is left.[17]

On the other hand, zero-based budgeting assumes that stipulations for the automatic review or termination of a particular resource decision are stated at the time of allocation. This procedure implies that all resources in the organization will be released if subsequent decisions do not renew a particular allocation. Obviously, the key point to judging which perspective is more realistic is the extent of control possible in the organization. The capacity for control is not confined to the principal. The issue becomes, if every player in the arena desired to change the present pattern of allocation, could they? In the heydays of the 1960s educators were sure it was an issue of purpose and will, now they wonder about nonpurposive complexity.[18] In any case, the issue of how much of the school allocation educators assume can be influenced should be decided beforehand.

Lump Sum versus Categorical

The final area needing prior understanding relates to the type of control placed on any budget decision. Lump sum allocations assign dollars or other resources to organizational units (e.g., departments) without stipulations about how the allocation is to be used. Categorical allocation assigns resources by functions to be accomplished. Either can be used as a decision rule within an arena (or combinations) but the issue needs to be clarified. The principal should understand the normal practice of the school system and decide the costs or benefits of being consistent with the larger system.

In summary, there are five general understandings about budget that should be agreed upon before actual allocative decisions take place. In the actual dynamics of a local school arena the principal should play a critical linking role.

THE PRINCIPAL AS THE POLITICAL LINK

Most important to this context is the role of the principal as *the* major player and link between the levels of school government. Those in the central office responsible for budget matters will probably expect to deal exclusively with the principal in all money matters. This makes the principal the translator and interpreter of the central office within the local school arena. It also means other arena players will expect the principal to have superior knowledge about budget matters. This situation is a blessing and a curse. The translator function is one of great power and control potential. However, it also carries the expectation that the principal will be in a position to anticipate the future. The reality of many situations is that the *central office*, despite the best efforts, may not be able to anticipate the future in terms of the school budget. In this situation, the principal may wish to let other arena players know the dilemma. Many school systems have had the experience of laying off personnel in March because of anticipated shortages and then hiring back in June because unexpected adjustments found money. The principal might use this type of example so that arena players see that the issue relates to state government as well as in school system and local school government.

The key role of linking to the central office revolves around establishing political understanding of the terms fair share and base. From the political viewpoints, a certain local school is in competition with other local schools and various sectors of the central office for available resources. Modern organization theory suggests there is a natural tendency for subunits of a bureaucracy to try to secure *more* resources even if they are not needed for actual operations.[19] The earlier discussions of general strategies to defend the present amount of resources or to inch forward by adding to existing programs or to attempt to gain resources by creating new programs have a special relevance to budget politics. The words *fair share* and *base* serve as markers in budgetary judgments of how well a particular local school is holding onto its allocated resources. Base indicates that those who deal with budget decisions expect some relatively steady point in what a school gets in resources (i.e., some point relatively free of cycle fluctuations year to year). The base is the general expectation among those who compete for and determine a local school budget that programs will be carried on at close to the going level of expenditures but it does not necessarily include all activities.[20] Having a particular program included in the school's base means more than getting it in the budget for a particular year. It means *"establishing the expectation that the expenditure will continue, that it is accepted as part of what will be done, and, therefore, it will not be subjected to intensive scrutiny"* (emphasis added).[21] The base is the expectation the principal hopes to establish as givens in the various account classifications of the operating budget. How much will a particular school receive automatically in supplies and equipment or plant maintenance? Notice that the principal does not have to be connected to the formal authority to decide particular allocations. The base is a state of mind that can also be established informally through a one-to-one contact with key actors in the district.

Fair share includes not only the base a local school has established but also the expectation about *what proportion* of other resources it will receive in comparison to other local schools. Many budget-related officials engaged in centralized allocations tend to lump all schools together (e.g., all secondary, all middle/junior, all elementary, all special education/

other) when discussing increases and decreases in proportion of funds. Fair share reflects how a particular school does in comparison to others in its category when assessing proportional increases and decreases. If the 1980s emphasize the growing scarcities in public education as expected, principals can expect the knee jerk reaction to across-the-board cuts. This reaction gives a vivid example of the distinction between equality and fairness. Obviously, the equal reduction of some amount of funds will have different impact on schools with different bases. Even in situations where there have been previous attempts to achieve proportionate equality, the cuts will have a varying impact on actual operations. For example, a standard ratio of 1:25 has a different meaning for a school where reduction means the actual number of students is 26 compared to a school where the actual number is 1,026. One school may be able to achieve a minimal critical mass by application of the ratio while another goes out of business because it cannot deliver the operation. This example hints at a possible battle a principal, trying to influence fair share, might engage in. A principal of a small school may try to persuade those in central allocation (formal and informal) that "ratio is one thing, but we must have additional compensation to be able to offer the same *quality* as big schools. It's only fair."

CASE: THE ZERO-BASED SHAKEOUT

After nearly seven months as a principal, Rick felt that he was beginning to understand the job. Contrary to what he had been told during his college coursework, most of the effort was interpersonal rather than organizational. If you could keep the folks happy, the school would take care of itself. The day-to-day administrative acts like scheduling and ordering materials were a snap. In fact, by just being competent as a principal he had established a favorable climate for change. Next year would be a great one at the school.

Rick sent out a form to the various departments requesting their input for next year's budget. They were asked to identify projects and programs that they would like to see funded and to give an estimate of the level of funding needed to do the job. When he reviewed the returned proposals, he was astounded at what he saw. If he were to pass on these requests to the superintendent his school would be at least 400 percent over budget. If there was one thing this superintendent got excited about it was being O.B.

The dilemma, as Rick saw it, was that there were both good and bad proposals mixed into the return. To place a dime in the English department, for instance, would be to throw the money away. All those folks wanted to do is build up that collection of books and plays. The math department, on the other hand, wanted to begin an innovative program that would have high visibility in the community. The two ideas were both asking for $20,000—clearly not reasonable.

As Rick worked with his calculator totaling up the various requests he was struck with the overall pattern of the requests. In general, every individual request was clearly too high for what was being proposed. Rick buzzed for his assistant. What the hell was going on, he wanted to know? The assistant principal, a fifty-year-old veteran at the school, responded that department heads always blew up the requests about 100 percent figuring that they'd settle for half. It was the way it was always done.

Rick pondered the situation as the day wore on. Obviously, he couldn't afford all of the proposals at the level requested nor did the department heads expect him to find that much money. What they did expect was that he would simply cut the requests by a percentage and make awards to the departments. The percentage would depend upon what was available to the school from the superintendent's office. In taking such an approach, Rick would be forced to treat all proposals in basically the same manner regardless of their merit or his own priorities for the school. To deviate from such an expected action might mean a lot of ill will on the part of those departments being shortchanged. Clearly, he was in a bind. Human relations would not carry that day.

Rick called the department heads together one week later, and announced that a new approach to budgeting was needed because the requests had far outstripped the monies available. He noted that 85 to 87 percent of all budget was in salaries, and that since the departments were of varying size, it was obvious that the concept of balance had not been maintained among programs in the past. He stated that the school could no longer afford to simply give incremental increases to each department or lump sum amounts to departments without clear indications of how the money will be spent.

Rather than a simple knee jerk reaction to this situation, rather than just cutting all proposals, Rick asked department heads to tie requests to programs. The school would move to a new budgeting concept known as zero-based budgeting. Within categories, each department head would be asked to identify priorities among programs and estimate funding needed. Three levels of funding should be projected; a bare-bones program, a satisfactory program, and an ideal program.

The department heads were obviously unfamiliar with the zero-based procedure and asked many questions about how this would work. Did they, someone asked, have to justify existing programs? Yes. What about those programs and activities that were required by law? Estimate what they cost and put them in the bare-bones request. Did this include athletics and other high-cost-but-vital programs? Yes. Were the teaching salaries exempt from this process? No.

During the next several weeks the school was in turmoil in developing its first zero-based budget. Department heads called numerous after school meetings and individual classroom teachers were asked to develop lists of materials needed for classes and projects. Slowly, major estimates came into focus in each department. The range of requests, from bare-bones to ideal was staggering. When each of the departmental budgets reached the office Rick was pleased with the efforts. If he were to impose a bare-bones budget he could return nearly $39,000 to the superintendent. Even giving each department most of its "satisfactory" proposals he could save a little money for some special projects. In addition, in looking at the ideal requests he could see that within two years he could easily fund all of the dreams of individual faculty members if he desired to. Also, if the superintendent were to ever have some extra money at the end of the school year, Rick's school would be ready with a legitimate list of needs.

Rick decided against revealing the total budget allocations to all department heads at once. He knew that because the allotments were unequal he could easily become embroiled in arguments about the worth of one program versus another. Rather, Rick called all department heads together and reviewed the procedures followed. All of them, he said, would receive more than a bare-bones budget. The department heads responded with knowing glances and cheerful comments. No department will have a completely satisfactory budget, reported Rick. The department heads groaned in unison but still in good humor. There will be some discrepancy among awards to individual departments because of the need to foster equity. The department heads showed their anxiety by shifting their positions and busying themselves with the rearrangement of papers and coffee cups. Rick then scheduled individual meetings with the department heads to discuss their programs and allotments.

In the meetings with department heads Rick was careful to review the procedure by which the allotments had been made. These were the department's figures, and Rick's role had simply been to determine how far the funding would stretch. Each department head was given something to show the department as a symbol of his or her ability to get resources and the funding was always in the order of departmental priority. In addition, Rick held back about 5 percent of the allocations and parcelled them out to those heads who really felt they had been treated unfairly.

Case Questions

1. What advantages were gained by using a zero-based budget format at Rick's school? What were the liabilities?
2. In what ways might Rick use ZBB to improve upward communication in budgetary matters?
3. What are the political implications for a budgetary system like ZBB that does not grant an automatic base or fair share?

4. In what other way might Rick have dealt with the historic precedent of automatically inflating budget requests?

NOTES

1. Aaron Wildavsky, *The Politics of the Budgetary Process* 2nd ed. (Boston: Little, Brown, 1974), p. 4.
2. Theodore Caplow, *How to Run Any Organization* (Hinsdale: Dryden Press, 1976), p. 17. Caplow says, "One predictor of a manager's eventual downfall is the failure to secure the organization's finances by the end of the honeymoon."
3. The authors are indebted to the anonymous reviewer that emphasized several of these points after reading an early draft of the manuscript.
4. In October 1965 President Lyndon Johnson mandated all federal agencies adopt PPBS. However, the concept of systematic budget to program analysis was utilized by the Bureau of the Budget and Rand Corporation in the early 1960s for historical overview; see Fremont Lyden and Ernest Miller, ed., *Program-Planning Budgeting* (Chicago: Markham, 1972), especially pp. 63–78.
5. Allen Schick, "The Road to PPB: The Stages of Budget Reform," *Public Administration Review* 26, no. 4 (December 1966): 114–126.
6. See Wildavsky, *The Politics of the Budgetary Process*, pp. 205–208, 223–227.
7. Harry Hartley, "Economic Rationality in Urban School Planning," unpublished paper of the National School Board Association, 1971.
8. Aaron Wildavsky, "The Political Economy of Efficiency: Cost Budget Analysis, Systems Analysis and Program Budgeting," *Public Administration Review* 26, no. 1 (December 1966), 36–51.
9. Reported in Stanley Elam and Gordon Swanson, eds., *Educational Planning in the United States* (Etasca, Ill.: Reacock, 1969).
10. *Ibid.*, p. 89.
11. *Ibid.*, p. 110; Mr. Beasley was from Northern Illinois University.
12. *Ibid.*, p. 172.
13. N. E. Long, *The Polity* (Chicago: Rand McNally, 1971), p. 193.
14. Florida State Department of Education, *A Guide: Internal Accounting for School Activities* (Tallahassee: State Department of Education, 1960), p. viii.
15. For further discussion of application within local schools see Ralph Kimbrough, *Administering Elementary Schools* (New York: Macmillan, 1968), pp. 349–365.
16. For a specific example of the decision dynamics surrounding this basic issue see David Wiles and Thomas Williams, "Implications for Decision Making Autonomy in the Metropolitan School Organization," *Midwest Journal of Public Administration* 7, no. 4 (October 1973): 245–260.
17. Wildavsky, *The Politics of the Budgetary Process*, pp. ix to xxiii, 1–10, 128–142.
18. A popular example of the issue is President Jimmy Carter's effort to reorganize the education sector and create a Department of Education. For theoretical arguments see Todd LaPorte, ed., *Organized Social Complexity* (Princeton: University Press 1975).

19. Either to fulfill actual operating needs or to enhance a buffer zone as protection against the rest of the organization—"work expands to make the job." See Anthony Downs, *Inside Bureaucracy* (Boston: Little, Brown, 1967).
20. Wildavsky, *The Politics of the Budgetary Process*, p. 16.
21. *Ibid.*

CHAPTER 8

Personnel Politics

The politics of personnel administration reflects different meanings. There is the political distinction between levels of school government—district decisions made through collective negotiations about personnel allocations mandate local school conditions and predetermine choices. However, an even more pronounced political distinction is based upon the contextual meaning of *personnel*. Personnel politics that emphasizes human contacts is different from the institutional interpretation of personnel administration. The principal's role in both contexts will be considered.

THE INSTITUTIONAL PERSPECTIVE

This view considers people only as they hold institutional roles and represent incumbents of an organization's positions. The institutional view of personnel administration assumes the assembly-line interpretation of local school governance and control. There is no controversy about the dominance of the institution's formal authority to make final decisions or that the role of the principal is at the pinnacle of power in relation to all other subordinates or clients within the school setting. The closest the traditional view comes to recognizing alternative perspectives of control and governance is in abstract references to the professional teacher's expertise and the need to promote morale by democratic administration. *The prostitution of these terms comes in the inherent contradiction between a perception of peers in choice (like the arena) and the traditional view.*

The crucial nature of personnel policy making is widely recognized.[1] Williams lists "seven basic areas of teacher personnel problems: staff selection, staff assignment, professional growth opportunities, supervision, teacher morale, evaluation of teacher performance, and merit rating."[2] Gibson and Hunt outline the personnel function as hiring, employment, and withdrawal.[3] Hiring includes requisition, recruitment, selection, and appointment. Employment includes placement, career development, promotion and transfer, personnel relations and services, rewards, and conditions of work. Withdrawal includes separation, benefits, exit interview, and position evaluation.

The institutional concept of personnel policy making is characterized by *the administrator as the sole final decider or holding veto power over any delegated process*. Discussion of several decision areas will highlight political implications of the hierarchical assumption.

The selection of staff gives "the principal a critical responsibility for selecting members whose talents will form a cohesive whole." [4] Williams infers the autonomy of faculty is a covert criterion of selection: "Teachers must realize that by the way they teach, appear, act and talk they are conditioning students to look with favor or disfavor on teaching as a career." [5]

Calculating teacher load demonstrates a second assumption of institutional personnel administration; it attempts to standardize policy choices for formula, standing operating procedures and other routines. An example of this thinking is represented in the following list.

1. The number of sections taught daily (or weekly).
2. The number of pupils taught.
3. The number of different preparations required.
4. The amount of time required for cooperations: study halls, activities, etc.
5. The length of the class period.
6. The nature of the subject and the consequent amount of time required for preparation, for marking papers and notebooks, and for arranging equipment, apparatus, and materials.
7. The personnel of the pupils taught: tractability and range of individual differences in ability, factors that are difficult to measure.
8. The age and maturity of the pupils taught and the consequent character of the subject matter.

Traditional administration assumes a workable formula for measuring teaching load in the junior and senior high schools:

$$TL = SC \left[CP - \frac{DUP}{10} + \frac{NP - 25CP}{100} \right] \left[\frac{PL + 50}{100} \right] + 0.6 \, PC \left[\frac{PL + 50}{100} \right]$$

TL   = units of teaching load per week.

SC   = subject coefficient used for giving relative weights to classes in different subject fields.

CP   = class periods spent in classroom per week.

DUP = number of class periods spent per week in classroom teaching classes for which the preparation is similar to that for some other section, not including the original section.

NP   = number of pupils in classes per week.

PC = number of class periods spent per week in supervision of the study hall, student activities, teachers' meetings, committee work, assisting in administrative or supervisory work, or other cooperations.

PL = gross length of class periods, in minutes.[6]

A final example of institutional assumptions about personal administration are the recommended practices to maintain high teacher morale. Techniques suggested are:

> Assigning at least one superior class to each teacher; developing a personal record folder for each teacher that records his contributions to the school and to its success; establishing a professional reading library, publicizing teacher achievements in the school and local papers; providing summer employment for summer school teaching, curriculum development, and guidance services; hiring aides to assist teachers in routine tasks; permitting pilot or experimental programs that are endorsed by the faculty; assigning a reasonable teaching load; and giving teachers opportunities for promotion to administrative positions.[7]

The worker position of the teacher is clearly inferred. It can be argued we have chosen the example of old-school personnel administration and that there are much more sophisticated methods of blending bureaucracy to policy making in personnel matters. In this sense, personnel administration reflects the larger questions of good educational administration. In the 1980s there seems a wide proliferation of specific strategies and tactics to facilitate or make more palatable the institutional stipulations about a perception of decision making. But the basic dilemma of circumventing superordinate-subordinate relations between the teachers and administrators remains. As long as the bureaucratic model defines policy making, the range of alternative decision postures is limited.

It can be hypothesized that the failure to adequately restructure institutional stipulations of bureaucratic control and governance led to the current overt challenges to the basic assumptions of decision making. *Today, the arena perspective of personnel administration represents the foremost challenge to the historical base of educational administration.* An increasing number of teachers are questioning the assumed correlation between professional and subordinate decision status. Unable to change the schools internally, teachers of the 1960s and 1970s attempted to redefine the meaning of professional by going outside the bureaucracy. The 1980s will see the *internal* focus of role redefinition.

Teaching provides a classic example of the political implications surrounding the traditional view of the personnel function in schools. The meaning of the term *professional* teacher has become a battleground of emotional and psychological definitions about decision role and purpose.

In the name of professionalism teachers have walked out of the classroom on strike. In the name of professionalism teachers have remained in the classroom in spite of strike demands. What causes dedicated teachers to disagree so violently about the philosophical meaning that underlies the whole teaching function? This situation is not a case of good and bad personnel, rather these individuals are caught in the vise of organizational dynamics that have roots into the very meanings of bureaucratic roles, administrative responsibility, and lay governance within public education in the United States. Collective negotiations cannot be written off as the result of new exotic societal changes in the 1960s and early 1970s that caused teachers to become militant. The seeds of misinterpretation, conflict, and controversy over the meaning of *professional teachers* had been planted in the school institutional structure at the turn of the century.

As mentioned in earlier chapters, tension between the ideal bureaucratic model and all types of actual social organizations is inherent. Factories, welfare agencies, fire departments, or schools are always somewhat different from their institutional explanations, and the difference is the human element. Using the bureaucratic model as one extreme, Etzioni describes *human element* at the other end of the authority continuum:

> We would like to suggest that in professional organizations the staff-expert line-manager correlation, insofar as such a correlation exists at all, is reversed.... managers in charge of professional organizations are in charge of secondary activities; they administer means to the major activity carried out by experts. The final internal decision is, functionally speaking, in the hands of the various professionals and their decision-making bodies.[8]

COLLECTIVE NEGOTIATIONS

The impact of master contracts hammered out in collective negotiations has had an undeniable effect upon the principalship and local school governance. The particulars of the master contract provide the principal and other local school players a solid piece of evidence about the type of system-level recognition of governance and control. Specifically the contractual *outcomes* of collective negotiations (whether called meet and confer or bargaining) indicate arena power relationships, the spirit of play, the pot that is competed for and, indirectly, what is considered smart political behavior.

Power relations between boards and teacher federations form a rough continuum of (1) total domination by one party (historically, the board), through (2) a zero-sum where both sides are locked in all out war for total win through (3) a sword-rattling brinksmanship of threat and hostile posture to (4) a mature utility-matching situation.[9] The contract will reflect the imperial or punitive nature of the teacher-board relationship. The preferred relation is called *mature* because both adversaries recognize the realities of give and take and that a mutual win is possible, but it also requires a mutual loss. More important, maturity means conscious recognition of a political peer arrangement in making educational decisions for the district (often called grudging respect). The local school arena will be influenced by the degree of political sophistication at the district level. The master contract will stipulate the key issues in personnel administration where local school to district relationships must be considered from a political perspective.

A second indicator of the district collective negotiation arrangement can be the inferences to spirit of bargaining. The following outline gives two general classifications of types of negotiating arrangements:

Spirit A	*Spirit B*
1. Board could act unilaterally without consultation with its employees.	1. Consultation with employees required under the good faith assumption.
2. Mutuality of interests and interdependency assumed.	2. Mutuality of interests and interdependency, plus divergency of interests and needs, are assumed.
3. Grievances and other personnel matters sometimes overlooked.	3. Grievances and other personnel concerns are considered important, and provisions are made in writing to handle them.
4. Much taken for granted.	4. Nothing taken for granted.
5. A day's work in teaching often puzzling to determine.	5. A day's work in teaching and responsibilities specifically defined.
6. One-way communications.	6. Two-way communications.
7. Narrow sphere of bargaining, often confined to economic matters only.	7. Parties may elect to bargain on a broad scale.
8. Superintendent represented teachers to the board and the board to teachers.	8. Both parties represented by expert representatives of their own choosing.
9. Board always had last word.	9. Impasse procedures provided neither party can be allowed to paralyze the bargaining process.
10. Courts finally resolved disputes; losers paid costs.	10. Third parties called in to intervene in resolution of disputes; costs shared equally.

11. Good faith not mandated.

11. Good faith bargaining mandated and assured legislatively and by written agreement.

12. Written personnel policies lacking specificity.

12. Written agreements set terms and conditions of personnel administration.

13. Divergencies between policy and practice often left unexplained.

13. Constant dialogue permits discussion of divergencies of policy to practice.

The types and number of personnel administration issues negotiated into a master contract gives a rough measure of the pot that can be played for in a particular school situation. In general, the more system-wide personnel stipulations, the less the area for bargaining within the local school. The following list gives an administrator's organization view[10] of issues that should be directly negotiated or advised by teachers. The "advisory consultation" list may also give a rough listing of possible pots in a local school arena.[11]

Items for Negotiation

1. Revised salary schedule.

2. Increased hospitalization benefits.

3. Reduced class size.

4. Compensation for committee work.

5. Increase in pay scale for summer school teaching and adult education classes.

6. Duty-free lunch periods.

7. Addition of paraprofessional personnel to give relief from clerical and other nonteaching duties.

8. Additional leave for conducting personal business.

Items for Advisory Consultation

1. Revision of policies and procedures on teacher assignments and transfer.

2. Review of leave of absence policies.

3. More teacher involvement in textbook selection and curriculum development.

4. Greater teacher participation in budget development and allocation of priorities.

5. Modification in procedures for handling pupil discipline problems.

6. Change in policies governing assignment of student teachers.

7. Establishment of a standing advisory committee on staff personnel administration.

8. Participation of teachers in reviewing reports of unsatisfactory teacher performance.

| 9. Increase in number of school holidays. | 9. Greater teacher involvement in planning of federally sponsored programs and projects. |
| 10. Terminal leave pay. | 10. Procedures for attendance at professional meetings. |

Finally, collective negotiation is important to this text because it has been a legitimate arena for overt political decision making. We can compare our strategies for playing local school poker with the results of experience drawn from the negotiating table. An administrator's[12] perception of smart negotiating behavior gives fifteen how-to-do-it guidelines:

1. Retain self-control. Negotiation sessions can be exasperating. The temptation may come to get angry and fight back when intemperate accusations are made or when the straw that broke the camel's back is hurled on the table.

2. Avoid off-the-record comments. Actually nothing is off the record. Innocently made remarks have a way of coming back to haunt their author. Be careful to say only what you are willing to have quoted.

3. Don't be overcandid. Inexperienced negotiators may, with the best of intentions, desire to lay the cards on the table face up in the mistaken notion that everybody fully understands the other and utter frankness is desired. Complete candor doesn't always serve the best interests of productive negotiation. This suggestion is not a plea for duplicity; rather, it is a recommendation for prudent and discriminating utterances.

4. Be long on listening. Usually a good listener makes a good negotiator. It is wise to let your adversaries do the talking, at least in the beginning.

5. Don't be afraid of a little heat. Discussions sometimes generate quite a bit of heat. Don't be afraid of it. It never hurts to let the opposition sound off even when you may be tempted to hit back.

6. Watch the voice level. A wise practice is to keep the pitch of the voice down even though the temptation may be strong to let it rise under the excitement of emotional stress.

7. Keep flexible. One of the skills of good negotiators is the ability to shift position a bit if the positive gain can thus be accomplished. An obstinate adherence to one position or point of view, regardless of the ultimate consequences of that rigidity, may be more of a deterrent than an advantage.

8. Refrain from giving a flat "no." Especially in the earlier stages of negotiation it is best to avoid giving a flat "no" answer to a proposition. It doesn't help to work yourself into a box by being totally negative too early in the game.

9. Give to get. Negotiation is the art of giving and getting. Concede a point to gain a concession. That's the name of the game.

10. Work on the easier items first. Settle the least controversial things first. Leave the tougher items until later in order to avoid an early deadlock.

11. Respect your adversary. Respect those who are seated on the opposite side of the table. Assume that their motives are as sincere as your own, at least until proven otherwise.

12. Be patient. If necessary, be willing to sit out tiresome tirades. Time has a way of being on the side of the patient negotiator.

13. Avoid waving red flags. Some statements irritate teachers and merely heighten their antipathies. Find out what these are and avoid their use.

14. Let the other side win some victories. Each team has to win some victories. A shut out may be a hollow gain in negotiation.

15. Negotiation is a way of life. Obvious resentment of the fact that negotiation is here to stay weakens the effectiveness of the negotiator. The better part of wisdom is to adjust to it and to become better prepared to use it as a tool of interstaff relations.

In conclusion, Nolte captures the flavor of how much the traditional view has been transformed.

> One gets little argument on the proposition that school personnel administration is not what it once was, but has changed. However, the proposition understates the case. It fails to make clear that the traditional "textbook" practice of education administration indigenous to America and in use for at least 135 years has been replaced by an entirely new and different process. Instead of a mere change in the process by which the schools are managed, a transformation has occurred.
>
> Differences between the old and the new processes of school personnel administration are so fundamental that they preclude the use of more familiar frameworks for assessing and predicting events. A new frame of reference is needed for understanding and assessing the administration of personnel in the schools.[13]

What the transformation of the institutional politics of personnel administration has become is competition between two educational organizations: the school system and the teacher federation. On either side, the human element is reduced to the skills of the negotiator (the principal may get guidance from another type of bargaining arena) or lofty statements about fighting to preserve the rights of the people (interchangeable labels of the professional teacher, the children, the public). The single most political characteristic of the institution perspective of personnel is that people decide *within organizational* arrangements.

COMMUNICATING WITH PEOPLE

From the standpoint of people within organizations, there are three regular causes of faulty communication. First, there can be a speaking-listening breakdown. Early communication models, such as those developed by Ryan,[14] described a communication system that consisted of a speaker, a message, and a receiver. Each of these components is necessary for complete communication. Distortion of communication in the system, called *noise* by Ryan, can be caused by either faulty transmission, the environment in which the message is transmitted, or faulty reception. Speaking-listening breakdowns can be either accidental or purposeful.

A second common cause of poor communication in organizations is an uncommon frame of reference between the sender and the receiver of the message. Individuals possess certain experiences, knowledges, and values that they use to encode and decode verbal communication. When the sender and the receiver do not see alike because of experience, knowledge, or values, communication is likely to be distorted. This understanding is especially important for the principal when trying to communicate with groups to which he or she does not belong.

Finally, in organizations many environmental barriers can and do impede effective communication. Examples of such environmental barriers might be the format for communicating (written versus face to face), the timing of communication, or the degree of confidentiality of the communication. Other environmental barriers may be primarily interpersonal in nature, such as the carryover effects of previous communication (especially when a principal has been elevated from within the teaching ranks).

A study of human communication patterns by Berlo has identified the following four predictors of faulty communication that can be used by administrators to anticipate probable communication breakdown:

1. the amount of competition the message has
2. the threats to status and ego that are involved
3. the uncertainty and error in what is expected
4. the number of links there are in the communication chain[15]

Other barriers to effective communication can evolve from language, values, perceptions, prejudices, and biases. The administrator should be aware that the following behaviors, in particular, reduce the possibility of clear and indepth communication:

1. an attempt to sell something in communication
2. a lack of trust from previous communication
3. a vested interest being communicated
4. a basic conflict of values among those communicating

5. prejudices against the sender or against the receiver
6. an emphasis on status among communicators
7. a rigid social structure
8. personal insecurity on the part of sender or receiver

Because communication is like an iceberg, with 85 percent of the real effort below the surface, the administrator must facilitate effective communication in an environmental context. There must be a concentrated effort to see communication in its totality. Wiles has outlined nine questions that can be used by the administrator to assess what is really happening in any communication encounter:

1. What does the speaker want to say?
2. What does the speaker want to conceal?
3. What does the speaker reveal without knowing it?
4. What does the listener want or expect to hear?
5. What will the listener's perception of the speaker let him hear?
6. What will the listener's experiences tell him the words mean?
7. What does the listener wish to conceal?
8. What does the emotional climate of the situation permit the speaker and listener to share?
9. What does the physical structure of the situation permit the speaker and listener to share? [16]

The administrator should also be aware that there will always be some degree of defensive behavior in any communication effort.

> Defensive behavior is defined as that behavior which occurs when an individual perceives a threat or anticipates a threat in the group. The person who behaves defensively, even though he gives some attention to the common task, devotes an appreciable portion of his energy to defending himself. Besides talking about the topic, he thinks about how he appears to others, how he can be seen more favorably, how he may win, dominate, impress, or escape punishment, and/or how he may avoid or mitigate a perceived or an anticipated attack.[17]

In general, establishing desired communication patterns in a school is a responsibility of the principal. Because he or she possesses the influence and primary power within the building, such responsibility cannot be abdicated. The authors recommend that the principal pursue a policy of authenticity and truthfulness as a means of promoting effective and desired communication in the school. The following behaviors would initiate such a pattern:

- Finding ways to be open, engaging in self-disclosure wherever possible. The principal may be consciously attempting to draw power and allegiance from some source other than status leadership or title authority.
- Exhibiting a willingness to be questioned. Most interpersonal perceptions are based on experience and information. To the degree that the principal can be open, he or she will encourage others to open themselves to questioning and exchange of information. The result will be fewer games and more accurate communication among participants.
- Entering into communication to learn and share, not to win or dominate. The administrator can set a pattern of desirable communication by sincerely seeking additional information or providing additional information when there is clearly no advantage to do so. Once school communication is perceived as a medium to learn and share, such learning and sharing will occur.
- Supporting other people who are venturing into openness. Real communication calls for varying degrees of trust, and teachers, parents, and students will look to the principal to set the tone for such trust.
- Listening for what is not said as well as what is said. The principal can increase effective communication in the school by demonstrating a sensitivity to the level and type of talk.

DEMOCRATIC ADMINISTRATION

Perhaps more important than any other discussion in this text is the question of whether democratic administration can be achieved in a competitive arena. The answer is both ethical and moral. It implies relations between people that distinguish the principal as Machiavelli versus an honorable player. *To talk of being democratic is not being wishy-washy or a weak administrator in a tough situation. It is a viable (and we feel preferable) way to govern a local school if understood in its political reality.*

The democratic emphasis was an outgrowth of the human relations movement in the 1930s when it was shown that variation of psychological and interpersonal factors could improve production in factories. Simply, it was found that people who are involved in ongoing decision processes that affect them will be more willing to accept (comply with) policy stipulations than those who are not allowed to participate.[18] The proof of improvement in organizational production was further rationalized by basic philosophical assumptions about the nature of man and what motivates him. Man was assumed to be a cooperative animal [19] who became human through, among other things, the ability to participate in projects involving mutual aid.[20]

Motivation of man is based upon satisfaction of a hierarchy of needs: animal survival needs (food, avoidance of pain, security) and human learned needs (self-actualization and psychological growth). Herzberg,[21] Maslow,[22] McGregor[23] and others have applied this satisfaction concept of motivation to organizational governance and control. A major conclusion of all the writers promoting this perspective of motivation was that the administrative structure could set the psychological climate of an organization based on which level of satisfaction was assumed important for individuals. If individuals are considered animals (e.g., subservient) then organizational motivation is restricted to survival need satisfactions. On the other hand, if individuals are considered *humans* within the organization, motivation is expanded to include psychological factors. McGregor demonstrates a general translation for the administrative perspective of subordinates in the bureaucracy by presenting two opposing sets of assumptions about the nature of man. Theory X postulates three basic assumptions:

1. The average human being has an inherent dislike for work and will avoid it if he or she can.
2. Because of this characteristic, most people must be coerced, controlled, directed, and threatened with punishment so that they will work toward the organization's goals.
3. The average human being prefers to be directed, prefers security, and avoids responsibility.

Theory Y embraces some different ideas:

1. Physical work and mental work are as natural as play, if they are satisfying.
2. People will exercise self-direction and self-control toward an organization's goals if they are committed to them.
3. Commitment is a function of rewards. The best rewards are satisfaction of ego and self-actualization.
4. The average person can learn to accept and seek responsibility. Avoidance of it and emphasis on security are learned and are not inherent characteristics.
5. Creativity, ingenuity, and imagination are widespread among people, and do not occur only in a select few.

The evolution of democratic administration is based upon the tenets of Theory Y, while the institutional arrangements of educational administration assume a Theory X focus. In the attempt to reconcile the inherent contradiction of Theory X and Y assumptions about the nature of

individuals in the organization, democratic administration became a pros-
tituted, misunderstood process. Many administrators saw democratic decision making as meaning *deny all* institutional expectations of governance
and control over subordinates. Participation and sharing meant negation of
all administrative responsibility for coordination and institutional accountability: a do-nothing, laissez-faire[24] approach.

Complete denial of the bureaucratic definition, which demands some
superordinate-subordinate responsibility, is no more realistic administration than assuming institutional stipulations are the only definitions of
governance. *Democratic decision making is a learned process, where all
people in an organization must be educated to accepting authority and
responsibility.*[25] Thus democratic governance and control arrangements
involve a conscious learning by administrators, teachers, students and all
others in a school. Much of the misunderstanding surrounding democratic
administration is tied to assuming that either democracy just happens in a
free environment or that only administrators must be resocialized. Neither
seems realistic for the arena/political perspective.

Fortunately, there have been several writers who have defined the
real meaning of democratic decision making that includes:

- conscious recognition of a balance between conflicting assumptions
  of motivation and satisfaction in bureaucratic governance
- conscious recognition that governance is a situational problem
- and conscious recognition that democracy within the bureaucracy
  is not a natural process, but a learned one.

In effect, the *operational* meaning of democracy is a "people" understanding of policy making that recognizes the institutional and personal constraints of the arena. Two writers who have given specific guidelines for
establishing democratic decision making are Kimball Wiles and Peter
Drucker.

In *Supervision for Better Schools*,[26] Wiles outlines the state of mind
that must be shared by staff and administrator if democratic policy making is to become a reality. The power-with approach is described as:

> If a faculty is governed by the situation, no one has power over any-
> one else. Decisions are made as to who will exercise which functions
> on the basis of skill and training... an executive decision is only a
> moment in the total process... it is the final statement of policy that
> the (administrator) must administer.[27]

It is clear that Wiles does not expect the administrator to give up his
or her institutional responsibilities.[28] However, he does stress that a climate
of power-with authority can be established for many decision situations.

Rather than removing the administrator from the decision process or taking away power, the principal can actually gain authority.

> The (administrator) participates in the discussion, exercises his full intelligence and gives the group the benefit of his best thinking. But his thinking is tested as carefully as is the thinking of any other member...he does not expect his ideas to be accepted as official rulings ...authority and responsibility are derived from function, not from delegation or position.... Authority is identified with training and information; it is used for "power with," not "power over." [29]

Although Wiles makes assumptions about the viability of consensus building and the rationality of a sequentially ordered problem solving approach, he acknowledges the dynamics of the political process always present. Institutional realities are recognized as demanding power-over implications for administrative governance. Wiles's basic theme is to establish interpersonal, informal value expectations of power-with arrangements when the situation permits. *The definition of appropriate situation depends upon the personal characteristics and group interactions within the organization.* Wiles sees decision making as a function of control and utilization of scarce resources (e.g., expertise, charisma, and interest). We differ from Wiles's perspective and the normative and descriptive approaches to administration in general [30] in the assumptions about the general nature of people making decisions within the bureaucracy. Wiles and other promoters of democratic administration assume trust and consensus (based upon logic) can be learned. We are more skeptical, for we assume bargaining occurs by competition and situational rationality.

Peter Drucker[31] promotes a different emphasis about democratic decision making but still recognizes the situational determination of balancing institutional goals with personal capabilities. Drucker, writing about business, says highly effective administrators cannot be distinguished by personal or interaction abilities except by studying the payoff or results of the arena.[32] Drucker argues that there is little correlation between a man's *effectiveness* and his intelligence, his imagination, or his knowledge. He does not recognize such a thing as an effective personality.

> Among the effective executives I have known there are extroverts and aloof, retiring men, some even morbidly shy. Some are eccentrics, others painfully correct conformists. Some are fat and some are lean. Some are worriers, some are relaxed. Some drink quite heavily, others are total abstainers. Some are men of great charm and warmth, some have no more personality than a frozen mackerel...some are scholars, others almost unlettered...there are people who use logic and analysis and others who rely mainly on perception and intuition.[33]

Drucker's radical bombardment on many conventional ideas of leadership is somewhat tempered by what effective executives do have in common.

> What all have in common is the practices that make effective whatever they are. And these practices are the same ... effectiveness, in other words, is a habit; that is a complex of practices. And practices can always be learned.[34]

The sources of Drucker's theory are the assumptions about the meaning of executive, worker, and effectiveness. The worker in many organizations can be distinguished on manual skills or knowledge. School staffs are knowledge workers. "For manual work, we need only efficiency; that is the ability to do things right *rather than the ability to get the right things done ... working on the right things is what makes knowledge work effective.*" [35] Drucker goes on to describe the role of the administrator. "The knowledge worker cannot be supervised (in the efficiency sense) closely or in detail. He can only be helped. But he must direct himself ... toward effectiveness." [36]

In education, the historical failure of boards and central offices to recognize the crucial distinction between manual versus knowledge work and evaluation by efficiency rather than product effectiveness has promoted the fight for teacher professionalism. The teacher organization, which formed outside the institutional school bureaucracy, is in itself a demonstration of the conflicting definitions of teacher as *subordinate worker* versus bargaining *peer*. Although not using terms *democratic administration*, Drucker does outline several principles of administrative effectiveness that assume staff competence as knowledge workers or professionals.

1. Knowledge work is not defined by quantity. Neither is knowledge work defined by its costs. Knowledge work is defined by its results.
2. Throughout knowledge organizations are people who manage no one and yet are executives (make normal decisions that have significant impact on the performance and results of the whole).
3. Effective executives build on strengths—their own, staff, the situation—not on weaknesses or impossibilities.
4. Effective executives gear efforts to results ... rather than with the work to be done, let alone with its techniques and tools.
5. Effective executives concentrate on a few major areas where superior performance will produce outstanding results.
6. Effective decisions are a matter of system—of the right steps in the right sequence—always a judgment of dissenting opinions rather than a consensus of facts.

Peter Drucker offers exciting ideas to the concept of democratic administration in education. Effectiveness is neither a laissez-faire or dogmatic authoritarian type of governance. Although Drucker's product emphasis is different from Kimball Wiles's, their assumptions of what type of subordinates inhabit school bureaucracies (professionals or knowledge workers) are similar. Consequently, both emphasize the basic tenet of democratic decision making. Their combined message is that the administrator must make every effort to set the type of organizational arena that expects real political meaning in words like authority *and* responsibility.

In summary, we feel the democratic theory of school governance is compatible with the political perspective. Power-with and product could be words for coalition formation and payoffs. The critical ingredient is the state of mind that fosters mutual respect and decency in the adversary relation of people competing for scarce resources.

WORKING WITH TEACHERS AS PEOPLE

The special group toward which administrative planning and organization should be directed is the teaching force. The 1970s witnessed enormous changes in the teaching profession including heavy unionization, a greater aggressiveness toward management, and a general maturing due to limited job mobility. The average classroom teacher will be older, more experienced, and more self-confident in the 1980s, and a more sophisticated relationship between principals and teachers is appropriate.

In spite of gains in extrinsic benefits during the past decade, teachers may not be any better at instruction in the classroom than they were ten years ago. The effect of endless curriculum innovations and accountability demands has been to lessen the teacher's enthusiasm for professional growth opportunities. It is interesting that a major survey of teacher-perceived needs for inservice, conducted in 1978, listed the same problems that have traditionally plagued public school teachers:[36]

1. ability to maintain order and help students with self discipline
2. ability to motivate student achievement
3. ability to apply appropriate evaluative techniques
4. ability to individualize instruction to meet varying needs
5. ability to use audio-visual materials in teaching
6. ability to provide instruction at various cognitive levels
7. ability to facilitate development of self-concept in students
8. ability to prepare teacher-made tests

9. ability to use observational techniques effectively in the classroom
10. ability to understand the interaction of school forces such as decision making and communication

It would seem that these particular needs of teachers could be met without great difficulty, but they continue to be perceived needs after years of inservice efforts by school districts.

If the principal is able to control teacher development activities and direct such inservice toward real problems in the school, the teaching staff will respond positively. At a minimum, the following preconditions should be in effect for planning inservice programs: (1) the teachers should be involved in the identification and articulation of their own training needs, (2) growth experiences for teachers should be individualized wherever possible, and (3) inservice activities should be planned at the school level, the proper unit for educational change.

The school-based staff development model developed by the Florida Department of Education lists nine hypotheses about planning inservice activities that have been supported by organized inquiry:[37]

1. Teacher attitudes are more likely to be influenced in school-based rather than college-based inservice programs.
2. School-based programs in which teachers participate as helpers to each other and planners of inservice activities tend to have greater success in accomplishing their objectives than do programs that are conducted by college or other personnel without the assistance of teachers.
3. School-based inservice programs that emphasize self-instruction by teachers have a strong record of effectiveness.
4. Inservice programs that have differentiated training experiences for different teachers (that is, individualized) are more likely to accomplish their objectives than are programs that have common activities for all participants.
5. Inservice education programs that place the teacher in active roles (constructing and generating materials, ideas, and behavior) are more likely to accomplish their objectives than are programs that place the teacher in a receptive role (accepting ideas and behavior prescriptions not of his or her own making).
6. Inservice education programs that emphasize demonstrations, supervised trials, and feedback are more likely to accomplish their goals than are programs in which the teachers are expected to store up ideas and behavior prescriptions for a future time.
7. Inservice education programs in which teachers share and provide mutual assistance to each other are more likely to accomplish their objectives than are programs in which each teacher does separate work.

8. Teachers are more likely to benefit from inservice education activities that are linked to a general effort of the school than they are from a single-shot program that is not a part of a general staff development plan.

9. Teachers are more likely to benefit from inservice programs in which they can choose goals and activities for themselves, as contrasted with programs in which the goals and activities are preplanned.

WORKING WITH PEOPLE IN AN INSTITUTIONAL CONTEXT

Caplow[38] provides several practical suggestions of how a principal should relate to the personal secretary, the assistant principal, the chairpersons of various departments or program clusters, and the rank and file of teachers. Although Caplow bases his suggested administrator activities on the assumption of a bureaucratic hierarchy, we feel he identifies critical points for the poker perspective of local school governance.

According to Caplow, the school secretary should be under the principal's direct and exclusive control. While the secretary should be under no obligation to other persons in management, it is equally important that the secretary does not acquire power over staff and other school managers. The daily access to information above makes the secretary's role one of power. The principal's function is to keep this power in check by constant surveillance. Caplow warns that managing *through* the secretary either leads to revolution or the principal's becoming a ceremonial figure.

For principals in large schools the relationship with assistant principals is crucial in personnel administration. There are usually problems in the principal-assistant principal relationship when there is more than one subordinate. Caplow feels the functional specialization of assistants (e.g., students versus curriculum building and so forth) causes natural battles for superiority. For this situation, he argues assistants should be kept unequal in formal influence and status attributes. Frequent meetings are suggested so that territorial disputes can be resolved early. Third, there should be an ambiguity in relations of principals to their assistants. *The desirable state of ambiguity is when each assistant considers himself or herself potentially superior, but fears to push the claim too far in a direct confrontation of interpersonal relation with the principal vis-á-vis a formal status.*

Caplow would also argue the principle of ambiguity for relations with department or program cluster chairpersons. However, he feels ambiguity with assistant principals is necessary so they will not assume too much authority, and ambiguity with chairs is to encourage them to accept responsibility. The larger the local school, the more power and responsibility must be delegated. However, Caplow notes that extent of delegation is related to the possibility of feudal type regimes and baronial welfare among and within the various departments or program areas.[39] Delegated power should be evaluated in relation to the principal's own power to (1) secure the local school finances, (2) evaluate the various departments objectively, (3) guarantee no inherent conflict of interest, and (4) remove a chairperson if necessary.[40]

The rank and file should be treated as a power structure. Pay particular attention to the shop steward teachers with ties to the system-wide federation. The principal should attempt to become the living symbol of the local school's collective identity. The image should be such that any honor or disgrace the principal incurs affects all school members. One of the toughest problems for many principals is finding the appropriate social role with the rank and file. Extraneous conversation necessary for human contact often creates the sociopsychological illusions of friendliness that has some relation to power. If sociability fails to relate to other power motives, Caplow believes, many hidden ambivalences are created. This condition is most likely in subordinates whose emotional vulnerability makes them express devotion to the principal. He argues "it is much better practice for the manager to measure the affection of subordinates by their compliance with his orders rather than their eagerness to fraternize with him (or her)." [41] Caplow states that this helps guard against "et tu Brute?"

While this text disagrees with the basic assumptions of managerial authority and power interest as Caplow describes them, we feel he identified crucial issues to be resolved in interpersonal relations. How actors work together within the arena is the key to the blend of persons to organizational perspectives of personnel administration politics.

THE SPECIAL CASE OF THE WOMAN ADMINISTRATOR

Women will present a unique political issue in the arena in the 1980s as they attempt to overcome minority status and issues of sexuality. Survival in an arena with shrinking resources during the 1980s will depend upon an understanding of this special case.

It is not our intent to imply a lesser significance to other minorities in school administration (racial or ethnic) or to equate women with other minorities. Rather, the woman in school administration holds a special minority status for two reasons. First, women in school administration represent the most recent example of a phenomenon that occurs when a "minority" is promoted for greater inclusion in governance roles. As blacks and other ethnic minorities have learned in earlier years, there seems to be a curious relation between the extent of public promotion of a minority and the actual results of gaining access and retaining employment. Women are finding that the increased promotion of affirmative action and equal opportunity employment during the past decade has resulted in a *smaller* percentage of women in school administration.[42] Many more women do become final candidates or gain temporary employment in newly created positions but the track record in securing conventional line positions has not been encouraging. This phenomenon of school governance will grow more pronounced in the scarcity of the 1980s. We will focus upon women as a minority because they will bear the two-edged brunt of what other specially classified groups have experienced: tokenism and "last hired, first fired."

The second reason we focus on the woman as "minority" is the special relation to concepts of organizational governance and control. Nowhere does the word *feminine* carry more sex role stereotyping than in consideration of decision making in competition or controversy.

One of the political dynamics that underscores the meaning of minority in personnel matters for specially classified groups is the tendency to separate appearance from reality or intent from actuality. Experience of blacks, Latinos, American Indians, and women has demonstrated that legal or formal stipulations of institutional compliance may actually result in *fewer* opportunities for minorities concerning employment or retention. The politics of the phenomena revolves around words such as *token* and *seniority*. The issue is whether formal processes designed to encourage minority representation by personnel administration have any relationship to actual results. Tokenism implies a minority is hired or retained as a symbolic gesture of mandated compliance. The selection of a single minority to *represent* institutional compliance is usually rationalized according to a lack of a qualified pool or as a righteous response to breaking the quota. The pool argument places the burden on acceptable advertisement and the minority applicant's ability to see opportunity for employment. The nonquota argument is that the minority must be considered, but the institution still has final choice. The operational impact of these mentalities often results in minority tokenism. Women selected for school administration in the 1980s may well face the token role, for the tendency becomes more pronounced under scarcity. Another dimension that may occur is the fragmentation of a single response to "who is a minority?" Even in the late 1970s there were indications of competition *between* women and blacks or blacks and Latinos for the minority label. These tendencies could reach full blown proportions by the mid 1980s.[43]

A second implication of the possible phenomena that formal recognition of minority may result in an actual diminishing of women administrators is the issue of "last hired, first fired." Again, other minorities have found that the initial securing of employment was only the preliminary bout to the real fight for retention. Again, scarcity promotes protection of the *core* employment structure and the seniority system is the key vehicle for the protection. Unions and federations derive their strength from the seniority system and cannot be counted on to support minorities that could split (by differentiating classification of the represented constituency) the uniform ranks. During the 1980s the hiring and retention of personnel on soft positions will become less covered by rhetoric and glossy promises than what occurred in the 1970s. Expectations of being a temporary filler may become a way of life for women and other minority players gaining access to the local school arena.

What does this say to the bargaining of the woman administrator? Simply, that the word *minority* highlights a special political issue that needs to be confronted in taking charge and maintaining control. If a woman is in some form of temporary arrangement to the local school arena her ability to play will be disadvantaged. *Political compensation should be attempted by deemphasizing the person and emphasizing the continuity of the institutional role.* The other special concern of the woman administrator is sexuality itself.

Several landmark efforts to discuss women in management have emphasized the unequality and differences of men and women in the same administrative roles. The open recognition of these differences should now be acceptable. *The woman is more than a minority in a majority power structure. The results of intensive socialization make her approach to questions of control and governance different. There are basic differences in men and women poker players when the game is deciding local school matters.* To avoid the risk of being labeled sexist, we turn to specific descriptions of women administrators to make the case. Margaret Hennig and Anne Jardim[44] point to several patterns of difference that make women have a special situation in school administration. First, women are more likely to see a job as what one does day-to-day, nine to five—a means of *surviving*.[45] With men a job usually relates to a task to be completed, a set of responsibilities, or assignments to be fulfilled. Men expressly relate the job of administrator to a career of advancement. Women separate the two issues entirely: a woman's career may not be directly linked to job performance in her mind.

Another difference is being a team player. Men are socialized to work together while women are taught to emphasize the individual as competitor.[46] However, the woman as competitor has a different perception of risk taking and winning than the man. Men see risk as loss or gain with the possibility of winning or losing. Opportunities always carry the risk of danger. Women see risk as entirely negative.[47] It means loss or ruin and is to be avoided as much as possible.

Finally, men and women have a different style when being judged in a subordinate role. Men reference their behavior to their boss's expectation of them while women behave according to their own self-concept. The man that refuses to adopt the boss's style does so with some sense of the price he will pay or some counterstrategy. Women act to "this is who I am—like it or leave it." [48] Hennig and Jardim summarize:

> ...boys learn flexibility, a way to get what one wants...a style that is unconscious—a far different thing from consciously attempting to win over authority figures...one by one...men learn to sit at meetings and put up with one another...to tolerate...and use one another to a degree that women often find incomprehensible...women tend to fall into the trap of "overemotionalism": intolerance (I don't like him or her and I can't work with either of them) or a painful vulnerability to criticism. [49]

One other note will be mentioned before discussing the women administrator as poker player in a local school arena. Four roles have been identified that purported to represent how women work with power in the organization: [50]

1. *the earth mother* ("I need to feel that you need me.")
2. *the manipulator* (our weapons are guilt, charm, anger, exclusion, and simply sensing and feeding a person's need, but with our own ends in mind)
3. *the workaholic* (we have difficulty saying this is the task, let's define it, let's be clear about your responsibility and mine)
4. *the egalitarian* (as long as a women doesn't act like a boss other people will work for her)

Several writers feel the roles are especially bothersome for women because women tend not to form hierarchies and have a nurturing mode that conflicts with the individual, achieving mode. There is a problem between the drive to relate and the drive to act when a woman is in a power (managerial) position.

Assuming women do approach the power dynamics of the political arena differently from men and find hierarchical relations unfamiliar, what does it mean? As the stability and continuities of past decision arrangements continue to erode under the force of scarcity, normal male-female differences are likely to erode. To be a male team player who knows the art of compromise is probably a winning style in a long-standing mature arena. But what of the arena that is in extreme crisis? The *person* who can offer a survival suggestion will be the winner there. We do not pretend to know what the 1980s will bring for those women in school administrator roles or the actual treatment they will receive as a viable equal member of the arena. However, uncertainty about school governance itself should break down much of the role stereotyping and pat decision relationships that other minorities have had to face in more stable times. We feel that the conventional socialization of *both males and females* will be disrupted for some time into the future. As educators of all sexes, races, and religions attempt to understand and cope with the coming changes we believe that labeling (such as earth mother) will die a natural death. In the late 1960s there was a pilot test in the big city ghetto schools that showed that minority success and administrative survival were a function of adapting to practical realities of specific governance situations.[51] The 1980s and 1990s should provide the changes necessary for a larger test of the same success-survival phenomenon.

CASE STORY: MIDDLE
MANAGEMENT FRUSTRATIONS

When the year had first begun the teachers had accepted hall duty between classes as a part of the job. That was before the Miller accident. Karen Miller, an attractive foreign language teacher, had simply been standing in the hall talking with a student when she was struck fully in the face by an elbow. The fact that two seniors were simply horsing around did little to console Mrs. Miller. The dental bills alone came to nearly four hundred dollars. Worse, the teachers served notice that they no longer intended to assume the role of police during or between classes.

As principal, Sam was in an immediate bind. Sure, the Miller accident was unfortunate... terrible, in fact. Without provocation Karen Miller had become one of some 20,000 teachers assaulted in schools each year. Perhaps Senator Birch Bayh had been right in issuing his famous observation that "the primary concern of many modern schools is no longer education, but preservation." Still, this high school had a nice population of kids in general, and the school was responsible for the students all day long. There was no way the teachers could quit monitoring the halls during the passing periods.

In a way it was lucky that this district was unionized, because monitoring the halls between classes was clearly in the contract. The teachers couldn't just walk out on that part of the job without jeopardizing the entire contract. After negotiating for months to get their new contract, the teachers weren't likely to throw it all away on this one incident. After all, Karen Miller had been fully covered by the school insurance policy.

Just to be sure, Sam had called up the superintendent, Larry Kinds. Larry had been interested in and concerned about Mrs. Miller, but thought that it would all blow over. That was Tuesday. Two days later (Thursday) was a different story entirely. Larry said that the teachers were really hopping over the incident and that they were going to make a major issue of it. Some Board members had been contacted and public sentiment was rising. Larry explained that he was having a particularly difficult time with several Board members and would appreciate it if Sam could handle this one at the school level. The superintendent, he explained, didn't need another battle at the moment.

On Friday the situation was out of control. Not only did the teachers stay in their rooms between classes, but a near catastrophe was avoided only by a stroke of luck. A sophomore passed out behind the lockers between third and fourth periods, and if his friends hadn't carried him to the office who knows what would have happened to him? It wasn't clear whether he had been on drugs or was genuinely sick. It didn't matter really; he could have died on the school premises.

Sam made a final and unsuccessful plea to the teachers before going to see Larry Kinds personally. During a terse and unproductive twenty minutes they wrestled with alternatives. Larry clearly favored ordering the teachers back out into the halls, but preferred that Sam do the ordering. Sam reported that two Board members had called him supporting the teacher's position and he really didn't feel secure issuing such an order without the superintendent's full support. It was obvious that inaction would only lead to greater confusion and potential for danger. It was finally decided that Board action was needed to clear the air. They would take it up with the Board Tuesday night.

Sam couldn't remember a Board meeting so well attended. Not only had the teachers and the union packed the room, but the newspapers had heard about it and half the town seemed to be there. The Board, in particular, seemed nervous and unnerved by the turnout. All this from a dumb elbow, thought Sam.

Larry Kinds finally introduced the problem after dealing with a number of routine tasks. His hopes that the public might get bored and go home had certainly been wishful thinking. Larry introduced the situation as a routine matter needing Board guidance and then turned to Sam to explain the events at the school. Hesitantly, Sam outlined the problem as he saw it. Twice he caught his voice quavering as he tried to describe the present condition at the school. The Board members whispered to one another and a general murmer drifted over the room. Finally, mercifully, the chairman called a recess.

During the break Larry, the chairman, and Sam huddled in a corner to discuss the proceedings. The chairman feared that the Board would support the teachers given the pressure of the moment. Larry, sensing he could no longer contain the momentum of the meeting requested a closed meeting so that the Board could deliberate in a rational manner on this important issue. When the general meeting convened, the room was cleared and the business of the Board resumed.

Larry asked each Board member in turn how they felt the Board should respond. By a 4–3 margin the Board indicated that this was a professional matter and one that seemingly was governed by the existing contract. Larry and Sam were to take control of the matter and work it out with the teachers. The general meeting was reconvened again and the

Board chairman announced the decision of the Board. A call for other business was made while a rather noisy audience responded to the Board's action. Turning to Sam, Larry whispered, "well, you've got your boundaries, buddy."

Sam approached school on Wednesday morning feeling as if he hadn't slept in weeks. He knew that there was no way he could force his teachers back into hall duty against their will. Still, he was fortunate because one of his teachers was an officer in the local association. If he could reach that teacher prior to the opening of school, perhaps they might reach a compromise. Failing such contact, he knew it would be a long day at the high school.

At ten minutes until eight Sam located his teacher in the lounge. Quietly and without fanfare Sam stated that he fully expected the union to take this matter up with the Board as a grievance, but hoped that the matter would be handled professionally and without jeopardizing the existing contract. The teacher, a fifteen-year veteran at the school, responded after considerable reflection, "You bet your ass we will, Sam."

Case Questions

1. Describe this case as it evolved in terms of boundary maintenance.

2. What kind of a strategy was the superintendent employing when he called for a closed session of the school board meeting? Did this action affect the decision boundary?

3. Obviously, the master contract played a role in this case. Did Sam do the right thing in using the contract as a communication vehicle to get the teachers back on hall duty?

4. Outline the next probable steps in this case from the standpoint of both the teachers and the administration.

NOTES

1. For example, Robert Fisk lists "obtaining, developing, and improving personnel" as one of four crucial categories of administrative behavior in "*The Task of Educational Administration*" in *Administrative Behavior in Education*, ed. R. F. Campbell and R. Gregg (New York: Harper, 1957), p. 211.
2. Stanley Williams, *Educational Administration in Secondary Schools* (New York: Holt, Rinehart and Winston, 1964), p. 124.
3. Oliver Gibson and Herold Hunt, *The School Personnel Administrator* (Boston: Houghton Mifflin, 1965), p. 87.
4. Williams, *Educational Administration*, p. 124.
5. *Ibid.*, p. 125.

6. From *Modern Administration of Secondary Schools* by Harl R. Douglass, © Copyright, 1963, 1954, by Ginn and Company (Xerox Corporation). Used with permission.
7. Williams, *Educational Administration*, pp. 146–147.
8. Amitai Etzioni, "Authority Structure and Organizational Effectiveness," *Administrative Science Quarterly* 4 (June 1959): 52.
9. Charles Perry and Westley Wildman, *The Impact of Collective Negotiations on Public Education* (Worthington: Charles Jones, 1970).
10. American Association of School Administrators, *The School Administrator and Negotiations* (Washington, D.C.: AASA, 1968), pp. 12–13.
11. Obviously, the list is not exhaustive. The authors also realize that certain situations exist where many more personnel items are decided within the local school and no advisory role exists for teachers.
12. American Association of School Administrators, *The School Administrator*, pp. 57–58.
13. M. Chester Nolte, *Status and Scope of Collective Bargaining in Public Education* (Eugene: ERIC Clearinghouse on Educational Management, 1970), p. 10.
14. Bryce Ryan, "A Study of Technological Diffusion," *Rural Sociology* 13 (September 1948): 273–285.
15. D. Berlo, "Avoiding Communication Breakdown," BNA Effective Communication Series (Rockville, Maryland: BNA Films, 1970), an extraction.
16. Kimball Wiles, *Supervision for Better Schools* 3rd ed. (Englewood Cliffs, N.J.: Prentice-Hall, 1967), p. 53.
17. J. R. Gibb, "Defense Level and Influence Potential in Small Groups," in *Leadership and Interpersonal Behavior*, ed. L. Petrullo and B. M. Bass (New York: Holt, Rinehart and Winston, 1961), p. 66.
18. Usually identified as the "Hawthorne Effect." See F. J. Roethlisberger and W. J. Dickson, *Management and the Worker* (Cambridge: Harvard University Press, 1939).
19. Ashley Montagu, *On Being Human* 2nd ed. (New York: Hawthorn Books, 1966).
20. Peter Kropotkin, *Mutual Aid, A Factor of Evolution* (London: Heinemann Limited, 1902).
21. Frederick Herzberg, *Work and the Nature of Man* (Cleveland: World, 1956).
22. A. H. Maslow, *Motivation and Personality* (New York: Harper & Row, 1954).
23. Douglas McGregor, *The Human Side of Enterprise* (New York: McGraw-Hill, 1960).
24. Fred Fiedler, *A Theory of Leadership Effectiveness* (New York: McGraw-Hill, 1967).
25. Edwin Bridges, "A Model for Shared Decision Making in the School Principalship," *Educational Administration Quarterly*, Winter 1967, pp. 49–61.
26. Kimball Wiles, *Supervision for Better Schools* 3rd ed. (Englewood Cliffs, N.J.: Prentice-Hall, 1967).
27. *Ibid.*, p. 39.
28. *Ibid.*, p. 47 for an example in curriculum development.
29. *Ibid.*, p. 40.
30. Chris Argyris, "Some Limits to Rational Man Organizational Theory," *Public Administration Review*, May/June 1973.
31. Peter F. Drucker, *The Effective Executive* (New York: Harper & Row, 1967).

32. *Ibid.*, p. 22.
33. From *The Effective Executive*, copyright © 1966, 1967 by Peter F. Drucker. Reprinted by permission of Harper & Row, Publishers, Inc., p. 22.
34. From *The Effective Executive*, copyright © 1966, 1967 by Peter F. Drucker. Reprinted by permission of Harper & Row, Publishers, Inc., p. 4.
35. *Ibid.*, p. 4.
36. Fred Pigge, "Teacher Competencies: Need Proficiency and Where Proficiency Was Developed," *Journal of Teacher Education* 29, no. 4 (July-August 1978). 70–76.
37. Gordon Lawrence, *Patterns of Effective Inservice Education*, monograph (Tallahassee: Florida State Department of Education, 1974).
38. Theodore Caplow, *How to Run Any Organization* (Hinsdale: Dryden Press, 1976), pp. 24–36. Based upon a military/business organization model, Caplow discusses the relation of the manager to personal assistant, headquarters staff, subordinate managers, and rank and file.
39. Inter- and intradepartment war over delegated power does not make the principal stronger because of a divide-and-conquer strategy. In fact, it increases the possibility of illegal coalitions against the principal.
40. Caplow, *How to Run Any Organization*, p. 29.
41. *Ibid.*, p. 34.
42. Patrick Bird, "Political and Programmatic Impact of Affirmative Action Policy" in *The Changing Politics of Education*, ed. Edith Mosher and Jennings Wagoner (Berkeley: McCutchan, 1978), pp. 282–293.
43. David Wiles, "Organizations Facing Retrenchment," in *The Changing Politics of Education*, ed. Edith Mosher and Jennings Wagoner (Berkeley: McCutchan, 1978), pp. 264–278.
44. Margaret Hennig and Anne Jardim, *The Managerial Women* (New York: Pocket Books, 1978). Originally printed by Doubleday in 1976.
45. *Ibid.*, pp. 33–34.
46. *Ibid.*, pp. 43–44.
47. *Ibid.*, p. 47.
48. *Ibid.*, p. 51.
49. *Ibid.*, pp. 52–53.
50. Sigue Hammer, "When Women Have Power Over Women," *Ms.*, September 1978, pp. 49–51, 93.
51. David Wiles, "Community Participation Demands and Administrative Response in Big City School Systems," *Education and Urban Society* 6, no. 4 (August 1974): 451–467.

CHAPTER 9

Curriculum, Instruction,
and Evaluation

The number of contrasting definitions of curriculum demonstrates the ambiguity of this policy-making area. Curriculum means a school's written course of study and other materials, the subject matter taught to the students, the courses offered in a school, planner experiences of the learners under school guidance, the program of education based upon planned objectives, and the theories and research of curriculum.[1] The political perspective notes that curricular issues may reflect the larger societal tensions more specifically and overtly than budget or personnel policy making.[2] During this century, national concern over immigration made curricular issues of both the Americanization and melting pot ideas. Nazi totalitarianism brought curricular concern for democracy as a way of life. The red menace brought anticommunism courses, Sputnik caused reemphasis on math and science, and debates on civil rights movements brought the ethnic studies curriculum revisions. The Latin root of the word curriculum means race courses, and up to 300 years ago, this definition emphasized the fixed and standard nature of the course. However, in recent time the race itself is a more accurate description of the agitated jockeying for position in the curriculum. "First vernacular languages, then physical science, then biological sciences have successfully fought their way into the curriculum. . . ."[3]

WHAT MAKES CURRICULUM POLITICAL?

The competitive nature of curriculum has focused on appeals to four different value bases: tradition, science, community, and individual judgment. Each value is promoted by policy bodies who have a vested interest in perpetuating a resource allocation stressing that value. Appeals to tradition assume ideas that stand the test of time (e.g., Great Books) are of most worth. Science assumes empirical rationality and systematic (behavioral) processes to define best curriculum. Appeal to community rests upon the philosophical purpose of schooling, while individual judgment is based upon assumptions of personal perceptions and uniqueness of each person in stating what is of most worth.

Since each appeal represents abstract and (if considered in terms of its internal logic) a rational basis of curriculum, it is futile to look at the rationalizations to understand curricular politics, except as symbolic ex post facto explanations of decisions.

There are actually two brands of curricular politics, one that occurs inside the schools among educators and the other that occurs between professionals and the community. The introduction of curriculum packages that occurred in the early 1960s is an example of the battles that rage behind the wall of professional expertise.

Although the lay public gained notice by their cries to catch up to the Russians in the space race (after Sputnik) the true pullers and haulers were two types of professional educators who fought for control of the school curriculum. A new breed of specialists who packaged curriculum were pitted against the traditional educator. The rationale of the curriculum specialists was that new packages would provide the necessary conditions for building *an empirical foundation* for the field of curriculum. Their policy rationale was

> only an individual with tunnel vision would subscribe to the belief that the best way to construct an educational program is to *develop individual subject matter curricula unrelated to a general plan and then allow prestige or publicity to determine those which are implement.*[4]

This way was the normal method of curriculum development based upon an add-on-mentality that operated when political pressure was felt. In effect, the new specialists were directly challenging the existing political structure that undergirded curriculum decisions. Sputnik, and the resulting public demand for something new to catch up legitimized the new breed of curriculum specialists, especially in the fields of math and science. In the 1960s it is estimated that the National Science Foundation and the United States Office of Education allocated well over *100 million dollars* in these areas. The package development spread to the social sciences and the arts and the alphabets: BSCS, SMSG, PSSC, MACOS (Man A Course of Study) are familiar to most educators. The implementation outlined the political battleground between the regular and specialist educators in curriculum policymaking. Read the anger and threat in the response of the American Association of School Administrators:

> Proponents of the "new" directors and staff of national curriculum projects, who were, for the most part college and university professors

of academic subjects—calling (in the 1960s) on teachers to teach subjects for which methods were not available....the academicans were ignorant of classroom and children's learning....they ignored warnings and pushed on overemphasizing the cognitive....they ignored institutional levels of curriculum that had been overlooked.... *the responsibility for action does not rest with curriculum specialists* ....they provide leadership on what *should be* but do not generally plan strategies or devise management techniques....*it is the chief administrator who has authority to act.*[5]

Scriven, in a slightly irreverent manner, evaluates programs such as SMSG as suffering from a "let's get back in our office and write up a good curriculum, and we'll give it to our teachers and they'll go into the classroom and use it" syndrome.[6] He points out that teachers felt threatened and resented new materials because the programmers (another name for the new specialists) never thought out the political implications. It may be Scriven's analysis of the present day situation is correct when he writes:

The reaction to SMSG programming illustrates the faddist tendencies in education so well that one must be very careful about it. You know, something comes on the scene, a bunch of idiots say it's going to cure all known educational diseases, everybody is terribly excited but secretly anxious as all hell because it's going to put them out of business and they have their own thing going. So we do a few tests, tremendous results, but is it the Hawthorne effect? We do a few more. The cheap boys' stuff is now flooding the market with rotten versions; it turns out they don't work so well. Ah! Relief! We can put it away. It was just another fad, so we say. We've been through that routine with at least six different innovations in education since the 1940s.[7]

Although many educators would hate to admit it, the pro and con reactions to the introduction of packages sound much like the words heard when civil service reform efforts clash with the ward-based patronage systems of the city political machine. Behind the rhetoric is the same clash for control between pronouncements of national expertise versus practical experience.

The second brand of curricular politics involves the educators and lay citizens.

Curricular politics goes to the heart of the schooling purpose and therefore this policy arena is often the most volatile and ugly of all educational decision making. Perhaps the only issue that the general public becomes more angry about than money spent (the famous California taxpayer's "revolt" against state subsidized public services) is the perception that a child is being warped or brainwashed by the schools. Many of the traditional curricular battles are infamous and some rage as hotly today as they did three decades ago. A partial list includes the theory of evolution, the communist menace, sex education, use of teaching machines, black studies, and competency testing. Public interest means that scrutiny of educational governance is most direct in this policy arena. Boards of Education are more inclined to directly intervene in curricular decision making than other areas. Principals are most likely to receive irate demands from citizens for action concerning curricular matters in the classroom and the library than other areas. Consequently, the political strategies and tactics of the administrator must be sophisticated in coping with curriculum issues particularly those that go to the heart of policy-making autonomy. The ability to handle self-appointed guardians of the public morality who want smut, anti-Christ, or communist literature removed from the bookshelves will determine whether a principal understands the political dynamics of local school administration. When values are involved so are emotions and confusion. When the clash of opposing values becomes too confused, Slater's discussion of United States culture is especially instructive.[8] Slater hypothesizes that the two cultures in the United States are inherently and absolutely opposite each other. These cultures are not rich versus poor, black versus white, or science versus humanism "but rather the opposition between the old scarcity-oriented technological culture which still predominates and the somewhat amorphous counterculture growing to challenge it." [9] The scarcity-oriented culture believes all gains have some loss so that any addition to a school's curriculum also means some deletion. The counterculture is inclined to view the world as being possible to gain without automatic loss. Slater would argue that the principal's detection of these basic value distinctions are at the core of handling a curricular controversy.

Slater also believes there is a fundamental distinction between the cultural centrists and those who believe there is a mosaic of diverse cultures. He notes:

> No meaningful compromise can be reached if the culture as a whole is not articulated in a coherent way ... centrists ... are still operating under the illusion that all Americans are playing by the same rules .... but this is not the case. Indeed, the moderates are increasingly despised by both radicals and conservatives as hypocritical, amoral and opportunistic-people who will take no stand and are only interested in their own careers.[10]

These are the cultural distinctions that underscore educators' debates over what is the core curriculum or what are the basic competencies. The political implication for such value confrontation gives a strong message to the local school principal. *If moral unity is gone, the only basis to balance conflicting curricular demands is a practical one. Specifically, if opposing value groups can be convinced that a significant moral issue is not at stake, a compromise might be reached.* Thus the symbolic politics of creating the impression of value consistency in the curriculum is being maintained at an abstract level while actual political compromise between competing groups does not address value positions at all. Does this conscious strategy to defuse value projections violate the ethical concerns for fairness, justice, and being up front? If the principal argues that democracy is a *learned* phenomenon that necessitates a certain state of mind, and further argues that the emotions of curricular politics negate the essential state of mind then there is no ethical conflict. If, however, the principal's actions are based upon making the institution work and giving the public a snow job by using Slater's arguments there is an issue of ethics.

In summary, two brands of curricular politics can affect the principal and the local school arena. One is inside the professional domain and centers on the meaning of expertise. Although we used the example of the new specialists versus the traditional educator, the principal should remember that the normal situation is a study of inherent conflict based upon discipline, specialty, and academic orientation. Normal curricular distinctions reflect the emphasis of arts versus sciences, vocational versus liberal arts, and so forth. Further, the growing scarcities of the 1980s are bringing these historical battles to the forefront of political concern.

The community brand of curricular politics reflects the restless and increasingly frustrated position of society in general. As educators tend to become a society of competing camps of opposing values, the possibility of operational consensus over curricular purpose diminishes. Further, the particular expressions of demands to alter the curriculum tend to lose their concrete meanings and be replaced by emotional rhetoric. In this political world, curricular consensus becomes an exercise of abstract symbolism while practical compromise strives to *deemphasize* moral identification with a particular issue.

THE PRINCIPAL AS A CURRICULUM LEADER

Throughout this chapter we have strongly inferred that the principal must assume greater political and ethical responsibilities as a curriculum developer. It is in this role that the principal in the 1980s can establish a new identity as a leader and carve out new roles that correspond to the changing conditions of the school. This assumption is not idle speculation, but an observation on the changing nature of the public school in the United States.

A leadership vacuum has been created in the school by events of the 1970s. Chief school officers, such as the superintendent and the assistant superintendent for instruction, are finding their time dominated by political responsibilities and fund-raising concerns. School Boards, likewise, are directing their attentions to managerial functions and responses to external stimuli. Supervisors have borne the brunt of curriculum development responsibilities in the 1970s; but, on the other hand, they are regularly discredited by professional teacher organizations. Their role in leading instructional improvement has been compromised by a management function, and is frequently the subject of attack during negotiations. To date, teachers as a group have been unable to provide the expertise needed for instructional planning and organization. Principals must choose whether to abdicate school planning responsibilities to commercial concerns and public pressure groups or to establish a new leadership identity.

Most principals are in the unique position to lead curriculum development efforts and, in doing so, can provide stability in an otherwise unstable political arena. The principal should master the following competencies in order to fulfill this role:

- produce and implement year-long plans focused on curriculum development and provide a schedule of steps toward completion
- define, with staff, common problems and help staff members with the solution of these problems
- evaluate the current educational trends and know the philosophical basis for these trends
- disseminate information on current innovations to staff members directly involved in the specific area of innovation
- coordinate curriculum development and evaluation for the grades found in the principal's school
- open channels of communication within professional staff that will allow the crossing of grade levels, ability levels, and individual discipline structures
- develop with staff behavioral objectives that will be measurable and compatible with subject areas
- help determine the integration of subject areas into total overall curriculum
- set up a system of information exchange among teachers
- plan budgetary allocations to insure that curriculum plans can be inaugurated and completed
- help and encourage teachers to be innovative and to accept different methods as long as they produce the desired outcomes
- be a primary resource person to teachers and students
- promote and encourage the direct involvement and participation of teachers in planning, implementing, and evaluating curriculum development
- use research and evaluation data in selecting and sequencing concepts for curriculum improvement
- provide a means for the continuous evaluation of existing programs

- determine the needs of the community and of individual pupils in planning and developing programs
- acknowledge the needs of special pupil and teacher groups in initiating and planning the curriculum
- communicate progress, plans, and problems to those members of the staff involved in the implementation of programs
- produce in printed form a description of the school's plan for improving the program of instruction
- provide vision in long-range planning

The following three stage curriculum development model (Table 9.1) may be useful in summarizing the leadership roles of the principal in improving school programs.[11]

TABLE 9.1 *A Model for Objective Progress in Curriculum Development*

Substantive-Content (Program)	Objective Study Area (Evaluation-Research)
STAGE ONE: DEVELOPMENT	
I. *Creative Generation:* the birth of the new	I. *Receptive Openness and Genuine Interaction:* tolerance for deviation
II. *Intellectural-Theoretical Conceptualization:* functional integration of ideas into an intelligible program worthy of trial	II. *Application of Systematic, Theoretical and Logical Criteria:* critical questions raised and answered tentatively Explicit statements required as to: A. basic educational objectives B. main program dimensions C. rationale for program D. possible evaluation techniques —potential techniques to be used in Step 3—Quality Control Evaluation
III. *Practical Implementation:* engineering conceptual program into operational form—a potential experimental program emerges	III. *Quality Control Evaluation:* continuing study of the engineering process and its effects A. How well is program functioning from moment to moment as a social process? B. To what degree are identifiable objectives being attained in short run? C. Modifications required in conceptual design of program— How does operating program compare with conceptual program?

TABLE 9.1 *Continued*

Substantive-Content (Program)	Objective Study Area (Evaluation-Research)
	D. Reconciliation of conceptual design with engineered reality
	E. Preliminary estimate of degree to which terminal objectives are attained
IV. *Definitive Description of Operating Program*	IV. Explicit reapplication of criteria questions in Step 2 above

STAGE TWO: FIELD RESEARCH

I. *Identification, Description, and Implementation of Sensible Alternative Programs:* summarizing and systematizing existent alternatives	I. A. *Abbreviated Application of Points 2, 3, and 4 in Stage 1:* alternative programs must also be describable and operational, and share important common objectives with experimental program
II. *Stable Implementation of Experimental and Alternative Programs:* conducting programs for purpose of scientific study	B. *Formulation of Testable Hypotheses:* relationship independent variables (programs and/or component parts), and dependent variables (learning outcomes and objectives)
III. *Maintenance of Experimental and Alternative Programs:* fidelity to engineered concepts and scientific needs	II. & III. *Formulation and Implementation of Experimental Design:* establishment of maximum scientific controls to test hypotheses
IV. *Interpretative Program Implications:* meaning for subsequent curriculum development	IV. *Acceptance or Rejection of Hypotheses:* conclusions of empirical data analysis

STAGE THREE: DISSEMINATION

I. *Communication, Display, Demonstration, Guidance, and Persuasion*	I. *Evaluation of Dissemination-Persuasion Process and Product:* analysis of transmittal procedures and results
A. expository-descriptive account of program and related research evaluation data	1. Fidelity with which the experimentally validated program and all related components are represented to, and understood by, interested educators
B. audio-visual depiction of program highlights	
C. behavioral demonstration (active communication) of program highlights	a. clarity of materials description
D. involvement of subjects in exploration of new program, considering both its advantages and disadvantages	b. role definitions for teachers and students
E. obtaining affective commit-	c. specification of educational objectives

ment to *trial usage* of program in local school

d. presentation of research-evaluation findings regarding program

e. inclusion of evaluation guidelines for application to local implementation

2. Extent to which transmitted program is, and can be adopted and retained in its prescribed form, within a local situation

a. purge dissemination procedures of any program features that are parochial, and not generalizable to all situations

3. Unanticipated problems created by gaps in the dissemination procedures

II. *Introduction and Maintenance of*
& *Program in New, Local Situation:*
III. incorporation of innovation into local school curriculum

A. future curriculum planning and policy

II. *Abbreviated Quality Control Evaluation:* samplings of points applied to determine the appropriateness of the operational program being disseminated to the local school situation

a. data revealing necessary local adjustments peculiar to a particular situation

1. conducted within local school, and primarily of local interest and help

III. Comparative analysis of outcomes where possible: field research type data, unique to a local school, is always desirable.

a. confirm that relationships generally established in Stage II, do prevail in local situations

THE ORGANIZATION OF THE CURRICULUM

A third factor of curricular politics is the formal organizational arrangement of a local school setting. The organizational view of the school sets strong parameters for the meaning of the curriculum. For example, think of the type of curriculum and instruction that would be compatible with Bidwell's perception of public education:

School systems are client-serving organizations, specifically vested with the moral and technical socialization of the young. The goal of any school system is to prepare its students for adult status by training them in the knowledge and skills and by indoctrinating them in the moral orientation which adult roles require.

School systems are (required) to produce uniform outcomes of a given level of quality. The source of this constraint is external and arises from the fact that school systems not only are client serving but also are agents of public welfare and, as such, must be responsible to the apparatus of government and to a public constituency. The constraining force of public constituencies is enhanced by the responsibility of school systems to use efficiently the public funds from which they are supported. The schools are responsible for a uniform product of certain quality. It sets a minimum, but not a maximum, level for student accomplishment. As for the minimum standard, all students must have acquired rudimentary competence for adult citizenship. Students also are to be prepared for differential roles, most notably in the occupational sphere. To provide services which have uniform outcomes means that the school system must routinize the variability of its service procedures and provide educational services which compromise coherent sequences of increasingly differentiated and demanding socialization tasks.[12]

In the organization of curriculum the atomistic arrangement of subjects is the most common. Although not championed by curriculum specialists for some time, the subject matter design continues to hold great popularity.[13] In contrast to the subject design is the broad fields organization of curriculum. Broad fields (e.g., language arts, social studies) are especially prevalent in local elementary schools. A third curriculum organization is called life activities or persistent life situations.[14] Priorities are established according to activities necessary to live life. A final design is known as the activity or experience curriculum. Problem solving is the key ingredient as the school is designed as life itself rather than preparation for life.

Obviously, the curricular orientation of a teacher or group of teachers will affect their decisions about issues of what is appropriate knowledge. A second type of organizational factor that affects curricular politics is the way instruction is carried out. Some of the obvious structures are the various graded school breakdowns that divide students and faculty. Plans for the twelve years of elementary and secondary schools range from 8-4 to 6-3-3 to 6-2-4 to 4-4-4 and 6-6 or 7-5.[15] The local school arena is affected by which grades are included or excluded by a particular scheme. Within the local school, the instructional organizations with the most impact on governance are the self-contained classroom and the department or cluster unit. The self-contained classroom assumes that one teacher (at the elementary level) is responsible for most subject matter. More important from a political standpoint, the self-contained classroom teacher can shut the door and virtually do whatever he or she pleases.

The department organization groups specialists together as subunits to consider curricular and instructional matters. The effect on the local school arena often is to make the department affiliation a natural coalition of other instructional organizations such as team teaching and to promote common vested interests among the faculty.

To this point, the translation of curricular politics to the role of the principal as leader seems to be apples and oranges. The political phenomenon seems characterized by the ambiguity of value-laden conflict, yet the preferred role and organizational arrangement of curriculum seems rationalistic. The key to resolving the apparent dilemma is *personal consistency*, which fixes efforts to improve educational programs to the particulars of a school situation. A brief historical explanation should help clarify the resolution.

A RECENT TRANSFORMATION

In the past twenty-five years, some of the leading educators have reversed their basic assumptions about which learning and knowledge underlies the meanings of curriculum and instruction. There is *a growing tendency to shift from standardized, uniform criteria to an emphasis on personal consistency*. Representative of the reflection on the past and the reorientation that is occurring is Jerome Bruner. Revisiting the Woods Hole conference on improving education in science and his famous text *The Process of Education* from the perspective of a decade later;[16] Bruner describes the late 1950s and early 1960s as innocent days where the "prevailing notion was that if you understood the structure of knowledge that ... by understanding some deep principles you could extrapolate to the particulars as needed." [17] Bruner further describes his most famous assumption that any subject could be taught in some honest form to any child at any stage of his or her development as an ideal whose pursuit was "probably the most important outcome in the great period of curriculum building in the sixties." [18] Educational reform of the 1960s was principally the reconstruction of curriculum that resulted in many successful efforts in mathematics, physics, chemistry, biology, and even some of the behavioral sciences. But by the 1970s the recognition that curriculum revision would not suffice without a more fundamental reordering of the entire educational system was apparent to Bruner. Classifying American education as a state of utter crisis, he stated, "by 1970 the concern was no longer to change schools from within by curriculum but to refit them altogether to the needs of society, to change them as institutions. It is no longer reform but revolution that has come to challenge us." [19] Bruner ended his revisit of the 1960s by asking for a moratorium, or at least a deemphasis on the structure of knowledge and an attempt to deal with fundamental value questions of the 1970s. He warned "reform of curriculum is not enough. Reform of the schools is probably not enough. The issue is one of man's capacity for creating a culture, society and technology that can not only feed him but keep him caring and belonging." [20]

In many ways the historical review by Bruner provides a concentrated perspective of curriculum policy making at the end of the 1970s. Today, educators still debate whether they are irrelevant as professionals or whether they promote a hidden curriculum that teaches subordination, regulation, stratification, and consumerism. However, the present concern for personal values such as caring and belonging may well be overridden by the expected scarcities of resources in the 1980s. As noted throughout this text, scarcities promote a tendency toward uniformity and a single school mentality to complex problems. In curriculum, the intellectual evolution from grand universal theories to concern for personal values may be further overridden by the practicalities of shortage. *The institutional position may well become that in which educators cannot afford the luxury of curricular debate or scrutiny of personal values.* If this condition occurs, individual educators in the local school arena may find a different consideration of curriculum occurring. Institutional concerns may avoid basic value issues and concentrate on practical decisions of economics and effects of shrinkage on the organizational structure. True consideration of curricular meanings may take on a nonschool function. In other words, the search for curricular values and resolving issues in accord with a striving for consistency may be a personal effort.

In summary, four factors define the stage for principal leadership in curricular politics. First, the inside politics within the professional ranks resembles the reform-patronage political continuum. There also seems to be regular pendulumlike emphases between those who wish to substitute technology and scientific curriculum and those who want traditional educator's practice and experience. Second, outsider curricular politics emphasize emotion and ideological expressions that make resolution of value conflicts very difficult, if not impossible.

Third, the historical evolution of serious thought about curriculum has seen the transformation from grand theories to a striving for personal consistencies. The scarcities of the 1980s may make the consideration of what knowledge is into a two-sphere thinking operation. Finally, the organization of curriculum and instruction within the local school shapes the arena of choice. Teachers invest in their knowledge and instructional styles and can be expected to bet their poker hand accordingly.

Two interrelated aspects of the school program directly involve curriculum and the principal as a major actor—supervision and teacher evaluation.

THE PRINCIPAL AS A SUPERVISOR

The conventional yardsticks of judging an organization's performance are found in the words efficiency and effectiveness. A local school is efficient if when *compared to other local schools,* its output is relatively high compared to its input. On the other hand, a local school is effective when it achieves its *own* goals.[21]

Both of these standard definitions fail to indicate much about how schools operate and how effectiveness or efficiency can be promoted. The critical dimension is how the local arena is shaped in terms of authority and power. If the arena resembles a hierarchy with the principal on top, the principles of direct supervision (borrowed from the assembly line) apply. If, on the other hand, the arena resembles a conglomerate of political regimes, then the principal must practice indirect supervision. The assumptions of governance and control are different in direct and indirect situations, and failure to adopt the correct supervisory mode can spell political disaster.

To show the wide variation between the hierarchy model and the conglomerate of organizational governance, the classic bureaucracy is defined as: (1) a division of labor based on functional specialization, (2) a well-defined hierarchy of authority, (3) a system of rules covering the rights and duties of employees, (4) a system of procedures for dealing with work situations, (5) impersonality of interpersonal relations, and (6) selection and promotion based on technical competence.

When these principles are translated into relations affecting people the following list emerges:

1. Competence is the criterion used for appointment.
2. Officials are appointed, not selected.
3. Salaries are fixed and paid directly by the organization, rather than determined in free-fee style.
4. Rank is recognized and respected.
5. The style of life is centered around the organization.
6. The career is exclusive; no other work is done.
7. Security is present in a tenure system.
8. Personal and organizational property are separated.[22]

In the bureaucratic model the institution is the *sole* source of authority to make policy. Legitimacy is in the position and the occupant of the role has the automatic authority of the institution.

The rules for *direct*, assembly line type supervision[23] in a hierarchy are:

1. set unmistakable goals
2. supervise the work more than the worker
3. demand perfect compliance to the essential rules and ignore violations of nonessential rules
4. reward sparingly but punish much more sparingly
5. give praise and criticism in private and understate it
6. listen to complaints sympathetically; never complain in turn
7. defend the faith—the manager is the natural custodian of the organization's sacred symbols and moral character
8. protect the differentiated status of subordinates (e.g., seniority)
9. take infinite pains to do the job right
10. retain final control

Obviously the direct supervision guidelines assume a classic bureaucracy decision world and not the world of the shifting political arena. The guidelines are unrealistic except for the special case where arena power arrangements are truly hierarchical and the principal desires that type of political arrangement. The potential realities of the 1980s and what is known about present school organizations make us favor the following principles of *indirect* supervision[24] as more politically realistic for the administrator.

1. Find and hold the purse strings. Curricular and instructional decisions affect allocation patterns like everything else.
2. Rely on personal and professional relationships with teachers and other subordinates to gain adequate information.
3. Do your homework and "roam the streets." Without the luxury of direct, firsthand knowledge of actual operations the principal must make extra efforts to find out what is going on.
4. Develop detailed plans and projections and, *above all*, refrain from attempting the impossible. Individuals and subunits of the school need to know their own expectations and that of others. Be open about this. Set goals that lie within reach and waste little effort on rhetorical exercises about the unattainable.
5. Reorganize drastically or not at all. The indirect supervisor cannot tinker or fine tune a person or department/program cluster. If an operating unit gives an unsatisfactory performance and cannot be improved the principal should make every effort to disband or remove it. If corrective measures are beyond the power of the principal then isolate and leave the problem alone.
6. Respect successful operations that are productive, even if some

aspects of their efforts seem crazy or unnecessary. All humans practice what Veblen called the "conscientious withdrawal of efficiency." [25] The principal should focus upon results.

7. Innovate boldly, but not often. As noted earlier all change efforts are costly, time consuming and likely to meet resistance or generate unintended effects. Since all efforts are potentially dangerous, go for broke. The best hedge against failure is extensive consultation and gaining consensus among key actors of the school arena.

The indirect supervision guidelines, coupled with earlier discussions of political strategy and tactic, provide the best posture for the local school principal. Before turning to the related topic of evaluation, a last word on the state of mind for supervision is appropriate. Calling back on earlier delineation of symbolic versus operational politics, there are distinct differences in what the motivation of a person or group means. One of the underlying premises of political theory is that demands upon a system cause stress and some type of adaptation. How demands and stress are interpreted is critical in the discussion of motivation and the state of mind for proper supervision. The *wrong* interpretation is shown in analogy of a donkey harnessed to a wagon and a carrot held in front of the animal. The motivation dilemma is that the donkey that never gets to eat will die but the one that does will stop pulling the wagon. From this interpretation, the administrative issue is how to get a donkey (person) to work endlessly for a reward that never comes. The conventional answer is *to create an artificial scarcity*, because the assumption is that only the continuous perception of scarcity will guarantee an excess of energy. The seduction of this state of mind is the evidence of success when its real life applications are viewed. People and societies that have deliberately made plentiful resources scarce have achieved successes in making certain scarce resources plentiful. However, the hidden cost of that success should be openly recognized in a theory of motivation. The process of creating artificial scarcities also tends to make people donkeys pursuing inaccessible carrots. Gratification becomes a *symbolic* striving, and the striving is for *things*. People who are motivated to produce for things and symbols can never be truly satisfied. They believe they are chasing a real carrot but only achieve images.

Perhaps the conscious creation of an artificial carrot can be rationalized as an emergency supervisory tool. However, the even more insidious message of this type of motivation is that, over time, the original real carrot can be removed completely and the donkey will keep on trotting. The means has become an end in itself and *processes* of doing something have to be reduced to some utilitarian value. As Slater notes, the right answer to "what are you doing?," can only be "nothing" if you are a child. [26] How many educators teach or administer exclusively for artificial carrots? How many pull the wagon and have forgotten why? There are some real lessons to be learned in what is glibly referred to as intrinsic motivation.

There are further implications of the wrong interpretation of motivation for curriculum and instructional practice. The postponement of gratification so that energy will be stored places high value on the norm of good behavior. Any activity or product with too much stimulation is dangerous because it generates desires and emotional response for wanting pleasure *now*. The carrot must remain a future expectation to guarantee being unattainable. Too much stimulation makes the carrot hard to see.

A second translation of the artificial scarcity is to promote the structure of inequality. Inequality is a means of creating artificial scarcity as those who are haves seek ways to promote their advantage. What motivation messages are educators giving when they say that kids will loaf if grades are eliminated?

The correct concept of motivation that underscores an appropriate supervisory state of mind does *not* rely on the creation of artificial scarcities within the local school arena. The core of the proper motivation is the recognition *that getting possessions and things generates, rather than reduces, scarcity*. Possessions can give emotional catharsis, but unlike true personal relationships they give nothing back.[27] It is not weak to talk of human values as the underpinnings of motivation any more than it is weak to discuss justice and fairness in governance. The local school can have an arena of cooperation and sharing that also meets the criterion of tough-minded utility matching under conditions of real resource scarcity. Likewise, it is possible to motivate professionals and deal with people by emphasizing values that make someone human and productive. Gaining personal respect in doing the job, caring for people and living with spontaneity, candor and play are essential ingredients to the proper motivation message. These may not be verbalized messages, especially if the supervisory situation would make words sound like preaching. The philosophy of lead by personal example has real meaning for this interpretation of motivation. *No matter how resources shrink and competition grows within the school system during the next decade, the possibility of achieving a human-oriented arena within the local school will remain.* The political sophistication necessary to maintain the boundary and resolve the rules for internal poker will also allow the capacity for achieving proper motivation and a supervisory climate.

EVALUATION

It seems correct that this text end with consideration of the principal and evaluation. The era of scarcity will promote demands for accountability and evidence that the public is getting their money's worth for educational services. The dilemma is that the popular perception of evaluation is some universal standard of objectivity, which can be applied in scientific fashion. But educational realities of learning, teaching, or governance do not lend themselves to the popular perception. Consequently, much of evaluation is symbolic show, where collection and analysis of evaluative information become elaborate efforts to create the image of classic rationality. Educators use generalization and central tendencies to cover for phenomena that may be more realistically portrayed as variability and discrete conditions. Educators look to institutional structures and operating procedures to enhance the objectivity image. No one has ever shown that a pleasing appearance or excellent compliance with school rules correlates to how children actually learn or whether a person can teach. General rating forms are often unreal but necessary to keep up the image. Educators recognize the frailties of national norming of achievement scores but promote their use as demonstration to the public (with a little creative application there is always a comparative base to present a favorable impression. As the Peace Corps used to say, the glass can be interpreted as half empty or half full). The issue is not whether the public will become aware of the distinction between symbol and reality in evaluation. Most of the public were students and observed first hand the continuing distinction (e.g., grades received versus knowledge gained). The fact remains that the public (and, in turn, the central office) has a vested interest in *not* recognizing symbol from ongoing realities. Evaluation should be approached as a political marker with particular relevance to the local school boundary issue. *Within the local school a faculty and principal can recognize that the declaration of teaching as an art or learning as an individual experience is not an apology but a statement of operational reality.* However, that recognition must be concurrent with the recognition that various audiences *outside* the arena demand standard presentations of comparative evaluation. A basic issue for local school resolution is the mix of evaluation as symbolic compliance to evaluation as a vehicle for operational improvement. This is no simple decision task, for some school systems have transformed the generation of evaluative evidence to a rationale for retrenching faculty. If this is the case, the evaluation criteria may be a key stipulation of the board-teacher federation master contract. These situations aggravate the ability of a principal to create a clear boundary between the arena and the environment. Without the boundary, much effort will be wasted trying to reconcile the inherent contradictions between symbolic and operational assumptions of evaluation.

Improving the School Program

Evaluation in schools might best be thought of as the basis for effective decision making about school programs. Quality programs in schools are dependent on good decision making, which results when alternatives are known. Knowing alternatives calls for valid and reliable information, and the availability of such information depends on a systematic way of providing it. Therefore, an evaluation program in a school is really nothing more than a way of providing information to guide decision making.

The historical track record of research and evaluation in schools is not particularly strong due to a number of conditions. Perhaps the greatest problem with most evaluation efforts is that they do not clearly address what is being evaluated. Another problem commonly found is that the results of evaluation programs are not fed back into the system for improvement. Finally, much educational research and evaluation is not statistically controlled, resulting in unreliable findings and interpretations.

While it is not within the scope of this book to address research design and statistical treatment of data, we do feel that there will be even greater expectations for school-based evaluation in the 1980s. This pressure for greater self-assessment will result from a number of forces. First, there is the ten-year-old accountability movement in the United States, which shows no sign of lessening. This movement began with California's landmark Stull Bill that set the tone for successive legislation:

> Each school district is required to adopt specific evaluation and assessment guidelines which shall include but not necessarily be limited to (a) the establishment of standards of expected student progress in each area of study and the techniques of assessment of that progress (b) assessment of certified personnel competence as it relates to the establishment standards.[28]

Subsequent legislative activity has led to other state-wide plans such as Virginia's Standards of Quality and the Florida Accountability Act.

A second force that will encourage school-based evaluation programs in the 1980s will be the fixed nature of school resources. A combination of failing school bonds, inflationary pressures on real dollar purchasing power, and lowered average daily attendance due to enrollment drops will enforce introspective evaluation. Should the various states adopt a voucher system or other mechanism that would speed the decline of public school enrollments, such school-based evaluation could become the criteria for the survival of the fittest.

It is to the advantage of the school principal to initiate school-based evaluation in the 1980s. Such actions will enhance his or her image as a person who is knowledgeable and in control. It is also important for the principal to determine the form of school-based evaluation. The more broadly based the school plan is, the greater the chance that it can make a significant contribution to program improvement.

A research and evaluation program could serve to answer those questions for which there is no available data. If, for instance, the school needs assessment fails to tell educators what they need to know about the effect of student self-esteem on achievement as measured by standardized tests, then an evaluation program should be established. Stufflebeam suggests an evaluation structure that is general to all types of evaluation and can guide the establishment of specific studies:

A. Focusing the Evaluation
1. Identify the major level(s) of decision making to be served, e.g. local, state, national
2. For each level of decision making, project the decision situations to be served and describe each one in terms of its locus, focus, timing, and composition of alternatives.
3. Define criteria for each decision situation by specifying variables for measurement and standards for use in the judgment of alternatives.
4. Define policies within which the evaluation must operate.

B. Collection of Information
1. Specify the source of the information to be collected.
2. Specify the instruments and the methods for collecting the needed information.
3. Specify the sampling procedure to be employed.
4. Specify the conditions and schedule for information collection.

C. Organization of Information
1. Specify a format for the information which is to be collected.
2. Specify a means for coding, organizing, storing, and retrieving information.

D. Analysis of Information
1. Specify an analytical procedure to be employed.
2. Specify a means for performing the analysis.

E. Reporting of Information
1. Define the audience for the evaluation report.
2. Specify a means for providing information to the audiences.
3. Specify the formats for evaluation reports and/or reporting sessions.
4. Schedule the reporting information.

F. Administration of the Evaluation
1. Summarize the evaluation schedule.
2. Define staff and resource requirements and plans for meeting those requirements.
3. Specify the means for meeting policy requirements for the conduct of the evaluation.
4. Evaluate the potential of the evaluation design for providing information which is valid, reliable, credible, timely, and pervasive.
5. Specify and schedule means of periodic updating of the evaluation design.
6. Provide a budget for the total evaluation program.[29]

It is useful for the administrator who is establishing an evaluation program to be able to distinguish among context evaluation, input evaluation, process evaluation, and product evaluation. Context evaluation seeks to define the operation context, to identify and assess needs in the context, and to identify and delineate problems underlying the needs. It is useful to those conducting evaluations in determining settings for educational programs. Input evaluation is used to assess system capabilities and the designs for implementing strategies. It is useful to those conducting evaluations in selecting sources of support and in programming change activities. Process evaluation is used to identify defects in procedural design or program implementation, and to maintain records of events and activities. It is useful for identifying procedural barriers and remaining alert to unanticipated blockage. Finally, product is used to relate outcome information to objectives and to context, input, and process information. Product evaluation is useful for decision making about the continuance, modification, or termination of school programs and activities.

For school-based research efforts there are some characteristics that are desirable. They can be used by the principal to review proposals and ongoing projects:

1. The problem should be clearly stated, limited, and be of real significance to the school.
2. If other studies have been conducted before in the area, they should be noted and their relationship to the proposed study drawn.
3. In quantifiable studies, where statistics may be applied, the variables to be controlled or manipulated should be identified in advance of the study.
4. A description of procedures to be followed should be made with enough clarity to be replicated by others at another time.
5. The particular group to be studied should be identified in terms of specific characteristics.
6. Any project report should note the school setting, describing among other things the organization, scale of operation, and any special influences.
7. Evaluation instruments used should be applicable to the purpose of the study. Self-esteem of students, for instance, is not readily measured by standardized achievement tests in reading.
8. Limitations of the study, and there are usually limitations, should be clearly stated.

In Figure 9.1 Roberts outlines the major decision points that may face the principal in developing school assessments.[30]

Research and evaluation, then, provides a back-up subsystem for planning and organization that provides situationally specific data to the prin-

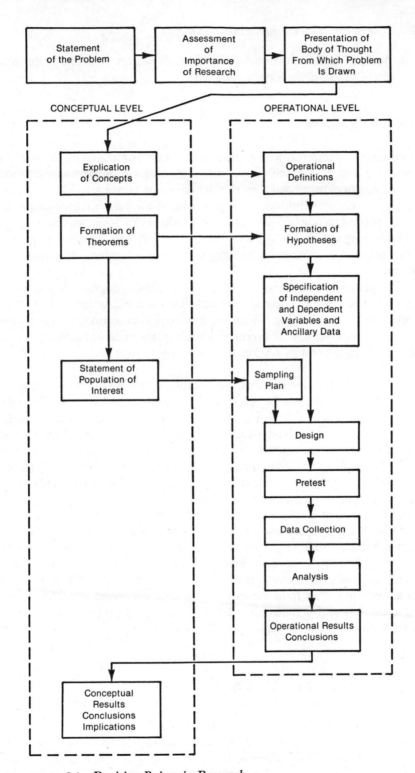

FIGURE 9.1 *Decision Points in Research*

cipal. Research and evaluation fill in information gaps vital to a systematic approach to planning and organization.

Providing a Rationale

By initiating a research and evaluation format for problem solving the principal prepares the school for meeting realistic evaluation demands. Such procedures bring order to the many events relating to idea development, goal setting, decision making, resource allocation, and evaluation. Such a procedure should also assist the members of the organization in understanding and explaining to others the mission of the school, sharing in the process of goal achievement, and comprehension of human and material resource usage.

The principal who plans and organizes school program development in a systematic manner has a responsibility to communicate with those affected by such planning. Without such communication, the plans derived from the data base will remain simply plans. The implementation of such plans are dependent on the actions of those persons who operate the school.

Several communication aids are useful in helping teachers, students, and parents in seeing the big picture of program development. The relationship of events and time, a crucial relationship, can be shared through the use of milestone charts (Table 9.2) or an events flow chart (Table 9.3). A slightly more sophisticated format for reporting progress can be developed from needs assessments and research data. Here, findings are translated into program development steps (Table 9.4) that identify the objective, time frame, personnel, resources, and expectations. Such program development steps, in clusters, can become the curriculum development plan for the school and also serve as the primary program evaluation schema. Such a communication device allows everyone in the school to understand how their personal behaviors tie in with the action of others.

Finally, the principal will need a master planning list (Table 9.5) that will allow him or her to monitor the various projects and activities occurring in the school. Such planning lists will be helpful in directing principal behavior on a day-to-day basis.

USING SYMBOLIC POLITICS

It should be clear that milestone charts, events flow charts, and planning checklists can do more than give practical guidance to users in personal evaluation efforts. These are also the vehicles of symbolic appearance that may well become some of the 1980s version of accountability if scarcity

TABLE 9.2

Milestone Chart

	Completion Date						
	1979				1980		
Milestones	Sept.	Oct.	Nov.	Dec.	Jan.	Feb.	Mar.
1. Review guidelines with State Department of Education June 7							
2. Identify the criteria for selecting a representative group of the school, community to serve as a task force	△13						
3. Identify the Education Task Force	△20						
4. Orientation for Education Task Force to guidelines and intent		△4					
5. Design a management system for processing the development of a plan		△6					
6. Identify special groups representing the school and community for involvement		△7					
7. Describe the scope and depth of the plan		△7					
8. Plan task for completing the philosophy stage		△7					
9. Appoint Task Force committees		△7					
10. Orientation for all special groups to guidelines, intent and management system		△11					
11. Collect data for the philosophy stage		△18					

Source: from Jon Wiles and Joseph Bondi, *Curriculum Development: A Guide to Practice* (Columbus, Ohio, Charles E. Merrill Publishing Company, 1979) p. 345. Used by permission of the publisher.

201

TABLE 9.3

Major Event	Starting Date	Completion Date
Hiring administrative staff (Project Director and secretary)	Notification of Funding Date	August 1
Overall planning	August 1	May 23
Recruiting three lead teachers and two counselors	Notification of Funding Date	August 1
Recruiting 12 teacher aides and 12 student tutors	August 1	August 17
Evaluating and selecting instructional materials	Notification of Funding Date	August
Purchasing instructional materials	August	August 17
Purchasing office supplies	August 1	June 30
Concentrated training of instructional staff	August 20	August 24
Inservice training of instructional staff	September 4	May 24
Pretesting of students in program	September 10	September 14
Posttesting of students in program	April 22	April 26
Interim testing of students in program	September	May
Working with parents and community groups	September 17	May 24
Disseminating information about program	August 1	June 29
Developing and implementing instructional program	August 1	May 24
Replicating project activities in other schools within LEA	August	Indefinitely
Demonstrating the project to interested observers and making available staff members as well as materials, equipment, and facilities which are relevant to the project	January	Indefinitely

Source: from Jon Wiles and Joseph Bondi, *Curriculum Development: A Guide to Practice* (Columbus, Ohio, Charles E. Merrill Publishing Company, 1979) p. 128. Used by permission of the publisher.

forces ugly confrontations. If this pessimistic projection occurs, administrators will need to know how to create the appropriate images of progress and accomplishment.

There are three types of evaluation formats that can be used to present an image of standard evaluation.[31] One format in an input evaluation lists characteristics of the learning environment but does not specify actual

TABLE 9.4 *School Projects Summary Data*

Objective (Project Number)	Responsibility	Anticipated Results	Completion Date	Resources
Elementary Gifted Program—event 15	Mr. Brighton, Case Elementary	Establish two gifted sections	February 1980	Training funds for staff development (budget item 134) Funds for materials acquisition (budget item 155)

TABLE 9.5　*Program Planning Checklist*

_____NEED ASSESSMENT COMPLETED	Formal—survey, interview, question-naire Informal—discussion, belief, etc. Directive—necessary mandate Other
_____GOALS DEVELOPED Start Date Established Target Date Projected (most likely time)	Goals Identified Goals Synthesized Mission Identified Mission Clarified Mission Accepted
_____MAJOR ACTIVITIES DELINEATED	All Possible Mission Objectives Synthesize All Objectives Convert to Product Statements Activities (Product Statement) 　Agreed Upon
_____RESPONSIBILITY CHARTED	Activities Stated Personnel (Human Resources) 　Identified Responsibility Allocated
_____ACTIVITIES ASSIGNED	Supervision Responsibility Accepted Work Accepted
_____TASKS IDENTIFIED	Work Detailed Target Date Set
_____EVENTS DELINEATED	Work Assigned Target Dates Set
_____TIME SCHEDULED	Event, Task, Activity, Time Com-bined Combined Time and Target Date 　Compared Time Adjusted When Necessary
_____MANUAL COMPLETED AND DISTRIBUTED	Mission, Activity, and Task Sheets 　Collated and Tabbed Responsibility Chart Entered Manual Duplicated
_____TIME SCHEDULES COMPLETED	Time Charts Developed Time Charts Centrally Posted

Source: from Jon Wiles and Joseph Bondi, *Curriculum Development: A Guide to Practice* (Columbus, Ohio, Charles E. Merrill Publishing Company, 1979) p. 127. Used with permission of the publisher.

processes or products of the environment. In this case, the local school might be profiled in terms of years of teacher experience, degrees earned, student data, number of books available, and so forth. The purpose is to present the school demographics without stating how that relates to criteria for evaluating. Two strategies can be presented: either profiling the local school as an exemplary learning environment or presenting the hard case. The second strategy is to lower expectations in the event actual results are demanded at a later date. Obviously, the input evaluation image is the least satisfactory local school presentation.

The next type of evaluative presentation is the process focus. This explains teaching/learning as interaction and deliberately avoids the relationship between processes and outcomes. This kind of evaluation can be used to demonstrate a school climate is open, that governance is democratic, or that teaching is indirect. In some cases, this is a sufficient presentation of evaluation.

The last type of symbolic evaluation is output, which will be the most prevalent demand during the 1980s as scarcities promote accountability. In desperate situations there may even be demands for a single criterion (e.g., student achievement scores against national norms) to evaluate the teaching-learning process. More likely, the output evaluation will demand demonstrations of multiple competencies. The type and extent of effort a principal and faculty put into meeting the symbolic needs of output evaluation depends upon the political intensity of particular demands. Hopefully, efforts can stop well short of teaching the test, juggling the statistics, or late reporting, which have been utilized in some local school situations. Perhaps the most important task for the principal is to get an *accurate* picture of the political consequences of a bad performance. The range of consequences can go from wink or sympathetic nod of a head through public chastisement to wholesale firing or transfer of all personnel. If the consequences are not dramatic the principal will have room to deal with real evaluation within the arena. If not, boundary maintenance becomes the first arena priority.

It may make many educators uncomfortable and angry to confront the hidden face of evaluation so bluntly. However, the 1980s may demand such recognition regardless of how it upsets past myths and prescriptions. However, even with the conscious focus on symbol, this does not necessarily negate or avoid the professional responsibility for evaluation. On the contrary, open recognition of the distinction of symbol to reality demands a personal accountability far more stringent than any institution could envision. It comes down to the person as an educator. It is relatively easy to play-act for others and feel righteous about beating an unfair game. It is quite another thing to be phoney to yourself or not feel embarrassed about the conscious negation of professional responsibilities. Operational evaluation is self-assessment. All the input, process, and output indicators that could be generated mean nothing without personal translation and specific use in individual diagnosis. Again, we are talking about a consciousness or state of mind. External enforcement attempts to get real information only lead to political posturing and a no-win situation, for experienced educators have learned (for survival) how to present an appearance. If a teacher or principal *wishes* to be an intellectual prostitute there is no way to alter that wish by external stimulus. People can silence another person but that does not mean they have beaten him or her. If a principal has read this far and recognizes the political realities of the local school arena (e.g., self-contained classroom, federation, coalitions) then the above statement is obvious. In the final analysis, operational evaluation turns upon the generation of personal respect and responsibility. A key ingredient in that generation is the political role of the local school principal in the 1980s.

CASE STORY: ADOPTING TEXTBOOKS

The Language Arts Review Committee had begun like many school committees. In the curriculum review rotation it had been time to select a reading text for the district and a district-wide committee of teachers and parents had been asked to serve on a committee to provide selection guidelines. It happened every year and such committees were regarded, at best, as a necessary evil. The usual product of such committee work had been the adoption of the latest fare from one of the big companies. Only in this case, the committee had taken its job a bit too seriously.

For some reason, and for the first time, the Language Arts Review Committee had employed an outside consultant to help them with the process of reviewing their needs. The consultant had been one of those process people from a nearby university and before anyone knew what was happening the committee had flow charts and behavioral goals for a wide range of activities related to language arts. In the context of this approach, the need to find individualized reading materials for students in the district seemed to be a mandate. The committee developed recommendations for a selection criterion that no single textbook or even system of reading could ever match. More disturbing, the Language Arts Review Committee included a large number of parents from one specific area of the city. In selecting the parent representatives, someone had just reached for a parent advisory list that was handy and the resulting composition of the committee was disproportionately ethnic.

Following the normal flow of district procedures, the Language Arts Review Committee brought its recommendations before the Principal's Advisory Group (PAG) as an intermediate step prior to going before the Board. Most of the principals were caught off guard by the candid flavor of the report and failed to grasp the implications of a criterion that demanded reading materials that could be meaningful to all students in the district. Only when they read the final recommendation that "reading materials for the district be developed by classroom teachers in the district with the advice and support of parent groups" did the principals understand the problem. The Language Arts Review Committee didn't want to buy textbooks next year. The PAG took the report under consideration by a 27–1 vote. The lone vote, as usual, coming from Jim Holmes, principal of Grayson Elementary School.

When the superintendent had found time to read the Language Arts Committee report, he had hit the ceiling. "What the hell was going on out there?" He immediately called for the chairperson of the committee and for Jim Holmes. In a thirty-five minute session the superintendent laid it on the line. The district had always used textbooks. They were written by experts who knew what in the hell they were doing. The textbooks in reading insured that the children in the district had a uniform experience. Besides, these company representatives had been generous to the district. They had provided free samples of all their selections for years. Did the teachers forget who had been supplying the beer for their opening social event each year?

The Language Arts Review Committee chairperson, a tenured librarian, responded to the superintendent's antics calmly. The teachers of the district, she reported, had found after considerable inquiry that no single textbook was appropriate to the needs of all the children in the district. For the most part the books were written at too high a level for average student use, they did not acknowledge the cultural diversity of students in this district, and they were impossibly expensive. Each year these commercial packages called for more supplemental purchases of software, machines, and films. The money expended on these programmed systems could be better spent on teacher-made materials.

After the chairperson had departed, the superintendent turned on Jim Holmes with a fury Jim had not previously seen: "These people are from your district," he observed. The district could not afford to get into truly individualized materials . . . . it would cost a fortune. And, the superintendent demanded, there was no way he was going to take that kind of recommendation to the Board. He suggested that Holmes talk to the committee.

Jim did meet with the committee the following week. What he found as "the superintendent's representative" was substantial documentation of the committee's recommendations. A readability analysis confirmed the charge that the books were impossibly high level for most students. Only one company had really integrated culturally aware pictures into their text, and that particular company had an extremely poor track record on achievement test gains in the Title I literature. Perhaps most significant, the teachers and parents were questioning the whole idea that an outside expert could do a better job of developing materials for the district than the teachers that taught in the district. Teacher professional judgment was being questioned in this case, and the community cultural identity was at stake. Reading, the teachers argued, was a component that related to many fields, not a technical skill.

No amount of reasoning could get the Language Arts Review Committee off the track, and Jim had the undesirable task of reporting the same to the superintendent. Jim Holmes, by himself, was caught among the entire administrative hierarchy, the book salesmen, the teachers, and the community. At stake was teacher morale, public confidence, a potential brush with the teachers' union, and his own credibility with the administration.

Case Questions

1. How might a superintendent or a principal structure review committees so that they don't become autonomous decision-making bodies?

2. In taking the report under consideration, the Principal's Advisory Group failed to make a definitive judgment on the report that might structure action by the LARC. Design a procedure that would make the PAG an evaluative mechanism in curriculum development.

3. Is there some action that the superintendent or Jim Holmes might have taken to meet the legitimate concerns of LARC?

4. Develop an ending to this case and describe why you think the case would end in this manner.

NOTES

1. Glenn Hass, Joseph Bondi, Jon Wiles, *Curriculum Planning: A New Approach* (Boston: Allyn and Bacon, 1974), pp. xvi–xvii.
2. William Pilder, "The Concept of Utility in Curriculum Discourse: 1918–1967," Ph.D. Dissertation, Ohio State University, 1968.
3. Frederick Wirt and Michael Kirst, *The Political Web of American Schools* (Boston: Little, Brown, 1972), p. 204.
4. Elliot Eisner, "Curriculum Development: A Foundation," in Elliot Eisner, *Confronting Curriculum Reform* (Boston: Little, Brown, 1971), p. 3.
5. American Association of School Administrators, *Curriculum Handbook for School Executives*, (Washington, D.C.: AASA, 1973), pp. 365–373.
6. Michael Scriven, "Comments on SMSG: Where We Are Today," in Eisner, *Confronting Curriculum Reform* (Boston: Little, Brown, 1971), p. 87.
7. *Ibid.*, p. 88.
8. Philip Slater, *The Pursuit of Loneliness* (Boston: Beacon, 1970), p. 97.
9. *Ibid.*, p. 97.

10. *Ibid.*, p. 101.
11. By Douglas E. Stone, University of South Florida. Used by permission.
12. Charles Bidwell, "The School as a Formal Organization," in *Handbook of Organization*, (ed. J. G. March (Chicago: Rand McNally, 1965), pp. 973–977, 1012–1013.
13. Perhaps the most famous was the Amidon Experiment. See Carl Hanson, *The Amidon Elementary School* (Englewood Cliffs, N.J.: Prentice-Hall, 1962).
14. For example, Florence Stratemeyer et al., *Developing a Curriculum for Modern Living* (New York: Teachers College Press, 1957).
15. Ralph Kimbrough, *Administering Elementary Schools* (New York: Macmillan, 1971), pp. 121–130.
16. Jerome Bruner, "The Process of Education Revisited," *Phi Delta Kappan*, September 1971, pp. 18–21.
17. *Ibid.*, p. 18.
18. *Ibid.*, p. 19.
19. *Ibid.*, p. 20.
20. *Ibid.*, p. 21.
21. Chester Barnard, *The Function of the Executive* (Cambridge: Harvard University Press, 1938).
22. Bidwell, "The School as a Formal Organization," p. 976.
23. Theodore Caplow, *How to Run Any Organization* (Hinsdale: Dryden Press, 1976), pp. 93–99.
24. *Ibid.*, pp. 101–102.
25. Veblen, *A Theory of the Leisure Class* (New York: Free Press, 1952). The popular television series M.A.S.H. is based upon the theme that outstanding results may be achieved by individuals and groups that some judge crazy. Also see Gary Steiner, *The Creative Organization* (Chicago: University of Chicago Press, 1965).
26. Slater, *The Pursuit of Loneliness*, pp. 88–91.
27. The analogy is that an alcoholic becomes malnourished *because* he or she obliterates the hunger.
28. California Assembly Bill 293, Chapter 361, Section 13403–13489 Education Code, enacted July, 1971.
29. Daniel L. Stufflebeam, "Toward a Science of Educational Evaluation," *Educational Technology*, July 30, 1968, p. 10.
30. Karlene H. Roberts, "Understanding Research: Some Thoughts on Evaluating Completed Educational Projects," from ERIC at Stanford, ED 032 759 26.
31. For detailed discussion of the realities of evaluation see J. Averch et al., *How Effective Is Schooling* (Santa Monica: The Rand Corporation, 1974).

CHAPTER IO

Practical Politics
in Review

Throughout this book we have presented a different perspective of school administration. Traditional presentations of educational administration are too general and create the dangerous illusion that the role of the principal is one of certainty and stability. We feel that the treatment of the role of the administrator should tie words to reality.

The reality is that education in the United States is in a transitional era. Blanket assumptions of resource adequacy, reason, stability, and predictability have vanished in the turmoil of the 1970s. In particular, the traditional arguments of educational cycles, where it is expected that things will improve if educators simply wait, do not seem reliable. The magnitude of problems facing public and private education in America, and the scale of observable systems breaks in the 1970s, suggest that the 1980s will be troubled times for school leaders.

These realities demand a new conceptualization and a new perspective of school administration. This book has attempted to introduce such a new way of thinking. The following set of statements summarizes the political perspective of school administration:

THE POLITICS OF SCHOOL ADMINISTRATION

The Arena

- Schools have a political dimension. This political dimension is best understood in terms of the allocation of resources and specific instances of decision making.
- Legitimacy and control in schools, under certain conditions, are situational phenomena.
- The primary concern of the school administrator in the local school center is making decisions.

- In the 1980s, such decision making will be conducted in an environment of scarcity characterized by adverse relations, shortages of desired commodities, and sanctions for wrong choices.
- Winning or losing in such an environment will not automatically be decided by administrative status.
- The school setting can be conceptualized as an arena where administrative actions can be studied and analyzed.
- The arena perspective, unlike the bureaucratic perspective of school operations, sees each decision-making event as unique and situationally determined.
- The arena perspective acknowledges the imprecise nature of the decision-making process in schools and demands a tolerance for ambiguity in understanding decision making.
- The arena perspective is issue oriented.
- The arena perspective, unlike systems, bureaucratic or small group consensus models of school administration, accounts for decision-making discrepancies. By emphasizing the situation and the issue of a particular decision, the arena perspective can account for all activity in the school.
- In the arena model of school administration, change is assumed to be as likely as stability.
- From the arena perspective, the principal's role of leadership is not viewed as stable or fixed. Rather, the role of the principal is defined by the issue involved and the choice situation.
- By perceiving the principal as one player in the arena, there is no need to overextend information and, therefore, classification of behavior.
- The way a principal plays is dependent upon how he or she views authority, the availability of resources, competition, and the utilization of resources.
- Because of such variability in perception, the principal's role is analogous to that of a poker player who must play each new hand according to the cards that have been dealt.
- We are concerned, above all else, with the ethical dimensions of such poker. To win is not an adequate criterion for poker when children's lives are at stake.
- An open recognition of both the realities of the political decision-making process and the possibility for excesses is necessary because administration is the ultimate safeguard of ethical concern.

Taking Charge

- The first task of a new school administrator is to be accepted into the new environment. The means of entry by the administrator (previous experience, type of move) determines the best course of action for early acceptance.

- In planning entry, the symbol and image of leadership will be at least as important as actual performance and behavior.
- The specific strategy most appropriate to use in taking charge depends upon the types of groups present, their perceptions of existing conditions, and the previous pattern of administration that is being inherited.
- Emphasizing creativity or a positive outlook through symbolic imagery may help the principal gain entrance into the arena. Climate control represents an effective means of indirectly encouraging these themes of leadership.

Maintaining Control

- To maintain control the principal must have an adaptive strategy. For strategy planning there must be a calculation of resources available, basic power structures, the dynamics of the organization, and the extent to which stability is valued in decision making.
- School administrators in large organizations must be aware of bureaucratic bargaining techniques that affect decision making. Among these techniques are quasi resolution, employing regulations to avoid uncertainty, stress-reduction decisions, and organizational learning to slow down the decision-making process.
- Strategies for decision making and maintaining control should be based upon whether the arena is stable (abundant resources, single pyramid of influence) or unstable (few resources, shifting power, challenge to authority).
- In stable arenas the general strategy in decision making is to act as a representative of particular interest groups rather than as an independent individual. Such representation should be conservative and protective of interests.
- In unstable arenas, the general strategy is to act as an individual rather than as a representative. Coalitions are formed according to what's at stake. Actions must be distinguished from intentions since posturing is common. Rules for decision making are particular to the game in question.
- To maintain control in unstable arenas, the principal must prevent the formation of rebellious coalitions. Other players must always see each other as unequals.
- In unstable arenas the principal should have a strategy for various climates such as crisis bargaining, brinksmanship, and utility matching. The principal's decision style should match the configuration of the arena.

Making Changes

- Change efforts in schools in the 1980s will be governed more by political practices than rational planning practices.
- Most changes in the 1980s will be part of a refining process rather than the creation of something new.
- The gap between planned change and the actual implementation of change will be increasingly dominated by the irrational world of payoffs and face saving. To be effective, a change agent will need to be a politician.
- In the 1980s, successful change will be demonstrated and promoted as an extension of existing conditions.
- Change in the 1980s, unlike that of the previous twenty years, will address stability. The mandates for goal clarity, wise use of resources, and accountability will force such direction.
- Protection of interests and existing reward systems will direct change in the 1980s. The control of resources, not new ideas, will be the prime mover of change efforts.
- To increase the stability of change efforts in the 1980s, principals should telegraph planned changes. Such a method structures the medium for communication about intended changes and will reduce the possibility of surprise and disruption in the arena.
- A major role of the principal in promoting desired change in the 1980s will be to protect the creative individual in the arena. The creative individual represents the future, regardless of present conditions.

THE APPLICATION OF PRACTICAL POLITICS

Boards of Education and Central Administration

- The relationship between the central office and the local school is political within an organizational context. The composition of the arena and the style of play and bargaining results from this relationship.
- One of the important tasks for the school principal is to monitor the multiple and shifting decision boundaries that affect the local school.
- The decision boundary of the local school arena determines the shape of competition for scarce resources and the rules for playing in the arena.
- Three critical variables determine the decision boundary between the local school and the central administration (or school board).

These variables are: the amount of upward looking, the threat of veto, and the guaranteed support systems for the local school.

- The key to building a successful relationship between the local school and the central administration is the identification of key individuals who control the flow of ideas and resources.
- Strategies for establishing and maintaining contact with the central office include image building and contingency strategies.
- The use of systems as a language is valuable in increasing upward communication. The use of systems language can help shape the arena by identifying where and how decisions are to be made.

Parents, Community Groups, and Students

- A secondary boundary for the school arena exists where parents, community, and students affect decisions. Parents are the key boundary actors in terms of political importance.
- Principals can take the initiative in establishing boundaries and building relationships with parents by identifying those areas *where* parent input is welcomed and *how* the parents should be included in decision making.
- Being able to promote effective small-group communication is a critical skill for building principals in working with parents, community groups, and students.
- In dealing with community interest groups it is useful to categorize groups according to *why* they wish to influence school decision making. Concerns for control cut across traditional classification continuums such as liberal-conservative.
- The role of students in the arena is more often a triggering factor in boundary formation than a participating decision group. There may be, however, a resurgence of the student power movement in the 1980s as performance pressures for graduation are increased.
- Principals can anticipate that culturally diverse students will be the first to demand inclusion in decision-making processes in the 1980s. By *initiating* program reviews the principal can satisfy early needs that are voiced.
- Principals should be willing to give ground to student power plays. As a rule, such pressure will be short term in nature and will fade quickly due to the transient nature of the school population.

Budget Politics

- The importance of budget issues cannot be overstated. The budget records the outcome of struggles over issues. Administrators in the local school center must become involved in budget matters.

- Being able to talk in the appropriate language is a powerful political advantage in budgetary matters. PPBS (Program Planning Budgeting System) or some modification of PPBS will continue as the major budget language in the 1980s.
- An important distinction to be made about centralized budget planning is whether its purpose is to instill a rational system-wide process or whether its implementation will reach the local school level.
- The control of data about the local school center can help the principal identify problems and indicate budget solutions. The management of data will help the principal appear convincingly knowledgeable about the local school and is critical in budgetary matters.
- Use of tabulated data and compartmentalized management systems can assist the principal in presenting strong arguments for specific budget needs and in coordinating long-range budget planning.
- Hoarding resources or posturing scarcity to gain budgetary concessions is *not* recommended for the 1980s. Unlike the past, such a condition, if discovered, will have strong political implications for the principal.
- The principal must remember that he or she is the link between levels of school government in budgetary matters. The principal serves as the translator and interpreter of budget policies.
- The categories of fair share and base are two dimensions of the budget that can be influenced informally by contact with key actors in the district.

Personnel Politics

- The principal's role in personnel politics is comprised of two dimensions: personnel administration and human relations.
- An arena perspective of personnel administration represents a direct challenge to the historical base of educational administrative theory. In the 1980s, teacher professionalism will be the issue that forces adoption of the arena perspective.
- Master contracts negotiated through collective bargaining will stipulate many of the key issues in personnel administration in the 1980s.
- For the administrator, communicating with others in the arena from a human perspective (noninstitutional) is essential to gaining influence and competing in the arena.
- The employment of democratic decision making within a competitive arena setting is a learned process where all people in the organization must be educated to accept both responsibility and authority.
- The operational meaning of democracy within a bureaucracy is an understanding of policy making that recognizes the institutional and personal constraints of the arena.

- For the most part, democratic administration will be a perceptual phenomenon on the part of the principal and others in the system. The administrator must set the educational arena so that democratic decision making can occur.

- Administrative planning and organization during the 1980s should be focused on the teaching force. Older, more experienced teaching staffs in the 1980s call for a more sophisticated relationship between administration and instruction. Such a new relationship can help break down the growing trend toward spheres of influence in education.

- Women in the 1980s present a special political issue in the arena. Women must address the tasks of taking charge, maintaining control, and relating to others in personnel matters with definite strategy. Overcoming minority status and issues of sexuality can be achieved by placing emphasis on the continuity of institutional roles. Demonstrating utility in decision-making situations is a necessity for survival in an arena with shrinking resources.

Curriculum, Instruction, and Evaluation

- The competitive nature of curriculum development makes it political. Such competition occurs within the school and outside the school. The issue in curriculum development is resource allocation.

- School boards are more inclined to directly intervene in curriculum decisions than in other areas of school operation. Teachers, parents, students, and citizens-at-large also feel free to cross boundaries for decisions on curriculum matters.

- The roles of curriculum developer and instructional leader provide the principal an opportunity to assume greater political and ethical responsibilities during the 1980s.

- The personal consistency of the principal in curriculum decision making mediates between the political phenomenon of value conflict and the preferred condition of rational organizational arrangements. As resource shortages become acute, this role will become more critical.

- Regardless of how competitive for resources education becomes in the next decade, there will remain the possibility for a human-oriented arena within the local school.

- There will be a greater expectation for school-based evaluation in the 1980s. It is to the principal's advantage to institute such local evaluation efforts. This action will enhance the principal's image and allow for some degree of control over the form of evaluation.

- A basic issue for local school resolution will be the mix of evaluation for symbolic compliance to assessment demands and as a vehicle for operational improvement.

- The use of graphs, charts, and summaries can help the principal communicate trends and decision points to teachers and parents. Such devices can also be used to project symbolic appearances in times of extreme scarcity or accountability pressures.
- Perhaps the most important task for the principal in evaluation is to get an accurate picture of the political consequences of a bad performance.
- Operational evaluation, for most principals, is self-assessment. In the final analysis, operational evaluation turns on the generation of personal respect and responsibility.

A FINAL OBSERVATION

During the development of this book we have constantly scanned the educational horizon for signs that these projections will prove short lived. To date, no major alteration of a social, economic, or political nature has presented itself to suggest a new day is coming for American education. While it would be our preference for a new set of cards to be dealt, it appears that we will be playing with the hand we now possess. For this reason, being aware of the game we are in is an operational necessity.

One major theme presents itself throughout this book as a ray of hope: the role of the principal in the local school center will shape the arenas of the 1980s. It will take strong and visionary administrators to keep the game ethical and the real priorities of education in mind. Our constant suggestions to be above board, to telegraph changes, to reach out to parents and community, to involve teachers, and to act in a consistent manner are really a plea for the stabilization of the school arena.

If school administrators don't model such stability through their actions in the 1980s, the implications for education in the United States are ominous.

Name Index

Subject Index